Challenging Canada

Challenging Canada

Dialogism and Narrative Techniques in Canadian Novels

GABRIELE HELMS

McGill-Queen's University Press
Montreal & Kingston · London · Ithaca

© McGill-Queen's University Press 2003
ISBN 0-7735-2587-4

Legal deposit third quarter 2003
Bibliothèque nationale du Québec

Printed in Canada on acid-free paper that is 100%
ancient forest free (100% post-consumer recycled),
processed chlorine free.

This book has been published with the help of a grant
from the Canadian Federation for the Humanities and
Social Sciences, through the Aid to Scholarly Publications programme, using funds provided by the Social
Sciences and Humanities Research Council of Canada.

McGill-Queen's University Press acknowledges the support of the Canada Council for the Arts for our publishing program. We also acknowledge the financial support
of the Government of Canada through the Book Publishing Industry Development Program (BPIDP) for our
publishing activities.

National Library of Canada Cataloguing in Publication

Helms, Gabriele, 1966–
    Challenging Canada : dialogism and narrative techniques in
Canadian novels / Gabriele Helms.

    Includes bibliographical references and index.
    ISBN 0-7735-2587-4

    1. Canadian literature (English) – Minority authors – History
and criticism.   2. Minorities in literature.   3. Narration
(Rhetoric).   4. Dialogism (Literary analysis).   5. Canadian
fiction (English) – 20th century – History and criticism.
I. Title.

PS8199.H44 2003   C810.9'920693   C2003-902719-8
PR9192.5.H42 2003

This book was typeset by True to Type in 10/12 Sabon.

For Bob

Contents

Acknowledgments

It gives me great pleasure to acknowledge the people who have participated in the dialogue of this project. To Sherrill Grace I owe my greatest thanks for introducing me to the work of Mikhail Bakhtin. Her intellectual support, boundless energy, and unconditional friendship have been invaluable over the years. I would also like to thank Ansgar Nünning, who taught me about constructivism and the intricacies of narrative theory in my early days at the University of Cologne and whose work and spirit have remained an inspiration over the years. I gratefully acknowledge the financial support of the Department of External Affairs and International Trade Canada, which enabled me to pursue a doctoral program in Canada.

Patience took on a whole new meaning when I was struggling with unforeseen delays. I am grateful that so many people encouraged me to keep going. For their support and generous contributions at various stages of this project, I thank my fellow writers, critics, and friends: Guy Beauregard, Lisa Chalykoff, Noel Currie, Janice Fiamengo, Margery Fee, Jane Flick, Matt James, Beth Janzen, Susanne Kohlgrüber, Jennifer Lawn, Daphne Marlatt, Joel Martineau, W.H. New, Nancy Pagh, Patricia Rodney, Chantal Scharrenbroich, Susanne Spekat, Margaret Sweatman, and Julie Walchli as well as the anonymous readers of the manuscript. Susanna Egan, Gitta Oldendorff, and Kevin Stewart have helped in more ways than I can list here; they were the friends who always knew what I needed the most. When the time came to get the manuscript ready for the press, Joanne Richardson was the thoughtful and patient editor any writer would hope for.

To my parents, Marlies and Karl-Heinz Helms, and my brother Michael, I am grateful for their never-faltering support and the many long-distance phone calls. And finally, I owe special thanks to Bob Shore, who always cared and without whom this book would have remained a folder on my computer.

Challenging Canada

1 Dialogism, Cultural Narratology, and Contemporary Canadian Novels: What's the Point?

> The study of verbal art can and must overcome the divorce between an abstract "formal" approach and an equally abstract "ideological" approach. Form and content in discourse are one, once we understand that verbal discourse is a social phenomenon – social throughout its entire range and in each and every of its factors, from the sound image to the furthest reaches of abstract meaning.
>
> Mikhail Bakhtin

Many contemporary Canadian novels call into question ideas of Canada as a benign and tolerant country, "a peaceable kingdom,"[1] a country without a history of oppression, violence, or discrimination. They give voice to those previously silenced and resituate those cast as outsiders, thereby exposing the myth of an innocent nation and challenging its hegemonic centre.[2] Such novels may speak of the internment of Japanese Canadians, sexual abuse and incest, the exploitation of women, the disenfranchisement of immigrant workers, residential schools, the Chinese Exclusion Act, and violence spurred by homophobia; consequently, they make for disturbing reading. However, the demands they place on their readers cannot simply be accounted for by their troubling content, whether that refers to the broad historical context or an individual character's story. The complexity of their narrative structures and the multiplicity of perspectives they incorporate further challenge their readers. It is this connection – between multiple voices in contemporary Canadian novels and the unspoken assumptions that inform *how* these voices are constituted and interrelated – that interests me. I wonder, for example, whether a particular kind of formal experimentation in contemporary Canadian novels exposes cultural hegemonies and which narrative strategies are most suited to challenging the generic conventions of the novel. How can these formal devices contribute to or impede the text's challenge to social hegemony and injustice? And what is the point of linking techniques with social issues and asking these questions?

Last things first. Mieke Bal's (1990, 729) seemingly offhand and simple but invaluable question – "what's the point?" – which she would like to see asked of all academic work, demands immediate attention.[3] The point of this study is to examine how and why many contemporary novels challenge Canada. As writers give voice to social discontent and often expose social injustice, they continually imagine and reimagine Canada in their texts. By paying attention to their representation of voices, we may gain insight into the ways we continually talk about Canada, the values that inform our own and others' cultural expressions. Of course, we are dealing with representations of Canada in these novels rather than with the thing in itself. Such conceptual caution, however, renders such representations no less meaningful or significant. After all, the series of representations "that cumulatively come to function in the place of an ever-retreating 'in-itself'" are all we have (Knowles 1995, 18). While I do not deny the existence of an ontological world, I believe that we cannot perceive anything that lies outside our own experience. As a result, we do not mirror "the" reality but construct models or versions of it.[4] Because I understand reality as a subject-dependent construction, the question of what Canada "really" is becomes irrelevant. From an epistemological perspective, I want instead to ask what we know about Canada and how we know it.

It is the idea of a nation called Canada that is the focus of this book. However, my interest lies not in attempting to tease out theoretical differences between country and nation, nation and state, nation-state and state-nation.[5] I am most concerned with the discursive production of Canada, and in that sense I think of "nation" as what Benedict Anderson (1983) refers to as an "imagined community." Although I focus on the social imaginary that has created the ideology, or national consciousness, of Canada since it became a nation-state, I am also interested in the discourses that helped to create Canada in the period leading up to Confederation. I use "Canada" as a shorthand for these concepts; when I use the term "First Nations," however, "Nations" indicates various indigenous communities.

As we encounter, in the fiction under discussion in this book, gendered, racialized, and classed visions of Canada that work to privilege dominant groups, especially those constituted as white, middle-class, male, and heterosexual, I suggest not treating these visions as self-explanatory, transparent, or natural. By examining them as socio-historical constructions and by recognizing that all constructions operate within fields of power relations, we can expose the interests they serve, their justifications, and their material effects.[6] Once we recognize that our notions of Canada, to borrow from Michel Foucault (1972, 25), "do not come about of themselves, but are always the result of a construction the rules of which must be known, and the justifications of which must be scrutinized," we can begin to de-essentialize Canada and make challenges possible. The categories we use to analyze these constructions, such as gender, race, class, and sexual orientation, are themselves socially constructed, contested, and contingent (Scott 1992, 36);[7] they may be most usefully conceptualized as intersections of systemic networks (Mohanty 1991, 13).[8] Recognizing the simultaneity of these relations in critical analyses and the need to situate them within specific socio-historical contexts allows for a reconceptualization of power, domination, and resistance. Such an understanding of constructions prepares the way for their renegotiation.

Contemporary constructions of Canada are, to say the least, multifaceted. And often they are ambivalent. For example, while its relations to its colonizer Britain have been described as postcolonial, Canada plays a double role as an "invader-settler colony" (Brydon 1995, 2) because "it has also been an agent of that [imperial] power in the control it has exercised over populations within Canada's boundaries" (Bennett 1993/94, 175). Various examples come to mind: the internal colonization of Aboriginal peoples, regional colonialism (e.g., vis-à-vis Quebec and the north), and differential treatment of ethnic and racial minorities. The double role of Canada, and of the Second World in general (Lawson 1991; Slemon 1990), has led to the exclusion of these literatures from studies of anti-colonialist practice because anti-colonialist resistance has often been seen as synonymous with Third World and Fourth World writing (Slemon 1990, 32–3; Lawson 1995, 22).[9] While I do not want to elide the differences between experiences of colonialism in Canada and countries of the Third and Fourth Worlds, I do agree that we need to discard the simple binaries – such as colonizer/colonized, Europe/its Others, First World/Third World, vocal/silent – at the heart of some postcolonial criticism in order to examine the double role and ambivalence of the middle ground (e.g., in the literatures of Canada). In other words, we need to engage with the problems that come with the "confused, contradictory, and deeply *ambivalent* position within the circulations of colonialist power and anticolonialist affect" of invader-settler cultures (Slemon 1995, 283). Provisional, locally situated, and historically grounded critical reading strategies allow me to read for and think through a transformative politics in those contemporary Canadian novels that challenge the consequences of colonialism and imagine non-repressive alternatives.

Only through the analysis and negotiation of these constructions, their values, norms, and truths, can we create levels of consensus that will allow us to interact socially. To participate in this process is everyone's responsibility. To think in terms of constructions does not lead to passivity, helplessness, or the removal of historical agency; on the contrary, it requires commitment and ongoing negotiation. Moreover, the multiple possibilities enabled by a constructivist approach, and the concomitant lack of certainty or single truth, do not lead us to relativism. To paraphrase W.H. New's reminder in *Borderlands* (1998, 32), we have a responsibility to discriminate among the versions of Canada circulating around us. Not all versions will be equal; some may indeed be dangerous. As we accept this responsibility, we also need to examine, expand, and revise the criteria we use for our assessment. What is crucial for my argument is that these constructions are always open-ended and provisional. Hence, they can be influenced, renegotiated, and changed. Rejecting essentialist notions about Canada allows people to challenge the hegemonic constructions that have gained currency and to imagine alternatives.

A number of critics of Canadian literature and culture have recently begun to focus their attention on some of the constructions that have informed our thinking about Canada to date. While these studies contributed to my thinking and at times overlap my interests in this book, none of them relies on the methodological frameworks proposed in the following chapters. I am thinking, for example, of Margaret Turner's *Imagining Culture* (1995), which studies how New World discursive conditions are represented in Canadian literature, and Marie Vautier's *New World Myth* (1998), which examines how contemporary Canadian novels destabilize the traditional use of myth as they rewrite historical events. The essays collected in *Painting the Maple* (Strong-Boag et al. 1998) focus, from a wide variety of disciplines, on the role of race and gender in the construction of Canada. But I am also thinking of W.H. New's interest in how "paradigms of boundary rhetoric" construct Canada in *Borderlands* (1998, 5); Peter Dickinson's *Here Is Queer* (1999), which examines the intersections of nationalism and sexuality in shaping Canadian literatures (1999); and Jonathan Kertzer's discussion in *Worrying the Nation* (1998) of how English-Canadian literature became established at a time when the concept of nation came under close scrutiny.

But why study literature, and in particular novels, to find out what we know about Canada? Because novels, and here I follow Edward Said (1993, 73), "are not reducible to a sociological current and cannot be done justice to aesthetically, culturally, and politically as subsidiary forms of class, ideology, or interest."[10] In other words, novels are not simply reflections of social attitudes, caught in a one-directional relationship; rather, novels themselves contribute significantly to cultural attitudes and references and thus help to consolidate social visions or encourage resistance. Literary texts, alongside newspapers,

TV programs, Web sites, and art exhibitions, for example, are cultural practices that defy the separation of "an isolated cultural sphere, believed to be freely and unconditionally available to weightless theoretical speculation and investigation" from "a political sphere, where the real struggle between interests is supposed to occur" (57).

To get at this "real struggle between interests" as it informs novels, I will primarily work with Mikhail Bakhtin's concept of dialogism. It will be instrumental in my discussions of how multiple voices are interrelated in contemporary Canadian novels and of how they can challenge constructions of Canada. In *Problems of Dostoevsky's Poetics*, Bakhtin (1984a, 6, 40) describes dialogism as the organizational principle of the polyphonic novel in which a "plurality of independent and unmerged voices and consciousnesses" are "juxtaposed contrapuntally." In this interplay of voices, no single monologic voice is allowed to unify or dominate; not even the narrator's views can constitute an ultimate authority. Working with Bakhtin's concepts, many critics have recognized that not only is dialogism the organizational principle of polyphony in the novel but that it also "embraces," in Anne Herrmann's words (1989, 4), "an ideological interrogation of literary practices." A polyphonically conceived fictional world is itself a content, a textuality constituted by ideological practices. To treat dialogism only as a literary device would diminish and depoliticize Bakhtin's approach. Only a few steps have been taken, however, towards a cultural criticism of literature, especially Canadian literature, that uses dialogism to consider formal practices within social contexts.[11] I believe that a cultural narratology[12] would enable us to recognize that narrative techniques are not neutral and transparent forms to be filled with content, and that dialogic relations in narrative structures are ideologically informed.

Although dialogism provides an effective methodological tool for the examination of ideological signification in narrative structures, I am not suggesting that every novel with a polyphonic narrative is necessarily ideologically subversive or that novels lacking such textual features are ideologically conservative. Many critics examining Bakhtin's writings have reminded their readers that concepts such as dialogism or carnival are not inherently subversive, liberating, or benevolent.[13] Similarly, narrative theorists have repeatedly argued against a package deal between forms and effects. Meir Sternberg (1982), in particular, coined the phrase "Proteus Principle" to theorize how the effect of formal patterns, given the wide range of possible contexts, can change drastically. Moreover, in their discussions of Canadian novels, Sylvia Söderlind and Glenn Deer have both come to the conclusion that what is rhetorically subversive is not always politically subversive or critical of authority.[14] The ideological propensity of narrative, rhetorical, or linguistic devices depends on the social and cultural practices within which they are embedded. In Susan Stanford Friedman's (1989, 180) words, narrative is "potentially polyvocal and polymorphous," and its meanings are therefore defined not by any intrinsic qualities but by its social uses. Moreover, dialogism has often been used as a means to explore the peaceful and harmonious interaction of voices. As a result, the elements of struggle, conflict, and power dynamics have been neglected. More recently, however, feminist critics in particular have suggested that one of the greatest strengths of the concept of dialogism lies in its potential to articulate resistance through a contextualized investigation of power relations.

The forms of dialogic relations that I examine most closely are informed by the desire for such resistance and transformative politics. Ultimately, the novels I discuss seem not to be satisfied with the temporary authorized transgressions found in parody but, rather, strive for more permanent change. I read these novels, therefore, as resistance literature that, as Barbara Harlow (1987, 28) has explained, "calls attention to itself, and to literature in general, as a political and politicized activity." According to Harlow, resistance writing sees itself "involved in a struggle against ascendant or dominant forms of ideological and cultural production," of which colonialism is only one example (28–9); however, as Stephen Slemon (1990, 36) points out, resistance is not something that is simply "there" and easily accessible in a text. To get at resistance one needs a carefully theorized strategy such as dialogism, which reminds us that resistance is produced and reproduced through readers who are situated within their own specific contexts. Resistance is always constructed through multiple ideological relations; in other words, it is always mediated.

Moreover, it is crucial to note that resistance literature is not merely reactive. Peter Hitchcock, in *Dialogics of the Oppressed* (1993, xvi), argues that multiple voicings and dialogism fracture the monolithic and monologic discourse of power and call into question what he refers to as "the 'logic' of omnisubjection."[15] Similarly, Godard (1990b, 195) has shown that we do not have to follow certain Foucauldian critics in their focus on the strategies of exclusion and containment, which enable hegemonic discourses to consolidate their power in the face of their own internal tensions and contradictions; instead, we can shift the focus to these internal tensions and examine how they enable the elaboration of new discursive formations. Dialogism allows us to theorize resistance not as a counter-effect to networks of power but, rather, from a position of struggle, radical action, and change within power relations. The counter-discourse of dialogic relations moves beyond opposition to, or reversal of, positions and explores how discourses are displaced and destabilized and how they are simultaneously connected and disassociated.[16] As Godard summarizes it, the dialogic "establishes a theory of a transformative practice grounded in critique and resistance" (198). At the same time, resistance is always necessarily embedded in the structures it seeks to undermine or subvert. The novels under consideration show varying degrees of complicity with systems of oppression even when they seem to show the most obvious resistance.

What kinds of struggle are inscribed in contemporary Canadian fiction? How is difference constructed in a multicultural society, and what do these constructions reveal about access to positions of power? Is the multiplicity of multiculturalism a form of liberal pluralism and/or of celebratory dialogism? Is dialogism a strategy for liberation from oppression and/or does it result in chaos, nihilism, and disintegration?[17] I am most concerned with the ritual invocation of liberal pluralism or heterogeneity, which too often disguises the perpetuation of exclusion. As Abdul JanMohamed and David Lloyd (1987, 9–10) have pointed out, pluralism is "enjoyed only by those who have already assimilated the values of the dominant culture. For this pluralism, ethnic or cultural difference is merely an exoticism, an indulgence which can be relished without in any significant way modifying the individual who is securely embedded in the protective body of dominant ideology." Pluralism can easily become a strategy to neutralize or defuse opposition by seeming to accept it; in Gayatri C. Spivak's words (1987, 107), "the putative center welcomes selective inhabitants of the margin in order better to exclude the margin." The idea of "unity in diversity" and what we may call "democratic discrimination" serve as examples here. The latter phrase echoes the work of Frances Henry and Carol Tator (1994) on "democratic racism"; democratic discrimination highlights the contradictory nature of simultaneously maintaining two apparently conflicting ideologies, such as those of democratic liberalism and racism (or other forms of discrimination). Because multiculturalism or pluralism paradigms usually exclude the concept of hierarchy, they fail to recognize that discrimination, whether racism, sexism, or classism, relates to the possession of politico-economic authority and to forms of resistance. Many of these discourses of pluralism tend towards harmonization without seriously questioning or changing the social relations within which they operate. Only when we work with a perspective that stresses difference as struggle can we counteract assimilation, cultural normalization, and strategies of containment. Hegemonic formations need to be destabilized through struggle in the in-between sites where movement and change can take place. The writers selected for *Challenging Canada* attempt to explore such sites for intervention as they reconstruct notions of Canada in their novels.

TOWARDS A CULTURAL NARRATOLOGY

At this point it is necessary to outline in more detail the methodological framework of cultural narratology. The term "cultural narratology" describes the place where dialogism and narrative theory meet, allowing the analysis of formal structures to be combined with a consideration of their ideological implications.[18] But can there be an alliance between narratology, presumably a largely formalist poetics, and an explicitly political/contextual/cultural criticism of which Bakhtin's dialogism is only one representative concept?[19] Let me phrase this challenge rather polemically: is not the supposedly scientific, descriptive, and value-free discourse of narratology the very antagonist of the apparently impressionistic, ideological, and mimetic approaches of political or cultural criticism? The polemics are dated, however, for the field of narrative theory has changed dramatically in the past fifteen years. What I propose, and here I follow Bal (1990, 728), is based on the recognition that "the often alleged opposition between historical and systematic analysis is a false one." What appears as an abyss between incompatible approaches, then, is not an ontological given but, rather, a self-created critical construction (Nünning 1994, 102). Such bridging of the abyss, or recognizing that there never was an abyss, has been central to contemporary critical approaches in narrative theory. While both Warhol (1999) and Bal (1995, 1999) have most recently seen their narratological analyses in terms of their "cultural use," and while Onega and Landa (1996, 12) use the term "cultural narratology" (albeit without developing it), it is still necessary to conceptualize a cultural narratology and to test its usefulness.[20]

How did we get to the point of rethinking narrative theory?[21] Tzvetan Todorov (1969, 10) has been credited with introducing the term "narratologie" to describe the systematic study of narrative structure in his *Grammaire du Décameron*: "Cet ouvrage relève d'une science qui n'existe pas encore, disons la NARRATOLOGIE, la science du récit" ("This study builds on a science that does not yet exist, let us say, NARRATOLOGY, the science of narration/narrative"). Three years before, Issue 8 of the journal *Communications* focused on "L'analyse structurale du récit" (the structural analysis of narrative texts), bringing together central essays by Roland Barthes, Umberto Eco, Gérard Genette, A.J. Greimas, Tzvetan Todorov, and others. The work of Ferdinand de Saussure and the Russian formalists in the 1920s, especially

Vladimir Propp's *Morphology of the Folktale* (1928, trans. 1958), had inspired scholars to produce a grammar of narrative by preparing typologies, taxonomies, and complex models. This structuralist hope for a "science" of literature that describes the systematics of literary forms and literary evolution informs, for example, the classical narratological work of Claude Lévi-Strauss (1958, trans. 1963), Eberhard Stanzel (1955, trans. 1979), Booth (1961), Greimas (1966, trans. 1983), and Genette (1972, trans. 1980). Both Shlomith Rimmon-Kenan (1983) and Mieke Bal (1985) further developed these models and provided widely used guides to a study of narrative that still was primarily structuralist in nature.

After a period of increasing concern about the validity of the structuralist narratological enterprise, especially under the influence of deconstruction, feminist criticism, postcolonial studies, psychoanalysis, and so on, Herman (1999a, 1) can talk about a "narratological renaissance" in the late 1990s, illustrated by a wide range of innovative narratological approaches in his collection of essays, *Narratologies* (whose plural form nicely captures this sense of growing multiplicity). Increasingly, critics have insisted that we cannot understand narratives simply by classifying their formal elements; rather, we need to examine the complex interplay between narrative forms and their contexts, and we need to do this from a diachronic perspective. Barthes's *S/Z* (1970, trans. 1974), although seemingly structuralist in its approach to Balzac's novella, constitutes an early example of such a rethinking as he shifts the attention from textual production and product to the role of the reader and the reading process. Another early example, and one particularly relevant to my own notion of cultural narratology, is Frederic Jameson's *The Political Unconscious* (1981). Jameson makes explicit the connection between form and context by viewing cultural artifacts as "socially symbolic acts" (20). For the Marxist critic Jameson, texts are representations of social classes and their ideological struggle. I, as well as many others working on cultural analyses, take seriously his slogan "Always historize!" but I am also indebted to his discussions of the "ideology of the form itself" (141).

Let me briefly mention the recent developments in narrative theory that have most significantly influenced my own thinking about narratives; namely, cognitive, rhetorical, and feminist developments. The cognitive dynamics of the reading process become the focus of attention, for instance, in Manfred Jahn's (1997, 1999) cognitive narratology. Drawing on linguistics and cognitive science, Jahn recognizes both the idiosyncrasies of individual reading experiences and readers' shared reliance on interpretive strategies. Monika Fludernik's (1996) "natural narratology" also draws on cognitive analyses and reception theory, but she further broadens her perspective by working with non-literary genres from a distinctly historical perspective. Similarly, Ansgar Nünning (1999, 69) proposes a "cognitive framework for the analysis of unreliable narration" in order to bridge the gap between narratology and cognitive theory. A rhetorical perspective on narratives characterizes the work of Peter J. Rabinowitz (1987), Adam Zachary Newton (1995), James Phelan (1996), and Michael Kearns (1999) as they develop ethics of reading, striving to understand how readers position themselves in relation to the texts they read.

Susan Sniader Lanser's attempt to bring together feminist criticism and narratology in "a feminist narratology" (1986) and later in "a feminist theory of voice" (1992) has been particularly influential in rethinking narrative theory and refiguring boundaries. Lanser's "Toward a Feminist Narratology" (1986), in which she proposes a paradigm shift in narratology,[22] is, moreover, a good example of how such rethinking was vehemently opposed. According to Nilli Diengott's (1988, 49) response to Lanser, for instance, there is no need for and no possibility of reconciling feminism and narratology; misguided attempts at reconciliation result from a lack of clarity in defining objects of study (47), from confusion as to where narratology belongs (44, 46), and from some feminists' desire to appropriate other fields of study (42, 50).[23] In spite of such early resistance, Lanser's work has inspired further critical refinement of feminist narratology and many studies that show its usefulness in critical readings of specific texts. "Why Don't Feminists 'Do' Narratology?" is the provocative question with which Robyn Warhol (1989), for instance, introduces *Gendered Interventions*, her study of Victorian novels. By proposing "a partial poetics of narrative discourse" that recognizes distancing and engaging narrators as conventions of narrative texts in nineteenth-century realist fiction (xv), she attempts to analyze "gendered differences in writing strategies" as well as to "expose the gender bias in literary theories" that have ignored the engaging narrator as a literary convention (24). Nevertheless she insists on the distinction between poetics and interpretation (viii). We still see the same distinction in Gerald Prince's (1995) work when he suggests that questions concerning contexts can be considered under the pragmatic aspect of narratology, thus reasserting the distinction between narratology and narratological criticism (i.e., between theoretical poetics and interpretation). While, according to Prince, narratologists should be able to recognize variable, extratextual determinants, they are not concerned with the determination of meanings but, rather, with what I would describe as a search for a universally valid model of description, thus maintaining clear boundaries of textuality.

Two new collections of essays, *Grenzüberschreitungen/Transcending Boundaries* (Grünzweig and Solbach 1999) and a special issue of *Narrative* edited by Emma Kafalenos (2001), seem less anxious about what, in their introduction, Grünzweig and Solbach call the recent "interpretative turn" of narratology (14). Indeed, as many of their contributors seem to suggest, models, examples, and analyses can never be thought outside of contexts. This shift is most obvious in the increasing attention paid to contexts of production and reception, but it is also clear with regard to the specific roles of readers and their "particular reading practices" (Lanser 2001, 155).

In Canadian contexts, the role of gender in narrative texts has been explored in a number of venues, such as the 1987 International Colloquium at Carleton, which resulted in a collection of essays on gender and narrativity (Rutland 1997). Issue 7 of *Tessera* (1989), a journal focusing on feminist literary theory in Canadian women's writing, was devoted to feminist narratology, looking closely at narrative strategies for analyzing and writing women's subjectivity. Two of *Tessera*'s editors, Kathy Mezei (1996) and Barbara Godard (1990a, 1997), have further explored feminist narratology, often drawing on Bakhtin's work in the process. While Mezei's edited collection, *Ambiguous Discourse* (1996), seems, in its exclusive focus on female writers, to suggest that questions about gender are intrinsically connected with the gender of authors, characters, and readers, recent criticism has attempted to tease out aspects of sex, gender, and sexuality (Lanser 1996, 1999) and has shifted attention towards how narratives contribute to our understanding of gender within culture (Robinson 1991; Nünning 1994; Warhol 1999).

What all of these new narratological approaches share is a search for methodological frameworks that allow them to examine the connections between narrative forms and the historically determined understandings of reality that inform them.[24] Generally speaking, these approaches have long parted with the purely mimetic concept of literature, in which literature is seen as a mirror of reality; instead, literary texts are recognized as "historical and cognitive events in their own right" (Schwarzbach, quoted in Nünning 1992, 199). Their relationship with society is reciprocal and dynamic:

On the one hand, literary texts are considered to be products of their contexts in that they take up the social problems and cultural knowledge of a particular time and, through specific literary means, comment upon as well as interpret them. On the other hand, it has been pointed out that, in turn, literary reality models influence society as they contribute to the development of new ways of perceiving, thinking, and feeling about the world. (Nünning 1992, 199, my translation)[25]

Nünning's (1992) discussion of eighteenth-century novels, based on the conceptual frameworks of narratology and New Historicism, illustrates how productive such (re)readings can be. Novels produce their own fictional worlds through specific narrative techniques. These techniques are themselves recognized as ways of constructing the experience of reality in language. Thus, they themselves are already content. The analysis of these textual practices can provide us with an understanding of historically determined moral conflicts, world views, habits of thought, and individual and collective reality models that can increase the specificity of our cultural analyses. If narrative techniques are formal means of inscribing socio-cultural experiences, then they cannot be timeless ideal types that have been handed down to narratologists in ready-to-use systems; instead, as Lanser (1992, 5) explains, they are historically determined and are the result of "complex and changing conventions that are themselves produced in and by the relations of power that implicate writer, reader, and text." Even the broadest elements of narration are thus ideologically charged, socially and historically variable, and sensitive to differences (23).

A cultural narratology recognizes these points. It studies "narrative forms in their relationship to the culture which generates them" (Onega and Landa 1996, 12), a culture that they, in turn, continue to shape. In its simultaneous focus on narrative strategies and the contexts of production and reception, acknowledging in particular the dynamic nature of the reading process, cultural narratology recognizes that readers' understandings of texts can be "various, contradictory, and immensely complex" (Warhol 1999, 354). And, what is more, it seeks to account for and understand such differences and to explore their ideological implications. Let me return once again to my earlier question: what's the point then of a cultural narratology that recognizes that ideology is located in narrative structures themselves? The point is that, once narrative forms are seen as socially constructed, novels become valuable sources for cultural studies because their narrative forms provide information about ideological concepts and world views. Thus, the kind of narratology conceptualized here is not an end in itself. In alliance with a cultural view, it enables us to identify and understand cultural experiences translated into, and meanings produced by, particular formal narrative practices – practices that are in no way confined to literature but that could include daily conversation and examples from anthropology, science, and visual arts as well as work in new electronic media.[26]

For this reason I introduce the term "cultural narratology" in order to set it apart from what, in 1990, Chatman (1990, 309, 310) called "contextualist narratology" – a phrase he used when criticizing a whole group of scholars who had "diverge[d] sharply from structuralist narratology" and focused *exclusively* on "the acts in the real world that generate literary narratives." Cultural narratology is probably most closely aligned with the cultural turn of Bal's rethinking of narratology, which is seen in her afterword to her second edition of *Narratology* (1995), entitled "Theses on the Use of Narratology for Cultural Analysis," and then further developed in *Double Exposure: The Subject of Cultural Analysis* (1996). Rather than follow Bal's (1999, 39) example and speak of "a narratological analysis of culture" or "a cultural analysis of narratives," I will continue to use the term "cultural narratology" with the intention of emphasizing its roots in narratology, a field that has been significantly changed by the developments of the last fifteen years. A cultural narratological framework holds two distinct promises: (1) the semanticizing of narrative forms will move narratology beyond its notorious a-historicity; and (2) by providing adequate descriptive tools, it will enable cultural critics to attend to the specific tools and strategies that are characteristic of narratives in a wide range of media.

MAKING IT WORK

As I bring together Canadian novels and cultural narratology, I am interested in explaining the texts' dialogic dynamics and thinking through some of their tensions. As I think with, and at times against, Bakhtin, I hope to show that dialogism is a useful critical tool for reading resistance literature. It is by no means the only one. Once one becomes attached to a particular critical approach, it can be difficult to look at the world in any other way. And for a long time now I have seen the world in terms of dialogism. In its specific theoretical focus then, this study cannot completely escape the colonizing gestures of critical theory;[27] however, I expect that my readings will prompt other critics to expand and challenge them, which is to say to engage them dialogically.

While *Challenging Canada* deals with English Canadian novels exclusively, it does not attempt to write a literary history, nor does it aim to present a homogeneous picture of contemporary Canadian fiction or Canadian society. The number and kinds of novels discussed do not warrant either ambition. No teleological model of Canada's maturation as reflected in its literature informs the following discussions. No central unifying theme will emerge that could replace those of the garrison, the mosaic, or the New World, to name only a few. What I hope to illustrate is that the framework of dialogism and cultural narratology allows me to articulate my understanding of these novels as resistance literature. My readings pay close attention to narrative techniques but show that they are most productively read within specific cultural contexts. These contexts are dynamic; consequently, I see my readings not as an act of containment but as a project of exploration.

The corpus is admittedly eclectic and open to the charge of arbitrariness. The seven novels were not selected because they are the most polyphonic contemporary Canadian fiction, because they are the "best" novels written in Canada in the last twenty years, or because they are all proven bestsellers. Actually, I ended up with some very popular (and now critically acclaimed) novels, such as Joy Kogawa's *Obasan*, which is taught in high school and university courses, as well as lesser-known, albeit award-winning, texts such as Margaret Sweatman's *Fox,* which merits more critical attention than it has received to date. Finally, the order in which I discuss the novels is not supposed to suggest a notion of linear progression or increasing excellence. The discussions in each chapter take different directions; at times they overlap and support each other, at other times they may seem contradictory.

One last word of caution. When we assert the existence of resistance literature, it is also important to examine closely and self-reflexively how we read and disseminate such texts (Mohanty 1991). In the process of working on and reworking this book, I have been reminded many times (most often when I have taught the novels under discussion) that reading and analyzing literature are subjective undertakings. My own readings are influenced by various shifting configurations within which I am situated in Canada – configurations determined by citizenship, language, age, race, class, and so on. At times "a deceptive insider," at other times "a deceptive outsider" to borrow Trinh T. Minh-ha's terms (1991, 74), I have watched myself shift back and forth between positions available to me, less concerned with determining once and for all where exactly I belong than with exploring everything I can be – on different occasions and in different places. As Smaro Kamboureli (2000, 22) observes in her musings on the hybridity of the diasporic critic, the "objective is ... to produce a space where her hybridity is articulated in a manner that does not cancel out any of its particularities." For me, this space is less an in-betweenness than the simultaneity of all possible insider/outsider positions. While I am wary taking self-positioning as a guarantee of authenticity (of both oneself and one's readings), it remains crucial in self-reflexive analyses that focus on narrative techniques and that recognize the importance of readers' decisions and their cultural contexts with regard to reading for dialogic relations. Self-positioning also remains an important pedagogical concern for classroom interaction.

In Chapter 2 I prepare the ground for the following readings. I introduce some of Bakhtin's crucial ideas about dialogism, situating my own approach within a selective overview of recent Bakhtin criticism. Struggle and conflict form the basis for my understanding of dialogic relations because I recognize that discourses always operate within relations of power. As a result, I am interested in an analysis of dialogic relations not only in order to describe the heterogeneity of voices but also in order to explore how the actual relations between them can expose dominant discourses and challenge them from positions of difference.

Chapters 3 to 6 explore the framework of dialogism and cultural narratology in relation to specific Canadian novels. In Chapter 3 I discuss the processes involved in telling and writing family history in Joy Kogawa's *Obasan* and Sky Lee's *Disappearing Moon Cafe*. The dialogic relations in these novels foreground the epistemological questions involved in rewriting history, and they emphasize its open-endedness. I argue that, in spite of their similarities, these novels employ dialogism to different ends: one is ultimately most interested in getting history right while the other simultaneously affirms and challenges individual and community history. Chapter 4 focuses on the processes of un/reading in Aritha van Herk's *Places Far from Ellesmere* and Daphne Marlatt's *Ana Historic*. The novels challenge the monologism of fixed categories and hegemonic discourses by recontextualizing them and offering alternative constructions. Dialogic relations operate, for example, at the level of genre conventions, in the interrelations of chronotopes and narrative strands, and in the quotation of documents. I am particularly interested in questioning the novels' gestures of strategic monologism within their polyphonic narratives. In Chapter 5 I analyze the contestatory textual politics in Jeannette Armstrong's *Slash* and Thomas King's *Green Grass, Running Water*. Through dialogic interaction among and within perspectives, and through a relational approach to oral storytelling and written narrative, both novels critique the false binary choices offered to Aboriginal peoples and inscribe a third position of self-determination. Margaret Sweatman's *Fox* provides the focus for Chapter 6, in which I examine how the performative operates as a counter-hegemonic strategy. Through the collage of voices that have been forgotten or obscured in traditional historiography, and through a recontextualization of familiar voices, *Fox* opens up sites for intervention and re-stages the Winnipeg General Strike of 1919. In Chapter 7 I conclude by suggesting additional novels that could expand the scope of this study, by raising previously unasked questions, and by indicating directions for further research within the methodological framework of dialogism and cultural narratology.

2 Dialogism: Yesterday's "Fave Rave" or Opportunity for Critical Intervention?

To say that Mikhail M. Bakhtin's writings have become popular in contemporary Western academic discourse over the last two decades is both a considerable understatement and an obvious simplification.[1] When Ken Hirschkop (1989a, 195) compiled his initial bibliography of critical literature on Bakhtin in 1989, he claimed – and possibly feared – that the Bakhtin snowball was about to turn into an avalanche. During the 1980s and early 1990s the interest in Bakhtin's work certainly took on remarkable proportions, a scenario that has variously being described as the "cult of Bakhtin," "a Bakhtin fad," or "the Baxtin industry" (Said in Williams 1989, 181; Malcuzynski 1990, 84; Morson 1986, 81). Now, at the beginning of another decade, we can confirm that we have moved beyond waxing stars and new fads. Bakhtinian criticism continues to thrive: from conference presentations to dissertations and literary journals (especially *Dialogism*), scholars raise new questions of familiar texts, edit previously unpublished material, and move Bakhtin's work into new contexts.

Appreciative characterizations of Bakhtin's ideas frequently include the adjectives "flexible," "suggestive," "ambitious," "ambiguous," and "generous." Such praise is not limited to studies in one single discipline; Bakhtin's concepts have created interest across many traditional disciplinary boundaries and figure in numerous interdisciplinary studies, such as literary criticism, linguistics, philosophy, psychology, ethnography, film studies, cultural studies, women's studies, and music.[2] Even within specific fields, the diversity of approaches is extremely broad. Within English studies, for instance,

Bakhtinian approaches have been used to analyze Gothic fiction (Howard 1994), contemporary drama (Keyssar 1991; Harvie and Knowles 1994), Victorian novels (Garrett 1980; Clark-Beattie 1985; W.V. Harris 1990; Shumway 1994), Victorian biography (Amigoni 1993), Medieval literature (Farrell 1995), the Classics (Branham 2001), Black women writers (Henderson 1989; Andrade 1990), poetry (M. Davidson 1983; Richter 1990), parody (Hutcheon 1989; Kuester 1992), and texts as diverse as the Bible (Reed 1993) and novels by James Joyce (Kershner 1989), Malcolm Lowry (Grace 1990), Leslie Marmon Silko (Krupat 1989), and Christa Wolf (Herrmann 1989). In these discussions, many labels have been attached to Bakhtin: he has been called a formalist, a semiotician, a Marxist, a neo-Kantian, a structuralist, and a postmodernist. A number of critics, such as Paul de Man (1983) and Robert Young (1985/86), early on expressed their dismay about Bakhtin's apparently unlimited applicability, while others have examined critically but enthusiastically the reasons for his remarkable popularity.

Any definitive label, however, seems to contradict Bakhtin's (1986, 155, 170) own belief in the open-endedness of all critical work, including his own, as well as his suspicion of "theoretism," that is, any method that considers systems in which every element has a place in a rigorous hierarchy as the only valuable form of knowledge (Morson and Emerson 1990, 27–8). As a result, Bakhtin (1986, 169–70) was critical of structuralist projects. A narratology that does not include a diachronic perspective and focuses on self-enclosed systems at the expense of context would exemplify the totalitarian assumptions he criticized. The sheer number of Bakhtin's writings and their often contradictory nature resist generalization, but critics have used labels to contain the heterogeneity of his ideas, to simplify his discourse, and, at least temporarily, to ease their own discomfort with its open-endedness and conceptual slipperiness.

In this book, I engage critically with Bakhtin's concept of dialogism in order to develop a politicized Bakhtinian approach to Canadian fiction. In participating in the circulation of Bakhtin's concepts, I do not wish to partake in "uncritical hero worship" or to perform "mechanical applications" of Bakhtin's ideas (Morson and Emerson 1989, 49). While something as fashionable in contemporary literary criticism as dialogism may trigger fears and warnings of superficial readings or careless appropriation – after all, Hitchcock has not warned us of dialogism as the "fave rave of the culturati" for nothing (1993, xii)[3] – I want to show that dialogism can be a valuable means for developing a cultural-narratological approach to Canadian fiction. Given the extensive critical work that Bakhtin's writings have elicited, it is tempting to read critics explaining or commenting on Bakhtin rather than to read Bakhtin's own work. Engaging with his long, repetitive, and often contradictory essays can be fascinating but also very discouraging. How much easier it is to go to a book about Bakhtin that neatly summarizes and categorizes his crucial ideas. While I think it is important to get some first-hand experience of Bakhtin's writings, I am not suggesting that the reader can thus find a way of returning to the original Bakhtin. As White (1987/88, 218–19) has said in his reply to Young's attack on Bakhtin criticism: "There is no repetition, no retreat, no anachronism, in short there is no going *back* to 'Bakhtin.' 'Bakhtin' *was not* in the forms in which he now is ... It is not we who return to 'Bakhtin.' It is 'Bakhtin' who now finds meaning amongst us." To emphasize the fact that his "Bakhtin" is an appropriated version and to resist the illusion of a close, unproblematic familiarity with "Bakhtin," White explains that he uses the single quotation marks "to signal his ['Bakhtin's'] alienation from and dismemberment in the current conflict of possession" (221). With this caveat in place, a familiarity with Bakhtin's works nevertheless provides important common ground for further discussion and enables both the reader and me to recognize my own as well as other critics' vested interests in engaging with Bakhtin.[4]

Bakhtin never actually used the word "dialogism" in his writings (Holquist 1990, 15). As I use and problematize the term "dialogism," I try to capture Bakhtin's wide-ranging thoughts on the topic of dialogic relations without draining the concept of its processual and unfinalizable nature. Initially, Bakhtin discussed dialogic relations in the context of Dostoevsky's novels, but he later expanded the concept to grapple with the novel as a genre, with language, epistemology, and even ontology. The main sources for Bakhtin's reflections on dialogism are *Problems of Dostoevsky's Poetics* (1984a), first published 1972 as the revised edition of the earlier *Problems of Dostoevsky's Creative Works* (1929); "Discourse in the Novel," originally published in 1975, in *The Dialogic Imagination* (1981); and "The Problem of the Text," first published in 1979, from *Speech Genres and Other Late Essays* (1986).[5]

Bakhtin (1981, 288) uses the term "heteroglossia" to indicate that language is always multilayered, stratified, and never unitary:

Actual social life and historical becoming create within an abstractly unitary national language a multitude of concrete worlds, a multitude of bounded verbal-ideological and social belief systems; within these various systems (identical in the abstract) are elements of language filled with various semantic and axiological content and each with its own different sound.

These languages develop out of the tension of conflicting centripetal and centrifugal forces in society: "alongside the centripetal forces, the centrifugal forces of language carry on their uninterrupted work; alongside verbal-ideological centralization and unification, the uninterrupted processes of decentralization and disunification go forward" (272). As Bakhtin explains, because languages develop out of these processes, they cannot be considered a neutral medium (294). On the microlevel, Bakhtin concludes that every single word is inherently dialogic; that is, "it is entangled, shot through with shared thoughts, points of view, alien value judgments and accents" (276). To use a word and make it our own, we have to appropriate it from someone else's discourse.

From this perspective, languages, even single words, are specific views of the world, ways of conceptualizing the world in words (291–2). It is as world views that these "'languages' of heteroglossia" enter the novel (291).[6] When Bakhtin describes the novel as "a microcosm of heteroglossia" (411), he makes explicit the connection between the social world of heteroglossia and its artistic representation in the novel.[7] The processes of language unification and decentralization reflected in the novel cannot be separated from the ongoing social and ideological struggle in society.[8] However, although the novel "orchestrates all its themes, the totality of the world of objects and ideas depicted and expressed in it" through heteroglossia (263), this mixing of languages is neither arbitrary nor unsystematic. Bakhtin insists repeatedly that the goal of the novelistic process is the creation of an "*artistic image of a language*," to be achieved through artistic consistency and careful organization (366). Bakhtin explains further that "the image of such a language in a novel is the image assumed by a set of social beliefs, the image of a social ideologeme that has fused with its own discourse, with its own language ... In the novel formal markers of languages, manners and styles are symbols for sets of social beliefs" (357). Heteroglossia can thus enter the novel in two ways: in the form of subjects and their languages and thus as a means of internal orchestration, or, if the novel seems to know only one language and style, as "dialogizing background," against which the world of the novel is set and which reminds the writer that the unitary language of the novel is neither self-evident nor incontestable (332).

To illustrate his notion of multiple languages and numerous voices within the novel, Bakhtin introduces the concept of "polyphony." He draws attention to the fact that he is employing an analogy between music and the novel: "We are transforming this metaphor [of polyphony and counterpoint] into the term 'polyphonic novel,' since we have not found a more appropriate label. It should not be forgotten, however, that the term has its origin in metaphor" (Bakhtin 1984a, 22). The voices (6), subjects (7), ideological positions (18), or consciousnesses (6), as Bakhtin variously refers to them, are characterized as "independent," "unmerged," "fully valid," "equally authoritative," "with equal rights," and "autonomous" (6, 7, 8).[9] Although Bakhtin emphasizes that the material brought together in the novel is heterogeneous, he insists that an element of similarity is also required to bring these voices into contact. He sees this crucial similarity in their dimension as specific views of the world (1981, 292–3). However, polyphony is not only a way of describing the existence of multiple voices. Bakhtin's pivotal interest in polyphony lies in using it to explore how these voices interact. Dialogism is the organizational principle governing how these voices coexist and interrelate:

The polyphonic novel is dialogic through and through. Dialogic relationships exist among all elements of novelistic structure; that is, they are juxtaposed contrapuntally. And this is so because dialogic relationships are a much broader phenomenon than mere rejoinders in a dialogue, laid out compositionally in the text; they are an almost universal phenomenon, permeating all human speech and all relationships and manifestations of human life – in general, everything that has meaning and significance. (1984a, 40)

Dialogic relationships, then, are possible not only among utterances or single words but also between language styles and social dialects – as long as they represent semantic positions or world views of speaking subjects (1984a, 184; 1986, 116). Dialogic relations cannot be understood in purely logical, linguistic, or psychological terms; rather, they manifest specific kinds of semantic relationships (1986, 118, 124). Such relationships cannot be established with things or objects; only voices, subjects, "*integral* positions," can engage in dialogue (138, 121). Because dialogic relations indicate semantic bonds, their analysis is not possible within traditional linguistics, by which Bakhtin means, especially, the work of Saussure and those influenced by him. Dialogic relations are the subject of a "metalinguistics" that deals with the realm of discourse, language in dialogical interaction, language in living totality (1984a, 181–3, 202). Some critics have followed Clark and Holquist (1984, 10) and Todorov (1984, 24) in calling this kind of linguistics "translinguistics" because "the term *meta-* has become so banal in the West" (Clark and Holquist 1984, 10). We may be more familiar today with the terms "pragmatics" and "social discourse analysis."

What kinds of interaction can actually take place between these voices? They may agree dialogically, modify, supplement, polemicize, parody, or contradict each other; but in all cases, they come into contact, which will not allow them to re-emerge unaffected (Bakhtin 1984a, 189). Such dialogic interaction obviously does not aim for resolution of differences in a dialectical synthesis because difference remains crucial for dialogic relations. Dialogism has no teleology and is not a problem that needs to be solved; it is not about winning battles or merely tolerating the conflict with other voices. Dialogic relations are actually constituted by struggle and open-endedness.

The value of meaningful dialogue as negotiated exchange is crucial for Bakhtin not only in his analysis of polyphony in the novel but also in his view of the world. Bakhtin (1984a, 69) rejects both relativism and dogmatism as either unnecessary or impossible positions and seeks instead a position that allows for a sense of moral responsibility. Ethical questions were at the forefront of his early writings in the 1920s, which have been published in *Art and Answerability* (1990) and *Toward a Philosophy of the Act* (1993); after his work on the development of the novel, especially on Dostoevsky and Rabelais, he returned to similar themes in his later essays (1986). Although these early and late phases of his writings have so far played only a limited role in critical studies, I believe that they can serve as a reminder of the crucial role of ethics in Bakhtin's work.

Needless to say, I must acknowledge, with Hirschkop (1989b, 3), that a term such as dialogism is itself dialogical. The meaning of this key term is constantly being negotiated, appropriated, and rewritten by critics in concrete socio-historical circumstances, just as it is within Bakhtin's own discourse. Where does that leave the critics? What do they make of the fact that dialogism, for Bakhtin, not only describes the nature of language but is also the principle of discourse and the universal axiom of human life? After all, Bakhtin (1984a, 252) explains that "to be means to communicate dialogically. When dialogue ends, everything ends. Thus dialogue, by its very essence, cannot and must not come to an end" (1984a, 252). If this is so, then how can dialogism function as a useful *differentia specifica* of novelistic discourse as well as an oppositional strategy in the fight against ideological unification in language and novelistic discourse? How can it be a useful category in the analysis of the novel if any utterance is already inherently dialogic? Cannot all novels consequently be called dialogic? I will engage with some of these issues as I proceed. For now, suffice it to say that dialogism is not as easily accessible a concept as some would have us believe: "There are no easy prescriptions for interpretation or quick fixes to be found in dialogism. It is no theoretical steroid" (Holquist 1990, 107). In my own appropriation of dialogism, I follow the lead of critics who have challenged Bakhtin's problematic all-encompassing notion of dialogism, rejecting it as a kind of master trope and, rather, exploring what Bakhtin left unsaid and undertheorized. Here I concur in particular with Bernstein's (1989, 199) approach: "Dialogism must be tested, not merely lauded. It must, by its very definition, be brought into our contentions as a participant without any guarantee or privilege, rather than as a kind of ultimate Court of Assizes under whose jurisdiction the debate proceeds and according to whose criteria the worthiness of the enterprise will be determined."

For such critical readers, liberal appropriations of Bakhtin's concepts, which often provide readings using Bakhtinian concepts but leave the ideas themselves unchallenged, are disconcerting.[10] Liberal versions of dialogism have emphasized notions of exchange, negotiation, agreement, and tolerance, focusing almost exclusively on the bright side of dialogism. A plurality of voices is envisioned as several well intentioned, equal partners experiencing peaceful, harmonious encounters. Terry Eagleton's (1989, 188) polemics expose, albeit in an exaggerated manner, the shallowness of liberal readings of Bakhtin: "It is very hard to believe that Bakhtin spilt so much ink just to inform us that we should listen attentively to one another, treat each other as whole persons, be prepared to be corrected and interrupted, realise that life is an endless unfinished process, that too much dogma makes you narrow-minded, that nobody has a monopoly of [sic] the truth and that life is so much richer than any of our little ideas about it." Critics of liberal Bakhtinian appropriations remind readers that power dynamics inform society and novelistic discourse at every level but that liberal readings are less interested in addressing inequalities and oppression than in securing the status quo of the ruling classes. It is important to remember that Bakhtin experienced authoritarian rule and marginalization within a historical context in which he was confronted with bleak and hostile social realities; what we know about his experiences of exile, imprisonment, and silencing sits uncomfortably with a liberal belief in individual freedom.

In Ann Jefferson's (1986, 174) words, critics need to take into account that dialogism is based on a "definition of discourse in relation to power itself." The struggle for power fuels the energies of both centrifugal and centripetal forces. Therefore, neither social context nor novelistic discourse can offer neutral playing fields. Consequently, subject positions in dialogic relations are inscribed along a vertical social axis so that dialogism inevitably operates with implicit principles of domination and subordination.[11] Seen in this light, dialogism describes more than friendly, mutually enriching encounters between different but equal voices. If discourse and power are indivisible, then narratives themselves are sites of social struggles, power struggles. However, while Bakhtin does not uphold pseudo-equality, neither does he explore the aspect of struggle in any detail.[12] Feminist criticism engaging with Bakhtin has drawn attention to the absence of struggle as Bakhtin's "blind spot" (Bauer 1988, 5).[13] The space in which the encounter, the struggle, the clash of voices takes place is hardly positive or neutral. It is contested ground that is at least ambivalent if not hostile.[14]

If we make explicit the connection between dialogic relations and power dynamics, then dialogism in a novel (and the criticism that discusses it) can help to explore how hegemonies are organized historically and to expose such dominant discourses in narratives; it can also function as a form of cultural critique that makes visible the social heterogeneity of voices and indicates potential resistance to dominant structures. Because, by calling attention to oppressive hierarchies of power, dialogism can become a strategy for combatting monologism, many critics believe that Bakhtin's categories are, in Robert Stam's (1989, 21) words, "especially appropriate for the analysis of opposition and marginal practices." Obviously, Bakhtin did not address himself to all forms of oppression, but he staked out a conceptual space for doing so. Feminists working with Bakhtin's concepts have been particularly interested, and successful, in exploring the space for oppositional practices.[15] Where Bakhtin seems to have missed or neglected the notion of masculine hegemony within social structures, feminist critics have intervened to explore whether and how dialogism can become a strategy to deprivilege and disclose the hegemony of patriarchal discursive practices and other oppressive ideologies, such as racism, (neo)colonialism, ethnocentrism, Eurocentrism, heterosexism, and classism.[16]

Unfortunately, very few critics working with the dialogic principle have acknowledged not only that "those in power do not usually engage in dialogue with those they oppress" (Mukherjee 1995a, 233) but also that it is probable (and often enough the reality) that the dominant voice will continue to dominate in spite of its willingness to engage in dialogue with oppositional voices. Yet this recognition seems crucial. In narratological terms, the relation between character(s) and narrator(s) is especially important here. While a character may serve as focalizer and so provide much of the information about his/her marginal perspective, the perspective of the narrator can easily domesticate that resistant perspective. The marginal voice can be included and heard, yet it may ultimately be appropriated or subordinated and dismissed. A critical understanding of dialogic relations needs to be suspicious of, and prepared to expose, strategies of domestication, absorption, and cultural normalization.

These challenges to Bakhtin's work suggest that we need to pay more attention to the implications and realities of conflict, contestation, and aggression when we explore dialogic relations. Emerson (1988, 514), for instance, finds Bakhtin's presumption of benevolence underlying all dialogic relations to be one of the most troubling aspects of his work.[17] More substantially, Gardiner (1992, 176) has noted Bakhtin's failure to grasp the realities of power structures and has consequently challenged his optimism about liberating struggles. One of the most provocative criticisms has come from Fogel (1989, 174), who has suggested that most dialogue is constrained and forced. If all initiation of dialogue takes the form of coerced speech, then disproportion and violence have to be recognized as constitutive of dialogue rather than as a perversion of it (179). To see dialogue primarily as a mode of conquest (Fogel 1985, 1989; Rabasa 1987, 147), however, questions Bakhtin's notions of friendly boundaries and encounters. As Morson and Emerson (1990, 470) point out, for Bakhtin the worst that the other in a dialogue can do is to fail to answer. As a result, Bakhtin's discussions of dialogic relations generally lack any mention of suffering, torture, or violence.[18] It must be noted, however, that these elements play a significant role in *Rabelais and His World* (1984b) – only to be banished again. Bakhtin seems to ignore the danger of carnivalistic violence because he is fascinated with the notion of a violence without pain. He is not so much concerned with the individual body or experience; rather, individuals are subsumed into the collective body of the people. Moreover, Bakhtin's indifference to dialogue in his study of Rabelais supports his problematic view of violence and makes it less relevant for my exploration of dialogic relations. His discussion of carnivalization and laughter in his revised book on Dostoevsky, which was written after the book on Rabelais, differs significantly from the latter. Both carnival and laughter are recharacterized here in less destructive and more positive terms.

Can dialogue and dialogic relationships actually become counterproductive in struggles in which voices try to be heard? If dialogic interaction always implies the threat of violence, and if voices are frequently absorbed or domesticated in the process, then how can it be safe for any oppositional voice to engage in dialogue? M. Pollock (1993, 238) has drawn attention to the potential problems and dangers "when the weaker voice allows the stronger one into its space." Because the dynamics of dialogue do not protect weaker voices, it seems necessary for marginal voices to control the space into which they invite dominant ones, which at times may result in their use of other forms of communication or silence as languages of transgression. While silence is conspicuously absent from Bakhtin's writings, it eventually needs to be theorized in dialogic relations. Silence can obviously be coerced, a sign of oppression and exclusion, but it may also represent a choice and function as a form of transgression and strategic resistance (Hitchcock 1993, 204; Cheung 1993, 20) or as a "weapon of authoritarian discourse" (Wall 1989, 211). As a voice in itself, silence also draws attention to Bakhtin's exclusive focus on linguistic expression (Hirschkop 1989b, 18); however, even if they are not expressed in words, voices and world views can be expressed dialogically.

Taking Fogel's skeptical view of dialogism one step further, Bernstein (1989, 200; 1992) has asked whether dialogism is or should be a universal desideratum at all. Unlike Bakhtin, he suggests that sometimes voices may not lead to stimulating exchanges but may sound like "intolerable babble" or noise (221); the dialogic nature of discourse may be experienced as entrapment and damnation rather than as liberation (208, 222). Such a predicament may indeed lead to rage, resentment, and violence as a means of controlling the inescapable. Dialogism as the *cause* of violence is an unfamiliar notion in the context of Bakhtin's work and criticism, but this recognition in itself may indicate to what extent readers have internalized Bakhtin's positive sentiments concerning liberating and enriching dialogic relations without acknowledging the negative.

Discussing the potential relevance of Bakhtin's theories within the history of the English language, Tony Crowley (1989) similarly problematizes the binary opposition implicit in Bakhtin's work between authoritarian monoglossia and pluralist heteroglossia. According to Bakhtin, if we desire a democratic, decentred social structure, then we will necessarily operate by enhancing dialogism. Crowley, however, speculates that, in certain contexts, a preference for dialogism and heteroglossia could be politically regressive (83). Bakhtin does not problematize the possibility of such a temporary suspension of heteroglossia for potentially beneficial centralizing tendencies. Although he acknowledges the simultaneity of both unifying and decentring forces, he dismisses institutional forms of ideological unification and organization.

When we resist sentimentalizing dialogism and simplifying communication, we have to acknowledge that dialogism is not inherently beneficial or life-enhancing. No cultural practice is liberating or repressive per se; its political effect is always determined by the concrete socio-historical context in which it operates and the uses to which it is put by historical agents.[19] While dialogism always signifies struggle, it may be a force of cultural resistance as well as a means of conquest. Instead of equating dialogism in an essentializing manner with liberation and monologism with totalitarian rule – which locks them into a mutually exclusive binary opposition – I suggest they need to be treated as principles that only achieve liberating or repressive effects once they are embedded in specific historical contexts. I am able, then, to concede that ruling forces at times adopt dialogic forms and oppressed groups resort to what I think of as strategic monologism.[20] Dialogism cannot be the monopoly of the oppressed (Hitchcock 1993, 1), nor can it free oppressed people by itself. As a critical tool it can be used within emancipatory practices and thus contribute to a process of historical transformation.[21]

To understand dialogism as such a critical tool leaves ample methodological leeway. Critics have analyzed dialogic relations in terms of themes, points of view, plots, rhetoric, reader responses, intertextual quotations, structural elements, and genre conventions.[22] The wide range of application is not surprising because Bakhtin (1984a, 40) himself emphasizes that *all* elements of novelistic discourse are juxtaposed dialogically. However, it is probably the concept of "voice" that people most often associate with Bakhtin's work. In spite of how frequently critics speak of the "multiplicity of voices" or "conflicting voices" in texts, the term itself remains remarkably ambiguous. Bakhtin himself uses "voice" interchangeably with terms such as "language," "subject," or "consciousness." In his notes for reworking the Dostoevsky book, he turns to the definition of voice yet again: "This includes height, range, timbre, aesthetic category (lyric, dramatic, etc.). It also includes a person's worldview and fate. A person enters into dialogue as an integral voice. He participates in it not only with his thoughts, but with his fate and with his entire individuality" (293). Bakhtin's consideration of both content and stylistic features differs from attempts in narrative theory to delineate the concept more narrowly.

Genette's (1980) distinction between voice as connected with the question of "who speaks?" and mood (or perspective or point of view) as connected with the question of "who sees?" continues to be the starting point of many discussions and definitions of narrative voice. This is not the place to rehearse in detail the limitation of this understanding. In my ensuing discussion of Canadian novels I follow Richard Aczel (1998, 495) in thinking of voice as a textual effect, best understood as the product of the interaction of reader and the "rhetorical organization of their [the voices'] constituent elements." To discuss voice, we need to do more than answer the question of "who speaks?" Aczel insists on the importance of stylistic expression

– "tone, idiom, diction, speech-style" (469) – in other words, the question of *how* the speech of both narrators and characters is constituted in narratives.

Moreover, we can appreciate, but also clarify, Bakhtin's complex notion of voice by distinguishing voice and perspective. Rather than following Genette's equation of narration = voice, focalization = perspective, I will use the term "perspective" to emphasize content (namely, the particular angle from which the narrated world is presented, a particular ideological position, a world view in the text). Such a perspective may be that of a character or a narrator, or it can be constituted through inserted genres in a montage-like narrative. Voice, on the other hand, shifts the focus to the narrative techniques used to constitute that perspective. However, voice is only one element to consider in the reconstruction of perspectives; in addition to speech and inside views, a character's/narrator's actions, as well as commentary by the narrator and other characters, need to be considered. In the readings that follow, I will move between the terms perspective and voice to emphasize both content and techniques as I examine what kinds of perspectives engage in dialogic relations, how these relations operate, and through what narrative techniques they are actualized as voices in the texts.

It is not sufficient, however, to describe dialogic relations by accounting for individual perspectives in a narrative text. We can only describe their complex dialogical interrelations when we consider the internal make-up of each perspective as well as the perspective structure of the whole text.[23] Since dialogism is a relational phenomenon describing the interaction between perspectives, it cannot be located at isolated points in the text; it has to be actualized in the process of reading. The reader brings together these perspectives and extends "these distantly separate ideas by means of a dotted line to the point of their dialogic intersection" (Bakhtin 1984a, 91). Even if a single phrase or comment may be an indication of or means for the realization of dialogic potential – for example, a double-voiced phrase – dialogic relations between voices can only be (re)constructed from the text as a whole.[24] Mere alternation of heterogeneous perspectives, narrative fragmentation, or the simple clash of rival voices do not in themselves guarantee dialogic relations.[25] Dialogism, in Paul Thibault's (1984, 113) words, "has the potential for re-defining the relations among 'voices,' for re-defining the interpretation of previous 'voices,' or even the set of rules according to which the discourse is to be interpreted." However, only if the coexistence of ideological positions at the level of the text as a whole is dynamic and confrontational can we actually talk of dialogic relations.

Finally, let me identify the two central narrative strategies that can create dialogic relations between voices: the interplay of multiple perspectives and the internal dialogization of one perspective. In a text that uses multiple perspectives, different voices are placed side by side, which creates perspective refraction of the narrated world along a horizontal axis (McHale 1987, 170). However, a character's perspective is not necessarily homogeneous. Internal dialogism describes a single perspective that is experienced as a mosaic of competing ideological positions.[26] Dialogization here occurs along a vertical axis that refracts a single character's consciousness. Bakhtin (1984a, 220) pays close attention to these interior dialogues in his discussion of Dostoevsky; he describes them as a number of conflicting voices within the limits of one consciousness. Although such microdialogues, according to Bakhtin, do not yet qualify as polyphony because there is no dialogue between unmerged consciousnesses, neither are they homophonic (220–1).[27] These two strategies are in no way mutually exclusive: novels with multiple perspectives frequently show internally dialogized perspectives as well. Under conditions of such dialogic interaction, double-voiced discourse – discourse with a twofold direction – arises: "It serves two speakers at the same time and expresses simultaneously two different intentions ... In such discourse there are two voices, two meanings and two expressions. And all the while these two voices are dialogically interrelated" (Bakhtin 1981, 324). In his book on Dostoevsky, Bakhtin (1984a, 199; see also 1981, 324–7) introduces a classification of different types of such double-voicing, which includes quotation, reaccentuation, parody, stylization, hidden dialogue, and incorporated genres. I will introduce each type of discourse as it becomes relevant in my discussions.

Problematizing the concept of dialogism has led me to believe that it is indeed more than a "fave rave" of the academic establishment. If we recognize conflict and antagonism not as disturbance but as conditions of dialogical relations, then we can examine the complex interrelations between dialogism in novels and their social contexts in order to understand the formation both of hegemonies and of resistance to hegemonies. The resolution of dialogic struggle would put such a project at risk. As a methodological tool for the discussion of ideological signification in narrative structure, dialogism can open up opportunities for critical interventions.

3 Storying Family History: Joy Kogawa's *Obasan* and Sky Lee's *Disappearing Moon Cafe*

By telling family histories, Joy Kogawa's *Obasan* (1981) and Sky Lee's *Disappearing Moon Cafe* (1990) examine the relationships between their female protagonists – Naomi Nakane and Kae Ying Woo, respectively – and other family and community members as they attempt to place these characters within their historical, geographical, and social contexts. The telling of history is not a simple, transparent process in these novels, however, for it also involves creating, challenging, constructing, and reconstructing histories. The novels focus not merely on what constitutes the families' histories but also, through dialogic relations, on how their histories are constructed, told, and written. To talk about Kogawa's and Lee's novels as storying family history may at first seem tautological, but I want to draw attention to the processes, strategies, and ideological as well as epistemological implications of creating family history in these texts.

A focus on history, especially Canada's treatment of Japanese Canadians during the Second World War and the protagonist's relationship with that past, characterizes much of the ever-growing criticism that has appeared since the publication of *Obasan*. On 22 September 1988, Prime Minister Brian Mulroney announced the Redress Agreement, which was negotiated with the National Association of Japanese Canadians. The settlement acknowledged the injustices committed against Japanese Canadians during and after the Second World War, offered symbolic financial compensation to individuals and the community, and provided for some forms of non-monetary compensation, such as clearance of conviction records, citizenship applications for those

unjustly expelled and their heirs, and the establishment of the Canadian Race Relations Foundation (Miki and Kobayashi 1991, 138–9).
Many critics who have focused on the role of history in Kogawa's
Obasan and the novel's relation to history point out that it was instrumental in influencing the Canadian government's settlement with
Japanese Canadians.[1] These critics have discussed Kogawa's novel as
an attempt to write revisionist history, that is, to challenge the dominant version of Canadian history by complementing and modifying it
from the perspective of Japanese Canadians.[2] In recent years, recognizing the popularity of *Obasan* in literary criticism and on high school
and university course syllabi, Scott McFarlane (1995a), Roy Miki
(1998), and Guy Beaurgard (2002) have begun the important work of
questioning what is at stake in this increasing institutionalization of a
single text and its treatment of history and race relations.

An analysis of the narrative strategies in *Obasan* shows not only that
the novel is an attempt at revisionist history but also that it problematizes the ontological and epistemological status of history itself.[3]
Hutcheon (1988b, 105–23) uses the term "historiographic metafiction" to describe novels that use "dates" and "facts" of official historiography but that, at the same time, undermine their claim to objectivity and authority because they cannot be reconciled with the
individual experiences and perceptions of the characters in the texts.
Historiographic metafiction thus self-reflexively problematizes the
ability to know the reality of those facts and dates. I consider *Obasan*
as an example of historiographic metafiction and argue that dialogic
relationships between the different perspectives of what happened to
Japanese Canadians during and after the Second World War expose
Kogawa's central strategy in her attempt to question traditional concepts of history and to display an infinite process of constructing new
versions of the past. The dialogic relations of the novel, with its frequent formal disruptions, achieve what Miki (1998, 117) describes as
"relativiz[ing] the reader's performance and draw[ing] her out of the
subjective limits ... of the text where minority perceptions are encountered in what could be thought of as their foreignicity." In *Obasan*
these processes go beyond the suspension of valorized oppositions and
infinite regress; they assert the need for political commitment even if,
or maybe because, history is recognized to be a construction.[4] While
Kanefsky (1996, 11, 15, 31, 16) sees "historical scepticism" and
"antiessentialist implications" as part of "systems of ambiguity and
distortion" and claims that they are "alienating, silencing, and politically crippling" for Naomi, I argue that, on the contrary, epistemological skepticism and an understanding of history as constructed provide
opportunities for commitment and change in *Obasan*.

Naomi Nakane is the homodiegetic narrator[5] in *Obasan* who relates the events of three days in September 1972, when she returns to Granton after her uncle's death, and her childhood experiences during the Second World War. However, the novel is not limited to displaying the subjectivity of Naomi's perception and her perspective. Dialogic interaction is conveyed by means of two techniques. First, Naomi's perspective is internally dialogized as she anticipates other people's views and their reactions and, thus, creates a microdialogue in her mind (Bakhtin 1984a, 74–5). Her consciousness appears as a mosaic of competing individual and collective perspectives; everything she observes is drawn into dialogue so that everything is projected against her and dialogically reflected in her. Second, in a montage-like fashion, the novel incorporates other genres, such as official and private letters, diary entries, telegrams, newspaper articles, conference papers, and a memorandum. As Bakhtin (1981, 321) says of such incorporated genres, they have their "own verbal and semantic forms for assimilating various aspects of reality"; each document offers a different discourse on the same subject. As the narrator incorporates these texts, the novel creates, in Shirley Geok-lin Lim's (1989, 244) words, "a fiction of sociological documentation." While it co-opts the discourses of these documents, Naomi's own responses to these texts are as important to the reader as are the documents themselves. In fact, as Smaro Kamboureli (2000, 176) suggests, if the novel has any revolutionary potential, it lies in "the way Naomi's character operates as a montage – not a 'synthesis' – of different historical discourses."

To analyze the dialogic relationships in *Obasan*, I first want to reconstruct Naomi's perspective as she has created and maintained it since her childhood. Second, I want to have a closer look at the documents that have been incorporated and how they function within Naomi's narration. At the beginning of the novel, Naomi's view of her world presents a coherent picture to her: her life is primarily defined by her work as a teacher and her visits to her family – her aunt and uncle – in Granton. However, doubts about her social status as an unmarried woman and, as a result, feelings of inferiority impinge upon this seamless picture of herself. To Naomi, her single status must be her own fault, the result of her insecurity:

Megumi Naomi Nakane. Born June 18, 1936, Vancouver, British Columbia. Marital status: Old Maid. Health: Fine, I suppose. Occupation: School teacher. I'm bored to death with teaching and ready to retire. What else would anyone want to know? Personality: Tense. Is that past or present tense? It's perpetual tense. I have the social graces of a common housefly. That's self-denigrating, isn't it. (Kogawa 1981, 7)

What initially sounds like the bureaucratic discourse found on an official form, with name, birth date, and place, quickly turns into parody when Naomi chooses the pejorative phrase "old maid" to describe her marital status. Casualness ("I suppose") mixes with frankness ("I'm bored to death.") and exasperation ("What else would anyone want to know?"), followed by Naomi's cynical wit in her wordplay on "tense." Her use of parody, in Bakhtin's (1981, 41–83) early sense of the word, introduces "the corrective of laughter" that exposes the limitations of the "serious word." How could the personal information on a form capture Naomi's personality, her perspective? It cannot. Instead, Naomi, without discrediting the attempt, lets the reader glimpse "beneath these categories a different and contradictory reality that is otherwise not captured in them" (59). The parodic distance she creates helps Naomi to protect the areas of her life that seem uncertain to her. Her childhood memories during and after the war, especially the unexplained absence of her mother (who never returned from a visit to Japan after the bombing of Pearl Harbor), are part of this uncertainty. When, as a child, Naomi tries to get answers to her questions about her mother, Obasan remains silent (Kogawa 1981, 26). Naomi's frustration over not knowing finally makes her imitate Obasan's seemingly successful manner. She believes, with Obasan, that silence is better than speech: "Some memories, too, might better be forgotten. Didn't Obasan once say, 'It is better to forget'?" (45). However, Naomi's nightmares, her memories of Old Man Gower's abuse, and her feelings of guilt about her mother's absence indicate that her silence leaves events and emotions unresolved.

The most important voice in Naomi's internal dialogue is that of Aunt Emily, who is an anti-racist activist living in Toronto. On her visits to Granton, she tries to show Naomi the necessity of a different way of life and a different way of dealing with the past; she challenges the attitudes that are at the basis of the static society in which Naomi lives. Aunt Emily is mostly interested in the injustices that the Japanese Canadians had to endure during the Second World War; she demands that these injustices be exposed and compensated. Emily's memories of the war differ significantly from the official versions of the past. She points out to Naomi that Japanese Canadians were dislocated from their positions of identity as Canadians because they were not recognized as Canadians and were thus denied their civil rights (33, 40; Jones 1990, 217–18). With the Order in Council PC 1486, passed on 25 February 1942, the minister of justice was given the power to remove all persons from a designated protected zone; however, this power was applied to only one group: "all persons of Japanese racial origin" (quoted in Miki and Kobayashi 1991, 23–4). The War

Measures Act legalized these racist government actions. Japanese Canadians were made into outcasts in their own country. No longer was their status based on citizenship or their birthplace; their racial background was inscribed as the marked position in an oppositional structure. They were made into "ethnic others," "enemy aliens" (24).

Naomi's ideal of silence is incompatible with Emily's way of thinking. Naomi listens to Emily's explanations without interest: "the very last thing in the world I was interested in talking about was our experiences during and after World War II" (Kogawa 1981, 33). One of her strategies to protect herself from Emily's influence is a critical parodic distance similar to the kind she applies to herself:

Dear Aunt Em is crusading still. In seven canonical words, she exhorts, cajoles, commands someone – herself? me? – to carry on the fight, to be a credit to the family, to strive onwards to the goal. She's the one with the vision ... Obasan's language remains deeply underground but Aunt Emily, BA, MA, is a word warrior. She's a crusader, a little old grey-haired Mighty Mouse, a Bachelor of Advanced Activists and General Practitioner of Just Causes. (31–2)

Naomi's attitude is ambivalent. Her doubts about the efficacy of Emily's attitudes and problem-solving strategies are mixed with a certain fear of her Aunt – "I never quite know when she'll explode" (34) – and her awareness that she is choosing the monologic way of resistance instead of confrontation. Naomi's refusal to confront other perspectives becomes obvious in her evaluation of the documents that Emily shows her after a conference visit earlier the same year, and which Naomi regards as proofs of an unchangeable past: "Crimes of history, I thought to myself, can stay in history. What we need is to concern ourselves with the injustices of today" (41). It is only when Naomi finds the collected documents in a parcel that Emily sent to her at Obasan's house that she becomes interested and curious enough to engage with them: "But on my lap, her papers are wind and fuel nudging my early morning thoughts to flame" (32). A photograph of herself and her mother, given to her by Obasan, starts the process of dialogic interaction in her mind (46). For the first time, Naomi is willing to accept the pain of memory in order to revive her feelings for her mother. She anticipates Emily's reaction to her hesitation in order to break down her own resistance:

The house in which we live is in Marpole ... It does not bear remembering. None of this bears remembering.

"You have to remember," Aunt Emily said. "You are your history. If you cut any of it off you're an amputee. Don't deny the past." ...

All right, Aunt Emily, all right! The house then – the house, if I must remember it today, was large and beautiful. (49–50)

The painful memory of her mother destroys the coherence of her perspective on the past, which Naomi has so skilfully constructed through her silence. She begins to realize that her memories are only "fragments of fragments" and "segments of stories" that need to be connected to each other (53).

Once the photo has triggered her engagement, Naomi is at least willing to look at Emily's diary, which is quoted in the novel the way Naomi found it among Emily's documents (80–110). Here the montage of the diary functions as a commentary because Emily's homodiegetic diary narration presents information about the internment and her own evacuation to which Naomi did not have prior access. It supplies explanations for some of Naomi's worries while creating others. Naomi does not explicitly comment on the diary and its effects on her, but she continues her own narrative of past events where Emily's narration ends. The reader may get the impression that the document has been cited without distortion. However, as Meir Sternberg (1982, 145) has explained, "Whatever the units involved, to quote is to mediate, to mediate is to frame, and to frame is to interfere and exploit." The reader has to remember that the moment the diary is incorporated into Naomi's story it is mediated and necessarily includes something new, namely, Naomi's understanding and evaluation of it as she incorporates it into her "story." As a result, the apparently unconnected texts develop diverse interactive relationships. Tension arises from Emily's original intention to address her diary to her sister, which can be considered the original external context of this text, while Naomi, on the other hand, uses the diary in the novel with explanatory and complementary intentions. In the new frame of Naomi's story, Emily's diary becomes double-voiced because it serves two speakers at the same time. Its inclusion in the novel introduces a new voice into Naomi's narrative, thereby stratifying the unity of the novel and intensifying its diversity of voices.

Two letters from the "Department of Labour, British Columbia Security Commission" (Kogawa 1981, 173), which explain the disappearance of Naomi's father and uncle and the departure of the rest of the family from Slocan, can also be analyzed as having commentary functions. When these letters were sent as orders carrying out the Order in Council, they enforced the eastward movement of Japanese Canadians. But while the letters are analeptic in the chronological sequence of the story (i.e., they explain past events), they are redirected to Naomi and repronounced as part of her narration (Jones 1990,

222): "The orders, given to Uncle and Father in 1945, reach me via Aunt Emily's package in 1972, twenty-seven years later. The delivery service is slow these days. Understanding is even slower" (Kogawa 1981, 172–3). Although these documents comment and explain the chronological and causal structure of the story, Naomi also exposes the contextual nature of such documentary evidence by redirecting and defamiliarizing it.

Let me turn to another type of incorporated genre. The newspaper clippings that Naomi finds in Emily's package report the departure of Japanese Canadians under "Canada's Japanese Repatriation Plan" (184–5); they function as a contrastive montage because here two or more passages are put side by side to clarify or expose each other. First, the articles that talk about the happy return of the Japanese to their homeland are contrasted with a telegram from a missionary in Slocan to Mackenzie King. In this telegram the return is qualified as a forced measurement of government politics and is described as "the cruellest cut of all," "expensive, inhuman and absolutely unnecessary" (184). However, the dialogic relations themselves have to be activated by the reader since Naomi does not explicitly explore the contrast. At this point, Naomi is not yet willing to deal with these documents as proof of a collective enforcement that has influenced her view of the past. Newspaper descriptions are still left intact and are viewed as factual accounts of reality. Naomi is as yet incapable of explicitly challenging these constructs of reality as particular readings of events.

The climax of her confrontation with the official documents is found in Chapter 29, when Naomi comes across an article describing the situation of deported field workers, which Emily has marked with an index card upon which is written: "Facts about evacuees in Alberta" (193). The article praises the Japanese Canadian workers as they are considered responsible for an increase in the production figures for Alberta's sugar beet fields. Naomi's first reaction reads as follows: "Facts about evacuees in Alberta? The fact is I never got used to it and I cannot, I cannot bear the memory" (194). The question itself is already a technique that signals the dialogic interaction that Naomi explores between her viewpoint and the one presented in the article. Not only does she repeat the words from the index card to reinforce its statement, but she also modifies the quote by turning it into a question. Naomi's own memories of her time on Mr Barker's farm reflect less the economic success than the difficult living conditions with which her family had to cope. Naomi quite explicitly resists the article's claim to truthfulness and its underlying collective reality model. Naomi shows in this contrastive montage that the facts of the article do not correspond with her own perspective: "'Grinning and happy' and all smiles standing around a pile of beets? That is one telling. It's not how it was" (197). Re-citing the caption, she begins to understand that such "facts" cannot be accounted for by the opposition of right versus wrong because they are always dependent on the observer's viewpoint, which is embedded within a historical context. From this point on, as Vautier (1998, 194) points out, "Naomi gradually takes over her aunt's expository function" as she integrates other documents into her own telling of her and her community's experience.

Naomi's attempt to create and maintain an alternative viewpoint on her own experience is mixed with her inner conflict about whether the ensuing pain would be worth the effort. The imagined conversation with Emily displays her conflict as the pressure and counter-pressure of remembering speech and forgetting silence:

Aunt Emily, are you a surgeon cutting at my scalp with your folders and your filing cards and your insistence on knowing all? The memory drains down the sides of my face, but it isn't enough, is it? It's your hands in my abdomen, pulling the growth from the lining of my walls, but bring back the anaesthetist turn on the ether clamp down the gas mask bring on the chloroform when will this operation be over Aunt Em?
  Is it so bad?
  Yes.
  Do I really mind?
  Yes, I mind, I mind everything. (Kogawa 1981, 194)

The coercion to speak, through the imaginary surgery Emily performs on Naomi, may be well intended on Emily's part and seen as necessary (Rose 1988, 223). But, as King-Kok Cheung (1993, 161) has rightfully pointed out, "read against the dream of the Grand Inquisitor, Naomi's pain suggests that even Emily's method may fall short." Emily may be guilty of not paying attention to Naomi's needs and inner speech. In addition, Naomi's resistance may already imply that she is suspicious of Emily's "unproblematized notion of Canada as a democracy" (Kamboureli 2000, 188). It does not come as a surprise that Naomi finally breaks her silence not in a face-to-face encounter with Emily but through her imagined dialogues.

In spite of her still existing doubts about the usefulness of the confrontation requested by Emily, Naomi's response to the condolence visit of Mr Barker, the family's former employer and landlord, shows how critical and self-confident she has become (Kogawa 1981, 221–6). For Naomi, his concern for their well-being comes too late, and the concern itself is patronizing: "'It was a terrible business what we did to our Japanese,' Mr Barker says. Ah, here we go again. 'Our Indians.' 'Our Japanese.' ... The comments are so incessant and always so well-intentioned" (225). Naomi's response indicates how much she resents the suggestion of being an outcast – in 1972 as well as in 1945. She refuses to accept Mr Barker's acknowledgment of past injury because his words reveal that he still sees Japanese Canadians as others – others that can be owned but that remain excluded from a Canadian "we." Naomi realizes that, if the record is to be set straight, if Japanese Canadians are to be recognized as Canadians, then they have to take action themselves. Her reflections on Mr Barker's visit end with her answering back to many of those insulting questions asked of Japanese Canadians: "Where do any of us come from in this cold country?" (226). And her response reaccentuates and thereby reclaims the "we" that Mr Barker so skilfully reserves for the white, Anglo majority. Naomi's response becomes a proclamation of the collective identity of Japanese Canadians:

Oh Canada, whether it is admitted or not, we come from you we come from you ... We come from the country that plucks its people out like weeds and flings them into the roadside ... We come from cemeteries full of skeletons with wild roses in their grinning teeth. We come from our untold tales that wait for their telling. We come from Canada, this land that is like every land, filled with the wise, the fearful, the compassionate, the corrupt. (226

Naomi's double-voiced response not only interacts dialogically with Mr Barker's previous comments, but its opening phrase "Oh Canada" also evokes the Canadian national anthem. Its sentiments, however, are not those of loyalty and devotion; rather, they are a lament. Parodic references to the anthem occur earlier in the novel as well. Naomi imagines the reply of B. Good, "the custodian in charge of all the property" (37), to a letter of inquiry by Aunt Emily: "Be good, my undesirable, my illegitimate children, be obedient, be servile, above all don't send me any letters of enquiry about your homes, while I stand on guard (over your property) in the true north strong, though you are not free. B. Good" (37). The allusions to the anthem show how its language and ideology can easily be used in the service of patriarchal and racist practices. Naomi uses the discourse of the anthem to show how a national symbol may purport to speak for a nation while its construction of that nation relies on the exclusion of its minorities. When Naomi and her friends sing the anthem as part of the Slocan school drill (156–7), it seems deeply ironic (Davidson 1993, 62–3). Again, the first person plural pronoun does not include these Japanese Canadian children: they cannot claim Canada as their "home." They have been made into "enemy aliens" and are told that Canadians with European ancestry have a right to think of themselves as "native" while immigrants from non-European countries and even Aboriginal peoples do not. When the children are expected to perform the ceremonies of their own exclusion, the anthem becomes a lament for a deeply racist country.[6]

The realization that there is "evidence for optimism" (Kogawa 1981, 199) in the dialogic confrontation and the modification of her own and other perspectives comes to Naomi when she finally understands that speech and silence do not have to remain mutually exclusive or paradoxical; rather, they are increasingly imagined as complementing each other (Cheung 1993, 165), which is not to say that the novel resolves the tension between them. Just as Naomi has learned to face Emily's documents about the war, so she realizes that constant questioning, accusing, and searching for guilt cannot to justice to her missed mother. Naomi can accept neither Obasan's absolute silence nor Emily's impatient speech and its claim to truthful documentation without reassessing them. As Betty Sasaki (1998, 125–6) points out in her discussion of different kinds of silences in the novel, since Obasan rarely speaks, Naomi focuses on nonverbal signs in Obasan's world (the objects around her, her behaviour); thus, Naomi manages not to speak *for* Obasan while helping her readers understand her silences. At the same time, Naomi recognizes "Aunt Emily's detachment from her personal pain that Naomi senses in the vehemence of her voice" (Kogawa 1981, 134). Naomi comes to accept the relationship between silence and speech as a "dialogic struggle" that is characterized by infinitely negotiated tension (Lim 1991, 242). This tension allows Naomi to find her own voice but also to retain her "ear" for the cultural registers of silence around her. In this way, the simple opposition of silence and speech, in which silence for a Western reader may be associated with passivity, repression, and fear, becomes untenable (Cheung 1993, 151; Sasaki 1998, 135); readers are invited to examine their own critical positioning as silence becomes a figure of speech, a language of agency and transgression throughout the novel.

Naomi is now able to listen to the two Japanese letters she found among Emily's documents, but whose content she does not know. The letters were written by her Grandmother Kato from Japan, and they relate what happened to Naomi's mother after the bombing of Nagasaki and why she did not return to her family. Naomi interacts with these letters by partly recounting their content in her own words and, at the same time, inserting original quotations. She is able at last to listen to her mother's "voice": "Mother. I am listening. Assist me to hear you" (Kogawa 1981, 240). The following chapter presents Naomi's hidden dialogue with her mother and is the climax of the internal dialogism in the novel. In a hidden dialogue, according to Bakhtin (1984a, 197), the statements of the second speaker are omitted, but the general sense is not violated; it seems as if Naomi's mother "is present invisibly." The readers do not actually read her mother's words, but they can see their traces in the influence on all of Naomi's remarks. On the basis of her new information, Naomi tries to restore the connection with her mother by anticipating her attitudes and reactions in her address.

Naomi seems to stand on firm ground at the end of the last chapter. She returns to the coulee, which she used to visit with her grandfather; her experience of the land is peaceful, beautiful, almost serene. A harmonious tension seems to have been reached: "water and stone dancing" (Kogawa 1981, 247). And it is no accident in this final scene that Naomi is wearing Aunt Emily's coat, which "is warmer than [her] jacket" (246). Better equipped with what Emily has given her – a coat but probably also her speech and activism – Naomi achieves a "personal transcendence" (79), which has led Arnold Davidson (1993, 22) to say that "*Obasan*, in its last chapter, comes dangerously close to over-resolution." But the novel does not end here. The postscript, another document presumably taken from Emily's package, is identified as an "excerpt from the memorandum sent by the co-operative committee on Japanese Canadians to the House and Senate of Canada, April 1946" (Kogawa 1981, 248–50). The excerpt is a ten-point argument against the plan the government devised after the war to return Japanese Canadians to Japan. The last move of the novel is, therefore, to place Naomi's personal narrative in a larger public context. Only this time it is not Naomi who is engaging with the text dialogically; instead, the document challenges the reader to activate its dialogic relations with the rest of the novel.

Because the excerpt emphasizes the political implications of Emily's narrative, it seems to pay a final tribute to Emily's position of political activism. However, while the novel foregrounds the political protest of Japanese Canadians, supported by the references to Ed Kitagawa, Jean Suzuki, and Gordon Nakayama in Kogawa's acknowledgment (n.p.), the excerpt is signed by James M. Finlay, Andrew Brewin, and Hugh MacMillan (250). The Cooperative Committee for Japanese Canadians, which was incorporated in June 1945, is only one example of the growing number of anti-deportation voices of the time. Alongside the legal battle of lawyers to halt the deportations, the Cooperative Committee and its allies organized an anti-deportation campaign that included fund-raising activities, distribution of pamphlets, organization of meetings, writing of letters to the prime minister and members of Parliament as well as numerous press statements (Sunahara 1981,

138). The public reaction opposing deportation orders was sponta-
neous and strong. The excerpt thus serves as a reminder of a time when
influential Canadians began to organize against racial discrimination,
and public opinion shifted when the time for change had come. However, the language used betrays the writers' indebtedness to the dominant ideology (Miki 1998, 116). Moreover, the excerpt also alludes to
the second uprooting of Japanese Canadians, which was the result of
"voluntary" repatriation and resettlement programs and was well
under way during the summer of 1946. Although the deportation
Orders in Council were ruled to be legal in December 1946, the policy
had already become unnecessary and, because of public protest, even
politically unwise.

Davidson (1993, 81) sees the fact that the Anglo Canadians who
signed the memorandum are set up as counterparts to the B. Goods of
the novel as "a reading directive in the form of a crucial question":
"Who represents the Anglo-Canadian reader in this text? The three
individuals who opposed mass deportation or, say, the custodian of
confiscated property, the misnamed functionary, B. Good?" Either
way, in the end it seems that Japanese Canadians are still *spoken for* in
Obasan, as Miki (1998, 117) has rightfully pointed out. What may
have seemed like a resolution of silence and speech in Naomi's character is undone in the final dialogic move at the end of the text. The political implications of the excerpt startle even contemporary readers; the
final document challenges Anglo-Canadian readers (1) to ask how it
was possible that Canada could adopt the "methods of Naziism"
depicted in Naomi's narrative and (2) to ensure that Canada will never
do so again (Kogawa 1981, 250).

The implicit notion of growth and maturity attributed to the reader is reinforced by the front cover of the Penguin edition, which
describes *Obasan* as "a moving novel of a time and suffering we have
tried to forget." As Scott McFarlane (1995a, 407) has argued convincingly, the "we" in this statement refers "to an imagined community made up of those possessing a homogenous 'Canadian memory,'"
thus re-enacting a process of exclusion but also of redemption. Since
the novel makes that memory more complete, this community can feel
in some way redeemed. By implication, this "we" does not include
Japanese Canadians who have never forgotten about the internment.
Moreover, I would add, it does not include others who lack that
homogeneous memory, such as postwar immigrants who may or may
not belong to visible minorities. For them, not being part of the "we"
can afford a distance that may not only be liberating (no guilt for
something they were not part of) but that may also make the book
more intriguing.

Obasan's montage-like narrative structure has at least two effects. First, Kogawa allows the reader to use the documents in order to reconstruct the perspectives that contribute to Naomi's inner conflict. Second, the montage creates a field of tension between the different viewpoints that challenges the quality of the documents themselves. Documents used as source material for traditional historiography are denied their claim to truthfulness. Through quotation the documents are recontextualized, which exposes them as readings of events embedded within a historical situation. Their underlying reality constructs are not simply "right" because they have a collective character. Actually, collectivity and homogeneity are ultimately seen as expressions of existing power structures and monologic control. St Andrews (1986, 31) has drawn attention to the fact that "history often silences the oppressed and glorifies its collective social memory." In her attempt to contrast this collective memory with an alternative view, Naomi exposes every description of reality and the past as an undertaking determined by subjective interests and conditions.[7] In the end, the homogeneity of the collective memory is itself unmasked as a construct based on subjective interests; it is therefore open to revision. *Obasan* presents the reader with a collection of documents about and from the past and with the narrator's attempt to find coherence in the diverging perspectives, which is only possible through dialogic relativization. Although the cited newspaper articles and government decrees cannot be changed insofar as they are material texts or insofar as their original effects are concerned, they can be made part of a contemporary dialogic confrontation. When they are introduced into a novel such as *Obasan*, they are moved out of their socio-historical vacuum and submitted to the unfinalizable and infinite dialogue of the text, which can have different effects for today's readers.

The novel itself has been part of the process of revising Canadian history. It was written in the late 1970s, a time when Japanese communities across Canada experienced a resurgence of pride and self-awareness with the lifting of the thirty-year ban on access to Second World War government files and the celebrations surrounding the 100-year-anniversary of the first Japanese immigrant to Canada, Manzo Nagano (Miki and Kobayashi 1991, 60–1). Japanese Canadians, not unlike Emily and Naomi, began to explore the ways in which language had been used to impose, enforce, and naturalize the Japanese difference as "essential" and how that difference had then been used to justify injustices. The need to contest the very discursive practices that had defined them, plus the confidence and courage resulting from organized community activity, enabled Japanese Canadians to tell their own stories, to break the silence, and to pursue a redress movement.

Where does fact end and fiction begin in this process? Through quotation, parody, double-voicing, and, thus, dialogic relations, fact and fiction seem to inform each other and to hold each other in suspension. As historiographic metafiction, *Obasan* provides a Japanese Canadian perspective on the events of the Second World War. Quotations from the novel were used by two politicians on Settlement Day to explain the seriousness and validity of the claims made by Japanese Canadians. In the House of Commons, Ed Broadbent, leader of the New Democratic Party, quoted Naomi's words in order to reinforce the notion that the injustices committed against Japanese Canadians were not abstract deeds but that they caused "profound, serious human suffering" and were "real experiences in real lives" (quoted in Miki and Kobayashi 1991, 148). Emily's manuscript, "The Story of the Nisei in Canada: A Struggle for Liberty," which is itself quoted from Kitagawa's writing, was cited by Gerry Weiner, minister of state for multiculturalism, in his press statement in order to explain that Japanese Canadians fought for acknowledgment of the injustice done to their people because they were loyal Canadians (150). The intertextuality does not stop here. In *Itsuka* (1992), her sequel to *Obsan*, Kogawa actually traces Naomi's involvement in the redress movement. This novel ends with a description of the events on Settlement Day, 22 September 1988 (271–9): "As I look down I can see Mr. Broadbent ... he rises and speaks and he's fighting to control his voice. 'They, as Canadian citizens, had done no wrong'" (275). The pervasiveness and infinite regress of quotations show that the dialogism of the narrative in *Obasan*, which I have only begun to explore, is part of a larger dialogic intertext in which the relations between novel and society are indeed dynamic and reciprocal.

"I've been waiting for this book, didn't know who would write it, a novel that explores our history, confirms the process of building a chinese canadian presence" (Wong 1990, 135). With these words Rita Wong opens her review of Lee's first novel *Disappearing Moon Cafe*. For Lien Chao (1997, 93), the novel confirms the important role of "the community's history in the development of its contemporary literature." Similar notions of assertion and agency characterize many reviews and discussions of the novel. Indeed, its paperback cover describes it as a "memorable and moving picture of a people's struggle for identity." I believe that the novel's achievement is due not just to the fact that it is written by a Chinese Canadian or that it tells particular kinds of stories; I contend that at least part of its achievement is due to the strategies Lee employs to organize it.

Chinese Canadian communities have been a vital force in Canada for a long time, but because of the severe racism Chinese Canadians have encountered, a confident, self-conscious, and critical voice capable of telling their stories is a recent phenomenon. The first Chinese workers came to British Columbia in 1858 when news reached California that gold had been found in the Fraser Valley and that there was a second Gold Mountain in North America.[8] During the period from 1881 to 1885, a larger number of Chinese workers, estimated at 15,700 to 18,000 (Li 1988, 17; Wickberg 1982, 22; Dawson 1991, 21), entered Canada directly from China: they were sought as cheap labourers for the construction of some of the most treacherous sections of the Canadian Pacific Railway in British Columbia. Chinese workers also contributed significantly to such other new industries as mining, land clearing, lumbering, salmon canning, and domestic service. Tolerated in times of need, these "sojourners" were no longer wanted once the railroad was completed and British Columbia was hit by economic difficulties (Li 1988, 26). Hidden behind what could be described as a utilitarian attitude, a wide range of exclusionary policies and discriminatory legislation was instituted, of which the imposition of a head tax upon every person of Chinese origin entering Canada – $50 in 1885, $100 in 1900, and $500 in 1903 – may now be the best known.[9] These measures culminated in 1923, when, on 1 July, the Canadian Parliament passed the Chinese Immigration Act, also known as the Chinese Exclusion Act, which almost completely stopped Chinese immigration to Canada.

Since immigration had always been geared towards a male workforce, Chinese communities in Canada were predominantly male. Women and children were usually left behind. With the introduction of head taxes, bringing over wives became a privilege of the economically successful merchant class. A wife became a status symbol in Chinatown.[10] In 1947 the act was finally repealed, and the right to vote was extended to the Chinese. It took another twenty years before Chinese immigration applications were judged by the same criteria as were those of other nationalities. As a result of the changed immigration policies, the Chinese population has increased substantially since 1967; a significant number of people have immigrated under the business immigration program that was introduced in 1978 and expanded in 1985. While the capital injected into the Canadian economy, particularly on the West Coast, has offset economic recession, increasing numbers of Chinese Canadians have again become the target of racial antagonism (Li 1992, 272–3).

Chinese communities have lived in and contributed to Canada for over 130 years, but discriminatory practices have led to their systematic marginalization, silencing, and exclusion in all sectors of social life during this period. With a growing interest in more diverse literatures and the establishment of more alternative publication houses, literary voices from the Chinese Canadian communities have finally been (allowed to be) heard. Over the past decade, anthologies such as Bennett Lee and Jim Wong-Chu's *Many-Mouthed Birds* (1991) and Andy Quan and Jim Wong-Chu's *Swallowing Clouds* (1999); autobiographical works such as Denise Chong's *The Concubine's Children* (1994), Evelyn Lau's *Runaway* (1989) and *Inside Out* (2001), and Wayson Choy's *Paper Shadows* (1999); and other writing by Choy, Larissa Lai, Terry Woo, Kevin Chong, and Fred Wah, to name but a few, have attracted much attention. Sky Lee explains the earlier lack of Chinese Canadian writers: "The silence is a reaction toward the very blatant, very violent racism the Chinese in Canada have endured ... I think the line of trust, in terms of communication, has been broken too often ... Our generation is the first generation to regain a voice" (quoted in M. Andrews 1990). In *Disappearing Moon Cafe*, Lee situates her fictional narrative of the Wong family within the carefully researched historical context of Chinese immigration to Canada and, in particular, of the Chinese Canadian community in Vancouver's Chinatown.[11]

If one is to understand the events that form the historical background in the narrative and how the text is "raced, classed, and sexed through relations of power, hegemony, oppression and resistance" (Schueller 1994, 4), then an awareness of socio-historical context is crucial to one's reading of *Disappearing Moon Cafe*. The "how" of this text is indeed intricate. *Disappearing Moon Cafe* performs double manoeuvres that may initially seem contradictory. It acknowledges a history of discrimination in Canada, but, by focusing on one Chinese Canadian family, it insists that characters need to take responsibility for their actions even if circumstances are not of their making. Although the Chinese Exclusion Act, for example, was imposed upon the Chinese population and had serious effects on the demographics of Chinatown, making it "ripe for incest" (147), this imposition cannot serve as a justification of incestuous relations. In other words, the novel does not just portray positive aspects of the Chinatown community; it is neither a nostalgic review of past hardships nor a present-day picture of a model minority. Sky Lee has spoken self-consciously of the fact that her novel may offend Chinese Canadians and that other Canadians may find it exotic (M. Andrews 1990; Lacey 1990).[12] As the novel powerfully asserts the presence of Chinese Canadians and their collective survival, it also challenges the homogeneity of the community by exposing its misogyny, greed, and secrets without, however, holding individuals exclusively responsible for their personal failures (Chao 1997, 121). For Maria Ng (1999), Lee's novel reinforces too many prejudices in its negative representations of Chinese immigrants. A contextual analysis of the text's dialogic relations shows, however, that Lee presents the reader with a highly complex portrayal of life in Chinatown – one that goes far beyond simply reinforcing stereotypes. *Disappearing Moon Cafe* both evokes a strong sense of community and challenges its motives.

Facing the table of contents and following a dedication and acknowledgments, Lee's *Disappearing Moon Cafe* provides the genealogical tree of "The Wong Family" (n.p.). Since the text on the back cover tells the reader that the novel "traces the lives and passionate loves of the women of the Wong family through four generations," this chart should provide some guidance through a complex family saga (Seaman 1991; Wong 1990, 135). However, what looks, at first glance, like a neat and straightforward visual aid to the history of the Wong family is not followed by a similarly transparent narrative. In keeping with conventions of genealogical research that trace a male-line descent from a common ancestor (FitzHugh 1985, 106, 117), the tree shows the earliest ancestor at the top and the descendants extending below, indicating marriages, children, and dates of birth and deaths. It should be noted, however, that the tree begins not with Gwei Chang or his ancestors but with the parents of Kelora, who was Wong Gwei Chang's first partner and who bore their son Ting An. Moreover, names and dates are only provided for those characters who, throughout the novel, will play a significant role in Kae's narration; for example, no names or dates are given for Ting An's wife or Song Ang's husband, for either wife or daughter of John, or for Kae's husband. Attention is directed to the end of the Wong family line through the following information for Suzie's child: "last Wong male died at birth 1950."

Indeed, the traditional genre of the family saga, driven by what Patricia Tobin has identified as the "genealogical imperative,"[13] is invoked, yet simultaneously undermined, in *Disappearing Moon Cafe* (Huggan 1994a). The narrative seems to pull away from the family tree, from its lines of descent, succession, linearity, and its traditional focus on the male line. The family history, which in ancestor research is understood as "identifying family members in the context of their physical and social environment" (Wright 1995, 3), is here informed instead by a focus on the women of the Wong family, by narrative juxtapositions, gaps, and contingencies. As the novel develops, the connections between the family tree and family history are sought out but also challenged and undermined. The novel does not seem interested in reproducing and transmitting the "correct" or "complete" knowledge of the Wong family history but, instead, draws attention to how this knowledge is produced. The question of male origin is ultimately displaced, as it is in the family tree, and the practices, discourses, and silences of the Wong family become the focus of attention. By dialogizing its narrative form, *Disappearing Moon Cafe* foregrounds the discontinuities of history, the differences and relations between members of the Wong family, and the affirmation of knowledge as perspective; thus, it explores the kind of genealogy that Foucault (1972, 10) describes as crucial to the writing of a general, non-foundational history.[14]

The novel is divided into a prologue, seven chapters, and an epilogue, all of which are further subdivided into a total of forty-nine sequences. The character whose perspective focuses each section is indicated by headings that usually consist of the respective name and a year. Only a small number of sections are headed by inserted genres (letters, telegram, phone call) or themes (babies, story, The Bones, Feeding the Dead). *Disappearing Moon Cafe* opens with a prologue that introduces Wong Gwei Chang, whose generation initiates the secrets and problems later explored by Kae. While five sections are headed by his name (the second most after Kae), they are relegated exclusively to the prologue and epilogue, a framing device to which I will return later. The time settings move between 1892, when Gwei Chang first encountered Kelora, and 1939, the year of his death. The four sections of the prologue serve primarily expository functions, creating an atmosphere while remaining vague about what the main narrative will involve. The prologue contextualizes the novel in three important ways. First, with a strong focus on memory, the notion of history is introduced as a subject-dependent construct rather than as a static fact (Lee 1990, 1, 7, 10). For example, the narrator tells us that Gwei Chang "played with his memories all day long. Or they played with him" (5); he wonders whether he could believe Chen because "Chen told him lots of strange, elusive stories, but who knows which ones were true and which ones were fragments of his own fantasy?" (7). Second, the prologue introduces information about the early immigration of Chinese workers to Canada. For instance, after coming initially for the gold rush (7), many Chinese men were hired as labourers for the CPR. Gwei Chang was sent by the Benevolent Association in Victoria to find the bones of those who died along the tracks of the railway; their bones were to be returned to Victoria and from there taken to China for proper burial (2, 16, 18; Wickberg 1982, 24). During his search he comes across several leftover work camp gangs. This historical information inspires many of the family stories told later in the novel. And third, the opening sections introduce complex relations between race, gender, and language through the relationship between

Kelora, a young Aboriginal woman who speaks Chinese, and Gwei Chang, an adult Chinese man who has immigrated to Canada. More specifically, the novel highlights the lost kinship between Chinese and Aboriginal peoples in British Columbia (Chao 1997, 96).

The first chapter introduces Kae Ying Woo, a thirty-six-year-old Chinese Canadian woman who is recovering from giving birth to her first child, Robert Man Jook Lee. Still in hospital, Kae frankly assesses her situation:

I'm so very disappointed. I've been brought up to believe in kinship, or those with whom we share. I thought that by applying attention to all the important events such as the births and the deaths, the intricate complexities of a family with chinese roots could be massaged into a suant, digestible unit. Like a herbal pill – I thought I could swallow it and my mind would become enlightened. (Lee 1990, 19)

Brought up with a strong belief that families assure people of their places in the community, Kae followed the path of the proper and perfect family woman: she got married and then had a child. Thus, she hoped to follow the "inevitable logic underlining life," ensuring a proper beginning and "a well-penned conclusion" of a life story that could indeed be massaged into a pill and swallowed (20). The linearity underlying this plan was to ensure order, enlightenment, and reassurance. All her life, Kae participated in this order by listening to and internalizing the family history just as it was told to her. Kae's "close scrape with death" during childbirth (21), however, has created a crisis – a threshold situation in which she needs to re-evaluate her life.[15] According to Bakhtin (1981, 248), time in the chronotope of the threshold seems to be without duration, almost instantaneous. It is not surprising then that the sections in which Kae participates as a character seem to have no duration; they are without specific time references, except when she decides to visit Hermia. Kae realizes two things: first, rather than bringing her fulfillment, giving birth leaves her feeling frustrated and trapped; second, the family history she was privy to was only one version of a multi-version history. In the hospital room, Kae's mother decides to share some of these other versions with her once she finds her grandson in good health. Paradoxically, "the story – the well-kept secret that [Kae] had actually unearthed years ago – finally begins to end for [her] with the birth of [her] son" (Lee 1990, 23). The crisis of giving birth forces Kae to rethink her situation and to explore the possibility of change so that her time of physical healing may also become a time of emotional and spiritual healing.

Instead of one family history, one coherent version massaged into a pill, the narrator Kae collects and presents multiple, often conflicting and contradictory, stories. This new approach to family history is born out of her realization that every history is always a particular history, someone's interested construction. She explicitly problematizes this concern throughout the narrative: if history can be told in so many different ways, then what is reality and truth (132, 191, 214)? How does history get constructed? Whose stories get included? Whose silences loom large (66, 145–6, 180)? The new approach to her family history is enacted through her gathering of all the stories she has heard and now retells. The narrative form of *Disappearing Moon Cafe* thus suggests an oral history of the Wong family, acknowledging "orality as a living tradition in the Chinese Canadian community and especially in women's subculture" (Chao 1997, 120). As an oral history, the narrative of forty-nine sections is appropriately organized, primarily through associative connections, and thus breaks away from chronological succession and notions of causality. In some sections, the narrator explicitly leads into the next one; some sections present a particular time or event from different characters' perspectives; some seem to be triggered by a single thought or memory; others do not share any obvious commonalities but may connect with later or previous sequences. While all sections somehow connect to members of the Wong family and their contexts, Kae only points out some of these connections. As the reader fills in the gaps and completes the connections between different stories – what Bakhtin (1984a, 91) has described as extending "a dotted line" between separate elements to the point of their interaction – the dialogic relations that are activated between perspectives undermine the discourse of the genealogical imperative. As, in concentric circles, the narrative seems to move closer to the question of Suzie's death, and, with it, to the end of the Wong lineage, it simultaneously expands and moves outward again. The gaps and interruptions, the secrets of what Kae has not known about the Wong family, are foregrounded. Discontinuity becomes the driving force of the narrative.

To argue that *Disappearing Moon Cafe* presents a recollected family history is also to raise the question of who narrates its stories, especially in sections in which Kae does not identify herself as the homodiegetic narrator. Some confusion exists in the criticism, which can be partly explained by a lack of terminological clarity as critics usually make no distinction between narration and focalization.[16] In the sections or parts of a section in which Kae does not identify herself as the narrator by referring to herself in the first person singular, the narrating instances nevertheless fulfill more than mere diegetic functions. They are not impersonal devices but, rather, become more or less personalized characters. A surplus of information allows for frequent privileged evaluations[17] and foreshadows explanations that allude to later events.[18] However, there are also many contextual references that provide important background information and that cannot be attributed to any of the other characters.[19] Moreover, the narrator exercises a synthesizing function because s/he provides many generalizations that seem to have no other source.[20] Rather than assuming various heterodiegetic narrators who are vaguely personalized but who cannot be identified, I argue that Kae is the narrator of these sections, too, because she retells the many stories she has been told and has gathered during her lifetime. In the telling, she is no longer foregrounded as a participant in the story. Although she does not refer to herself, the observations and explanations provided are consistent with her perspective, knowledge, and background. This approach would account for her omniscience, her knowledge of times, places, and events when and where she was not present. Through this narratological manoeuvre, the novel maintains some of the qualities of an oral history. As Hermia so poignantly asks of Kae at the round-table in "Feeding the Dead": "Do you mean that this story isn't a story of several generations, but of one individual thinking collectively?" (Lee 1990, 189). As the collector and teller of her family stories, Kae, indeed, becomes the individual thinking collectively, the orchestrator of dialogic relations, the mediator of double-voiced tellings. This reading supports Chao's (1997, 119) notion of the collective self as a powerful narrative paradigm in Chinese Canadian literature.

While Kae may thus be identified as the only narrator (with the exception of Suzie, who will be discussed later), focalizers shift much more frequently. Not only does Kae act as focalizer, most explicitly in those sections where she foregrounds her own presence, but the character whose perspective is the focus of one sequence often acts as focalizer within that section. Thus, perspectives of family members are established not only through the narrator's perspective but also through their own experiences. Yet the text literally refuses to make final statements about any character's perspective. The frequent shifts in time, place, and focalization keep their positions from materializing permanently. Kae's history of the Wong family is a collection of pieces that continuously shift in their relation to each other; as each story is told, it has already begun to change. At times, Kae herself makes self-conscious comments regarding the processual nature of her storying; the reader must continuously adjust and readjust the connections between the many perspectives the text presents.

Let me take a closer look at how some of the perspectives relate to each other. Mui Lan is introduced as the proprietress of the successful

Disappearing Moon Cafe in Vancouver's Chinatown; she came to Canada in 1911 as the "merchant's wife," bringing with her their sixteen-year-old son Choy Fuk. Initially a warm and optimistic woman, proud of her husband's overseas prosperity, Mui Lan begins to feel distant from him and misses the supportive community of women she enjoyed in her village in China. Only through the stories related primarily in the prologue and through some later references can the reader infer some of the reasons why she feels that Gwei Chang seems distant: he is more concerned with the memory of Kelora and the life he left behind.[21] Mui Lan adjusts to the lonely life in Chinatown by becoming increasingly cold, noisy, and demanding. However, she can only enjoy the economic success that becomes her life's new goal when the continuation of both the family and its good name can be assured. To her distress, after over five years of marriage, her daughter-in-law Fong Mei, whom she selected and brought to Canada to be Choy Fuk's wife, is still without children. Mui Lan's determination to have a grandson justifies the use of all means, whether secrets, lies, or blackmail. Her final offer to Fong Mei is double-voiced, a threat cloaked in a promise:

"I know a woman's heart! What woman would deny that yearning for a baby son, or even a baby girl to begin with ... Well, now you have the opportunity. All you need to do is give up your old man for a few days, and soon you'll have a son – and with him, security, prestige, honour, and the glowing warmth of a family to look after your old age. What could be easier? And where's the harm in that?" she asked innocently. (Lee 1990, 62)

If Fong Mei follows her mother-in-law's advice, she will let her husband have an affair with another woman who will bear a child that Choy Fuk and herself can later pass off as their own. While Mui Lan reads Fong Mei's body movements – her nodding – as agreement and sees her as worn down by her mother-in-law's attacks on her self-esteem and dignity, a shift in focalizers allows the reader access to how Fong Mei experiences the situation. What looks like agreement to Mui Lan is barely contained aggression: "By now, Fong Mei was all but cried out. She still kneeled on the floor, covered in a cold sweat, as if drained from some kind of wasted exertion ... Suddenly, she realized that there was rage as well. *So, it was rage, pushing her body beyond its limits! Rage that made her body shudder with icy fear*" (60, emphasis added). In the free indirect discourse, emphasized here by italics, the narrator's voice recedes, and the feelings of the character Fong Mei are foregrounded.[22] (Some reviewers have criticized Lee for too often using exclamation marks to indicate these transitions to free indirect discourse.) These are the first indications that the once quiet, obedient, and fearful woman who was married to Choy Fuk at seventeen, and who learned that to live in her in-laws' household meant to be silent and invisible, has changed into someone capable of trying to turn someone else's rules and decisions to her own advantage. And all the while Mui Lan still believes that Fong Mei's humiliation could not be worse. The change is captured in the following section attributed to Fong Mei:

She had changed these past six months. Where the loathsome living arrangement that Mui Lan had forced her into had once made her blood boil, it in fact suited her now. Fong Mei no longer felt like she was a part of somebody else's plans. *And quite truthfully*, Fong Mei had never borne any malice towards *that poor, unfortunate waitress-woman ... Pitiful thing – just a sore bag who didn't seem to have enough gumption or sagacity to manipulate a better life for herself.* (91–2, emphasis added)

Fong Mei is now able to assert her own sense of self. In doing so, however, she employs Mui Lan's very own strategies; she finds solace in reminding herself of the waitress's social inferiority, which we see in the lines focalized by her.

Choy Fuk pretends to comply with his mother's scheme to keep himself and his wife out of trouble. From his perspective (94–104), the reader learns that he feels no sympathy for Fong Mei's initial reservations because "he was a man. And it was not for a man to withhold his vital life-force stream on the spiteful whim of a barren wife. So what if he enjoyed the woman? What could be more natural for a man?" (96). Only through his perspective do we learn about the pressures he feels when, after six months, Song Ang is still not pregnant: "How can I face my mother, huh? How can I dare show my face in Chinatown, huh?" (102).[23] When it is revealed in Ting An's section that he was involved with Fong Mei, and when readers learn that both Song Ang and Fong Mei had babies in 1926, they, having the advantage of dramatic irony, can connect and fill the silences by actualizing the unspoken tensions between the perspectives presented: what is never actually said is that Choy Fuk is sterile, which means that both the waitress and Fong Mei must have been with someone else in order to get pregnant. Since this information remains unknown, there is initial worry when Keeman, Song Ang's son, wants to be involved with Beatrice as they are presumably both Choy Fuk's children. However, as it turns out, neither of these children is his. By relating the individual stories to each other, the reader is able to relativize their claims: what is one character's truth is another's lie; what is one character's gain is another's loss.

Suzie's perspective is the one that clashes most harshly with those of other family members in *Disappearing Moon Cafe*. It is Kae's "unwholesome curiosity surrounding her demise" (191) that drives her to tell Suzie's story – the story everybody else in her family has relentlessly tried to silence. According to the official family version, with which Kae opens her narrative, Suzie had "died of pneumonia as a young woman, when [Kae] was still a baby. She didn't ever marry or multiply" (19). Only when Suzie is pregnant and determined to marry Morgan, who unbeknownst to her is her half-brother, are the secrets and lies so skilfully constructed and protected by the previous generations of Mui Lan and Fong Mei exposed. Not only does suicide need to be kept a secret as it is usually considered a disgrace in Chinese culture, but what remains to be inferred by the reader is that previous wrongdoings will come to light and taint the family honour.

The first of the three sections headed by Suzie's name (171–3) directly relates to the previous one, in which Suzie promises Beatrice to behave well and to stay away from Morgan when she remains at the house alone while the family takes a trip to San Francisco to find Mui Lan. The reader learns from Suzie, however, what Beatrice does not know: that she did not keep her promise. The dialogic engagement between these two perspectives is further heightened by the dialogic format of Suzie's revelations themselves. She picks up on her final comment to Beatrice regarding Morgan – "we just talk" (170) — and begins the next section: "I wanted to tell you how we talked, my dear sister. Just saying that Morgan and I talked was a lie, flat and purposely kept so" (171). The direct addresses to her sister ("my antimatter twin," "Sister," "Bea," "my dearest" [171, 173]) and the frequent, increasingly desperate and pleading questions create the impression of Beatrice's presence as interlocutor. Suzie's guilty explanations not only respond to Bea's earlier trusting statement – "I believe you" (170) – but also anticipate her immediate disapproval and disappointment. The questions and accusations she expects from her sister shape the way she attempts to explain and apologize for "how we got out of control" · (173). This section interacts dialogically with Beatrice's and other earlier sections but is also internally dialogized as Suzie anticipates Beatrice's unspoken words within the hidden dialogue.

The second section under Suzie's name chronicles the events after she has announced to her mother that she and Morgan are expecting a child and that they want to get married (193–208). Confusion grows over the question of who is related to whom (Beatrice to Keeman or Suzie to Morgan). According to the official family history, Suzie is Choy Fuk's daughter, but the reader has learned that she is indeed Ting An's child and, therefore, Morgan's half-sister. The confusion climaxes when Suzie relates her experience of giving birth prematurely. In this threshold situation the tense shifts to the present, and Suzie's narrative alternates between talking about herself in the first and third person: "Suzie is on the verge of death again; her labour long and hard. Suzie is worn out, gasping for air; I got slurped in. 'I can't take any more,' my dark, clammy moan ... I am drifting, drifting up high. There in the dark room, near the window, my body on a narrow bed" (206). The threshold experience of birth, its horror and pain, makes Suzie experience herself as internally split, which leads to another form of doubling.

In the last section that Suzie narrates and focalizes, she describes her state after having returned home (211–13). Again, there is a strong sense of doubling between what she is able to do – having lost all sense of time, without the basic skills of getting dressed and feeding herself – and how she wants to appear to others, especially to Bea and Keeman: that is, as a woman in control. Only through Kae's letter to Hermia announcing her decision to come for a visit does the narrative tell the reader indirectly of Suzie's suicide shortly after (214–16).

To give Suzie a voice of her own, to make her a homodiegetic narrator in these important sequences, counteracts the previous silencing of her story by her family. Chao (1997, 100) sees Suzie's suicide as "sending a strong protest against societal control of women's reproduction in the institution of marriage and legitimacy." As a narrator, she constitutes herself as a subject, no longer the object of someone else's narration. The strategy validates Suzie's perspective within a complex set of stories that have silenced her. While Kae's ventriloquizing of Suzie's voice may be seen as problematic, I believe it is more important to recognize Kae's willingness as a narrator to take the risk of losing control over all the voices involved, including her own.[24] Moreover, the strategy of making Suzie her own narrator dramatically exposes the devastating effects of the family's secrets and lies. While it seems that everybody else's stories focus on dispersing more lies and secrets, Suzie's sections exert a centripetal pull in the novel, solving the family puzzle for Kae. However, knowledge of her story also has the opposite effect for her: it ultimately dissolves the family history, unravels its artificial unity, and enables Kae to accept family history as a space of dispersion, allowing her finally to move away from her family and go to Hong Kong to be reunited with Hermia and possibly to start a new life.

Kae's perspective engages with the stories of other family members in three ways. First, she relates experiences from her own past, especially with Morgan and Hermia and as a new mother in 1986. Dialogic relations also operate within these stories when her present narrating self comments on her past experiencing self. This is particularly pronounced when she talks about her experiences with Morgan (Lee 1990, 41, 64–70). Second, through her commentary, for example on Mui Lan (31), Fong Mei (37–38, 154), Beatrice (145–6), and Morgan (136, 159), she explicitly establishes dialogic relations between her own perspective and those of her relatives, which evaluate, contextualize, and challenge theirs. And third, in her self-reflexive and metanarrative comments she problematizes her role as writer and family chronicler. By retelling and thereby engaging with her family's stories, Kae initially searches for answers, authenticity, origins, and the true family history, all of which she sees as diametrically opposed to the lies, secrets, masks, and silences of her family as she has known it. As she explores the relations between the stories of her relatives, their temporalities and localities, her preconceived dualisms break down and boundaries blur. As her own genealogy acknowledges and follows shifts, disruptions, and gaps, Kae begins to approach history differently: history is always made up of a collection of stories, and only through their dialogic interrelations does a provisional history emerge.

Rather than dwelling on written sources of history as does *Obasan*, *Disappearing Moon Cafe* engages with the fictionality and the transience of a family's oral tradition (Hutcheon 1990, 91). The challenge of the novel's narrative form lies in finding a format or structure in print that allows for the transition from oral history into written text. The novel tackles this problem by combining the centrifugal pull of the complex family stories and their multiple focalizers with the centripetal force of the narrator Kae, who is both part of the family history and its orchestrator. Kae's exploration does not pretend to be objective, neutral, or uninterested. By foregrounding her role as family historian, the novel/Kae acknowledges that her selections of stories and their orchestration is tied to her agenda in the production of a history of the Wong family.

The dialogic structure resulting from Kae's orchestration is displayed in miniature in the section "Feeding the Dead" (185–90). As she contemplates the advantages and disadvantages of being a writer, Kae asks herself rather cynically – in a parody of the opening lines of Elizabeth Barrett Browning's "Sonnet XLIII" (1992, 41) – at the end of the preceding section: "How many ways are there to tell stories? Let me count the ways! For example, love is a fragile subject matter, too easily corrupted, often beaten dead. Let's take an opinion poll: the many and varied ways to destroy love! Oh, come on! We should be very good at it. It'd be fun!" (Lee 1990, 185). In "Feeding the Dead" Kae literally stages a poll of the people involved in her family history, bringing together some family members already dead (Suzanne, Fong Mei, Mui Lan) and others still alive (Beatrice, Chi, Morgan, Hermia, herself). The section employs a technique used in classical Chinese literature to enable wronged souls to return to settle the score (Chao 1997, 100) and combines elements from a Bakhtinian dialogue of the dead, Chinese mourning rituals, and stage directions for a movie scene. To create this unique hybrid section, Kae orchestrates all of the characters including herself, their voices, and their statements by introducing, framing, and evaluating them, albeit rather cryptically (as should be expected from a movie script).[25] In spite of her role as orchestrator, she cannot remove herself from the personal involvement with the other characters and therefore still feels "obliged" to Fong Mei (Lee 1990, 187). Many of the comments are organized through anacrisis, the rhetorical device Bakhtin (1984a, 110) describes as one person's word provoking someone else's. Suzie's first observation, for instance, ends with the question: "how else do you think she [Fong Mei] could have had three of us over eight years?" (Lee 1990, 185), which Kae herself answers "'I would say jealousy,' referring to Ting An" (186); thus, she expands Suzie's comments by speculating on Ting An's perspective. Beatrice responds by commenting on the nature of love as one of the driving forces in people's lives. In turn, her warning that it also carries some danger is answered by Chi, who undermines Beatrice's warning: "since when has that ever stopped anyone?" (186). Moreover, Chi disagrees fundamentally by questioning the very possibility of love: "maybe it's just something which people have invented to torture themselves with" (186). Spoken as a general comment, Morgan understands it as addressed to him, an attempt to blame him for what happened to Suzie. Regardless of the others' comments, Fong Mei is mostly interested in explaining her past actions in order to justify sacrificing her daughters for family position and money, male lineage, and her personal revenge on Mui Lan and Choy Fuk. In spite of Fong Mei's attempt to redeem herself in the eyes of her daughters, Suzie does not believe her mother's explanations, seeing only empty rhetoric in her words. Desperately trying to break free, she breaks down: "Knot after knot after knot! ... All this bondage we volunteer on ourselves! Untie them! Untie me! Don't tie any more!" (189).

In addition to creating a film scenario, in this fascinating section Kae stages several dialogues with the dead. Bakhtin (1984a, 112, 140) has described dialogues of the dead as characteristic of the Menippean satire; they allow the characters to be freed from all positions and obligations of ordinary life so that they can reveal themselves with unlimited freedom. The living women are joined by the dead: Fong Mei herself announces that she speaks "from beyond the grave" (Lee 1990,

187), with the hindsight that this gives her. The women are seated around "a timeless circular table" (187); while situated firmly in their own chronotopes, these women can cross time barriers to be reunited. Together they are part of "a classic scenario of wailing women huddled together to 'feed the dead'" (188). Both wailing and food presentations are part of traditional Chinese death rituals. Loud wailing as an expression of grief publicly announces the death and, at the same time, mitigates the emotional shock (Watson 1988, 12). Moreover, ritual weeping and wailing function to reaffirm the cohesion and solidarity of the family group.[26] Food presentations are an indispensable feature of the funerary rites, for they help the dead to make the transition from corpse to ancestor and facilitate the reciprocal relationship between the living and the dead (Watson 1988, 13; Thompson 1988, 73–4).[27] Supplying food becomes a concrete expression of the continuing relationship between the living and the dead, but it also serves to maintain, construct, and reconstruct social networks (Thompson 1988, 74), particularly, in Lee's novel, the network of women.[28]

Although Kae evokes these funeral rites to rehearse the formal family status and the relations among the women of the family, she also plays with them. She quotes the women's chant:

Mui Lan lived a lie, so Fong Mei got sly.
Suzie slipped away; Beatrice made to stay,
Kae to tell the story,
all that's left of
vainglory. (Lee 1990, 188)

The women's vanity and hypocrisy are relentlessly exposed and mocked in these lines. The chant may bring together the four generations of women, but its nursery-rhyme quality so trivializes their actions and histories that it inevitably questions the notion of communal grieving and the possibility of reciprocal relations. Moreover, Kae self-reflexively includes herself as narrator in this chant, thereby further undermining conventions of realism. The question remains: who or what is being mourned and who or what is being fed in "Feeding the Dead"? Is it, metaphorically speaking, the death of love since Kae wanted to explore "the many and varied ways to destroy love" (185)? Are all the dead women of the family mourned in this section (i.e., Mui Lan, Fong Mei, and Suzie)? I believe that this section, by presenting another threshold situation, actually stages Suzie's belated death rituals because the women believe that "her spirit is the most restless, most at risk" (189).

Finally, the connections between the prologue and the epilogue and their relationship with the intervening seven chapters also deserve closer attention. The epilogue constructs a frame for the novel by returning to Gwei Chang's relationship with Kelora and by picking up on earlier motifs. Chao (1997, 97) points out that Gwei Chang's "final remorse before death" concerning his son also "brings home a self-imposed criticism of racial phobia in the Chinese community." The epilogue ends with Gwei Chang's imagined conversation with Kelora, remembering their closeness and intimacy. On their own, the prologue and the epilogue seem to enforce a frame for the narrative – one that reaffirms the male lineage of the Wong family, focusing in particular on the patriarch himself. Although five sections are attributed to Gwei Chang, they are not situated within the central chapters of the novel but, rather, are at the margins of the text. In relation to the seven central chapters that tell of the women's agency within the family and the internally destructive powers of the family history, the epilogue seems to have displaced the man who used to be in control. However, Gwei Chang's death does not bring to an end the dispersion of the family history; instead, his death, which is associated with the "New Moon" (Lee 1990, 217), signifies both beauty and transformation.

So far I have emphasized the centrifugal pressure of *Disappearing Moon Cafe* (i.e., the differences between its stories and the dialogic relations between them). I would now like to look at how Lee uses language to create a sense of coherence and community between the characters of the Wong family and within their immediate context (i.e., Chinatown). Some critics have identified Lee's often documentary-style use of language, especially the literal translation of Chinese idioms and colloquialisms (e.g., the vulgarity of swearing), as grounding the narratives of this Chinese Canadian family.[29] While Lee does not incorporate passages in Chinese, she does employ idiomatic Chinese structures and transposes them into English. Although she can still attract an English-speaking audience, she nevertheless disrupts that dominant language through the translation effect, which Godard (1990a, 158) describes as writing "in structures of thought and language from their [minority writers'] native tongue transposed into English."[30] As a result of this linguistic strategy, the writing becomes double-voiced as it clashes with linguistic norms.

Language plays a significant role throughout the novel, which is foregrounded in the prologue when Gwei Chang and Kelora first talk and he expresses surprise at her ability to speak Chinese. Ting An is repeatedly singled out as the person in the Wong family who has the best knowledge of English and who, moreover, is local-born, which qualifies him to deal with the white community. Kae frankly admits that she does not speak Chinese; she requires the help of her friend

Hermia to translate letters exchanged between her grandmother Fong Mei and her sister. A closer examination of the terms used to distinguish Chinese Canadians in Chinatown from the primarily Anglo-Celtic majority in the rest of Vancouver and Canada shows a clear demarcation between "us" and "them" – a demarcation that marks the other, "them," as being constructed from the perspective of the Chinese Canadian characters.

The dominant community, repeatedly referred to not only as those responsible for the making of laws and policies but also as health care providers (Lee 1990, 204, 208), are most frequently referred to as "ghosts" (35, 42, 54, 107, 112, 219, 225), "barbarians" (61), and "devils" (24, 34, 61, 113); these terms are often modified by the adjective "white." Vancouver, the West Coast, and Canada are referred to as "wilderness" (61), "frontier" (61), and "backwash bush" (30). These phrases can most often be attributed to the focalizers Mui Lan, Fong Mei, Morgan, and Ting An; less often they characterize Kae's perspective. The Chinese Canadian characters speak of themselves and are referred to by the narrator as "Tang People" (25, 61, 73, 79), "yellow people" (70), and "Chinaman/Chinamen." While the phrase "Tang People" was originally chosen by Chinese Canadians as being indicative of their origin,[31] the other two phrases were commonly used by non-Chinese Canadians as derogatory terms. Phrases like "yellow people" and "yellow substratum" were frequently used in such newspapers as the *Colonist* to talk about the Chinese, especially in connection with the "yellow peril" – an idea that gained much attention in the wake of Japan's successes in the Russo-Japanese War (Roy 1989, 181–2, 123).[32] When these phrases are used pejoratively in *Disappearing Moon Cafe*, they are set off by quotation marks: "chink" (Lee 1990, 130, 172), "Iron-Chink" machine (169),[33] and "Chinaman" (76, 97). At least three times white youths use these words in a provocative manner, and once a white woman addresses a Chinese man as a "Chinaman" during a business interaction (76). In these cases the quotation marks function as explicit markers of the distance from which the narrator cites these phrases.

In other instances, however, the word "Chinaman" is used without quotation marks (2, 3, 6, 7, 14, 221, 223).[34] There may be two explanations for this usage. Within social discourse of the time, the racist trope "John Chinaman" had become naturalized to the extent that it appeared not only in newspaper articles but also in political speeches and official reports.[35] The concept of an essentialized "John Chinaman" not only symbolized a Chinese person's alien status in the community but also functioned as an image of all Chinese men and women from China by collapsing all class, gender, family status, or other divisions within the Chinese Canadian community (Anderson 1991, 37, 71; Chao 1995, 335, 338). The novel exposes the phrase's racist usages but also attempts to reappropriate it. The phrase itself becomes double-voiced because it becomes subject to the evaluation of Chinese Canadians who expropriate it and use it according to their own intentions.[36] These examples of internally dialogized words are particularly powerful because their double-voicedness is emphasized by the retention of their racist overtones.[37] Through these double-voicings at the level of the word, the novel further extends its process of dialogization to engage perspectives otherwise not directly represented – those of the dominant white community. For Kae, there is no undivided place or position from which to speak. She is both insider and outsider – in Canada, in China, and, in particular, in the Chinese Canadian community. Kae is aware of her positioning as a member of her community and family as well as of the narrator in the novel. While she may overestimate her role ("I am the resolution to this story" [209]), she breaks the silence of her family, her Chinatown community, and the dominant culture.

Joy Kogawa and Sky Lee resort to strategies shared by many writers in colonized spaces: "fragmenting the homogeneous structures that smooth over differences; decentring the language, complementing one voice with another from a different space, including the silences previously excluded; foregrounding the problematic nature of language itself" (Brydon 1987, 105). In *Obasan* and *Disappearing Moon Cafe*, these narrative techniques create dialogic relations between multiple perspectives. In both novels these perspectives do not interact on a level playing field; various forms of hierarchies and oppression inform the contexts within which they operate. While *Obasan* and *Disappearing Moon Cafe* employ dialogism as their guiding narrative strategy, and while it is tempting to read these novels as "firsts" in their respective literary traditions (thus emphasizing their similarities), it is important to highlight that dialogic relations work in these novels in different ways and, I believe, with slightly different purposes.

Both novels manage to stay largely within the conventions of realism but also succeed in contesting them through their overlap with history, auto/biography, and storytelling. The historiographic metafiction of *Obasan* focuses on the written products of history and incorporates other genres, government documents, newspaper reports, and official letters to expose and ultimately to challenge a hegemonic history (one written in and supported by these documents) that serves the dominant discourse. Lee, on the other hand, chooses not to reiterate discourses that have encouraged her family's and community's silences but, rather, prefers to speak her own silences through the storytelling of her fictional Chinese Canadian family (Chalykoff 1994, 26). While *Disappearing Moon Cafe* may also be thought of as historiographic metafiction, its focus is the exploration of oral history as it looks inward – into the stories of the Chinese Canadian community in Vancouver in general and into the stories of the fictional Wong family in particular. While Kogawa challenges the notion that a written document represents a fact that is irreversibly fixed, Lee suggests that the oral is no more fictional than the written is factual.

In their attempts to reconstruct, reconsider, and challenge versions of history, Naomi and Kae are aware that they are reconfiguring their own identities. To story their family's histories is always also to story their own identities. While *Obasan* is the private interior narrative of Naomi rendered into public discourse through Kogawa's novel (Davey 1993, 111), *Disappearing Moon Cafe*'s protagonist Kae is a writer who reflects critically on her own orchestration of stories, the construction of history through stories, and the shaping of her own identity through this process. Although this metafictional element is consistent throughout the novel, it remains obscure and problematic because, as readers, we cannot be sure whether the novel Kae is writing is the novel we read or whether what we read is Kae's preliminary collection of stories.

And yet, a crucial difference emerges in the way the novels conceptualize history. While it would be difficult to reduce *Obasan* to Aunt Emily's position, her approach to history nevertheless seems to dominate the novel. According to Emily, it is possible "to get the facts straight" (Kogawa 1981, 183) so that once Japanese Canadians speak out, the right version of history can be written. Although Emily calls for a revisionist history, her reliance on "rightness" does not challenge the concept of history itself (Davey 1993, 103). Moreover, on the grounds of a universal humanism that insists on the equal standing of all as it seeks out the commonalities among races rather than deploying a discourse of difference (Kogawa 1984, 21), the novel seems to challenge, but does not, as Frank Davey (1993, 112) would have it, implicitly accept, the injustices committed against Japanese Canadians.

Lee's *Disappearing Moon Cafe*, on the other hand, uses dialogism to a different end. Difference and particularity are crucial in the stories of the Wong family, which Kae orchestrates. She self-consciously presents her family history as one configuration of history only; she understands and enacts genealogy as dispersion rather than as a return to origins. The novel relies not so much on a continuous drive to get things "right" as it does on holding dual impulses in suspense. The stories are at times constructive and at times disintegrative; they explain and obscure. Kae's orchestration both affirms and challenges a sense of community. Family history is important but cannot be considered transparent. Reconstructing the stories of other family members helps to shape Kae's own sense of self while simultaneously undermining it. She is always both insider and outsider in the stories she tells as well as in the family of which she is a part.

Lee activates, or, better, she asks the reader to activate the dialogic tensions between the stories. As a result, the dialogic struggles I have just outlined contribute to the performative quality of her novel. The predominant mode of storytelling allows her to write a fictional oral history that functions as a strategy of revision "supplemented by historical interruption" (McFarlane 1995b, 26). At this point of interruption, it provisionally stages the subjectivities of its protagonists through race, gender, and class in the Chinese Canadian community. I believe that this performative aspect in Lee's novel resists attempts to make the workings of the novel transparent. Any story told in the novel is dialogically related to all the others so that any comment on an isolated incident or a single character within a particular story becomes reductive.

That the dialogic relations of *Obasan* and *Disappearing Moon Cafe* have such different effects may be related to the time of their publication and the present situation of Japanese and Chinese Canadian communities. *Obasan* was published at a time when discussions leading to the 1982 Charter of Rights were well under way. The constitutional affirmation of equality among Canada's constituent groups set the tone for many formerly subordinated groups, enabling them "to seek recognition of, and restitution for, the past," which for many meant organizing redress movements (James 1995, 14). *Obasan* is informed by and has contributed to the redress movement of Japanese Canadian communities. By exposing the consequences of the injustices committed against Japanese Canadians – the loss of community, the repression of memory, the psychological problems – the novel enacts "a form of recuperation and of exorcism" (Omatsu 1992, 171). Within the novel, the investigation of Naomi's psychological trauma requires that Aunt Emily's involvement be placed within a broader social movement; similarly, the redress movement enabled and, indeed, required Kogawa to break a personal silence and to bear witness to the official racism of the past (Kogawa 1984, 24; Cheung 1993, 153). The negotiation of the settlement in 1988 gave the Japanese Canadian community a new authority to speak on constitutional civil liberties, which became evident in its contributions to the parliamentary hearings on the Charlottetown constitutional proposals. As Omatsu (1992, 169–70) comments on the Redress Settlement: "we are learning that the potential for flexing our political muscle is limited only by our inability to see beyond our own backyards."

The redress movement of Chinese Canadians has drawn less attention than has that of Japanese Canadians. The insistence on symbolic financial compensation for the imposition of a head tax between 1895 and 1923 has been strong, but their claims, together with those of seven other redress organizations, were rejected in December 1994 by Minister of Secretary of State for Multiculturalism Sheila Finestone. While recognizing the historical contexts that have contributed to the Chinese Canadian community's situation today, Lee seems more interested in understanding how the collective self and individual family members worked within these parameters. Therefore, *Disappearing Moon Cafe* takes a close look at the Chinese Canadian community itself. It seems particularly appropriate that the fictional Disappearing Moon Cafe is located at "50 East Pender Street" (Lee 1990, 23) where today we find Vancouver's Chinese Cultural Centre. The dominant discourses within the community are exposed, and its internal heterogeneity is foregrounded. Resisting the essentialization of the community, Lee reaffirms internal differences in a genealogy of dispersion. The novel may not seem to be obviously informed by the effects of the Charter of Rights, but that impression may be wrong as the affirmation of equal status may well have encouraged Lee's close, critical examination of the Chinese Canadian community.

4 Processes of Un/reading in Daphne Marlatt's *Ana Historic* and Aritha van Herk's *Places Far from Ellesmere*

In one of her imagined conversations with her mother Ina in *Ana Historic*, Annie tries to explain what it means to her to tell a story: "if i'm telling a story i'm untelling it. untelling the real" (Marlatt 1988, 141). Unlike Ina, who believes that "you can't rewrite what's been written" (142), Annie not only untells and rewrites what has been written, but she also speaks the silence of what has not been written. Similarly, the narrator of *Places Far from Ellesmere* takes Leo Tolstoy's *Anna Karenin* to Ellesmere Island in order to set Anna free and to imagine her unwritten story: "knowing that this story, all that is written, can be un/read, uninscribed" (van Herk 1990, 113). The process of un/reading is a recurrent motif in Aritha van Herk's *Places Far from Ellesmere* (1990) and Daphne Marlatt's *Ana Historic* (1988). Both texts challenge fixed categories of reality, fiction, genre, gender, sexuality, and social discourse, showing how they have determined representations of women in history and literature. In their attempt to cross established borders, they deconstruct naturalized categories and offer alternative constructions from new perspectives. These two actions, a double movement textually marked by the slash, are performed simultaneously in what Marlatt has described as fiction theory. Her definition is a helpful starting point in my readings of *Ana Historic* and *Places Far from Ellesmere*. "Fiction theory," Marlatt explains, is

a corrective lens which helps us see *through* the fiction we've been conditioned to take for the real, fictions which have not only constructed woman's "place" in patriarchal society but have constructed the very "nature" of woman (always that which has been). fiction *theory* deconstructs these fictions while *fiction* theory, conscious of itself as fiction, offers a new angle on the "real," one that looks from inside out rather than outside in (the difference between woman as subject and woman as object). (Marlatt et al. 1986, 9)

In this chapter I explore the un/readings that these texts perform. I examine in detail Marlatt's and van Herk's play with genre conventions, the interaction of their narratives, their use of incorporated documents, the relationships between women and nature, and their orchestration of endings. I try to determine to what extent dialogism is used in Marlatt's and van Herk's texts to expose hegemonic discourses and, at the same time, to inscribe counter-discourses.

According to its title, *Ana Historic* is a novel, but many of its characteristics defamiliarize that label: a lack of linear plot development, fragmentary paragraphs, unusual diction, blank pages, unnumbered pages, divider pages that use white space to foreground single lines, arbitrary headings, italicized paragraphs, and an acknowledgment page that lists eleven source texts, to name only a few. On one of the divider pages the reader is told explicitly that "a book of interruptions is not a novel" (Marlatt 1988, 37). Does that mean that *Ana Historic* is not a book of interruptions or that it is not a novel after all? Paradoxically, it is both a novel and a work full of interruptions. Marlatt challenges the reader's familiar ways of seeing and being seen and, through "dialogic play," sharpens her awareness of what novelistic discourse legitimizes (Lowry 1991, 85). In an interview with George Bowering, Marlatt (1989, 104) explains that, in *Ana Historic*, she tries to "deconstruct the novel" in its conventional form, particularly by undermining the novel's sense of continuity, which is linked to a plot that is traditionally dominated by one central line of development to which everything else is subordinated. To settle the debate over whether *Ana Historic* is or is not a novel seems ultimately unimportant.[1] Marlatt's implied adherence to novelistic convention, indicated by the subtitle, serves as her point of departure and drives the subversive gestures of *Ana Historic*.

Van Herk pursues similar goals of generic subversion but chooses a different strategy. Readers who think of genres as products – given, fixed, and natural – may want to describe *Places Far from Ellesmere* as a "genreless book" (Thomas 1991, 70; Goldman 1993, 31); traditional categories do not apply, and "geografictione" – the term coined by van Herk for the subtitle – may not be part of the critic's vocabulary.[2] Unlike Marlatt, van Herk does not challenge generic conventions of the novel from within the literary tradition; rather, she introduces a new term. She has identified "genre" as one of the tools of a patriarchal literary tradition and seeks to transgress its generic conventions, to refuse the reader the comfort of categories, and thus to reinscribe genre as a process in which the reader is actively engaged (van Herk 1991, 38; Manera 1995, 87). For van Herk, crossing familiar genre boundaries and inscribing a new generic location becomes a political act (Buss 1993, 197); she is prepared to accept the cost of marginalization in exchange for its liberating effects:

Cross-boundary writing asserts some powerful reconstructivities ... By estranging themselves from the safety zone of genre, [such texts] participate in their own marginalization ... their refusal of an authenticating space permits them to question the persistent locations of race, gender, nation, and language. "To ... inhabit the border country of frontiers and margins robs discourse of a conciliatory conclusion" (Chambers, 116). It is as refugees from conciliation that such writing locates its praxis, in exchange for the freedom to question the master/piece and the concomitant time/piece of linear and structural narrative that such palimpsesticism offers. (van Herk 1993, 16–17)

But what is a geografictione? The term combines geography, fiction, and the ending "e," which, in many Indo-European languages, marks the feminine form. Rather than a modifier-head structure, in which geography modifies fiction, van Herk (1990, 40) indicates the reversibility of its components when her narrator comments on Edberg: "Edberg: this place, this village and its environs. A fiction of geography/geography of fiction: coming together in people and landscape and the harboured designation of fickle memory." Van Herk (1992, 54–68) has developed the connection between geography and fiction in "Mapping as Metaphor: The Cartographer's Revision." She argues here that "mapping, like language, is creation more than representation, and so it is not illogical to think of fiction as cartography" (58). Specifically referring to Places Far from Ellesmere, van Herk (1996, 129) has suggested that it may be "a book masquerading as a map, or more accurately, a map masquerading as a book." Because geography always relies on an observer, it will always be a subject-dependent fiction rather than an objective fact; in turn, by telling stories, fiction tries to provide a map for experience, subjectivity, and nation.[3] The term "geografictione" therefore describes a literary genre (as the subtitle indicates) and a place ("This geografictione, this Ellesmere" [van Herk 1990, 113]). The perspective from which the mutual implications of geography and fiction are explored is that of a woman, as the feminine ending of geografictione already suggests. Van Herk foregrounds the idea that geography, mapping, and fiction cannot be neutral/neuter; as the narrator realizes in her explorations, all

three discourses, as she knows them, have been written by men, while
the perspectives of women have been silenced and marginalized. *Places
Far from Ellesmere* opens up the spaces of interconnection between
place and fiction in order to inscribe alternatives.

Van Herk's geografictione is divided into four sections that focus on
four different places: Edberg, Edmonton, Calgary, and Ellesmere. The
second subtitle, "explorations on site," raises a number of interesting
issues. The common understanding of exploration as a systematic
investigation of unfamiliar, unknown regions for scientific purposes is
both evoked and undermined in van Herk's geografictione. The obser-
vational character of the first three sections suggests such a project of
investigation on location, which is focused on sight (an obvious play
on "site"), but the narrator seems to reconstruct these sites from memory, through association. They become "mnemonic reading[s]" (van
Herk 1996, 130). No scientific purposes drive the narrative; instead,
the narrator explores places as they relate to her own life, her personal experiences, her memories, her "landscapes of the mind" (Porteous
1990). In the narrator's attempt to write her own experience, the discourses of geography and history become closely connected. The
matrix of place and time becomes a way of understanding experience
– a notion that Bakhtin, dissatisfied with the way aspects of time and
place had been treated separately in literary criticism, explores through
the concept of the "chronotope." The chronotope captures the "intrinsic connectedness of temporal and spatial relationships that are artistically expressed in literature" (Bakhtin 1981, 84), and meaning is only
possible "through the gates of the chronotope" (258). I propose that
the four sections of *Places Far from Ellesmere* relate to each other dialogically through their respective chronotopes.[4]

A number of observations support such a relational reading. In the
reconstruction of the exploration sites, explicit references to the other
locations show how each section is informed by and reflects on others
in the narrator's experience.[5] The ongoing reconfiguration of places
occurs as the narrator (and reader) reads towards and then back
through Ellesmere. The title itself suggests a relational focus: *Places Far
from Ellesmere*. While the head of the phrase is "places," these places
are considered and situated in relation to one particular site, Ellesmere.
"Far" itself implies the interdependent place/time matrix of the
chronotope; "far" indicates distance and remoteness not only in spatial but also in temporal terms.

In the first three sections the narrator establishes different chronotopes by associating each city with a time in her life: Edberg with childhood and teens, Edmonton with university years, Calgary with work
and adult life. She explores these places by reading them through

already existing maps and creating her own map as she goes along. Although these maps may not be adequate as referential guides, they operate as ways to organize, orient, and control the personal, social, and cultural experiences of the narrator (Huggan 1994b, 14). The narrator contemplates the question of representation and the status of maps. Maps can be neither objective nor totally exact; they are resemblances of the environment and function, therefore, not as copies but as models of reality. Can such a map then be considered factual, the narrator wonders? Or "is it all an elaborate fabrication" (van Herk 1990, 15)? Comparing her memory of Edberg to other people's recollections, she realizes that there are "other originals" (37): "their versions negate yours" (37–8). The narrator creates two kinds of maps, the boundaries of which increasingly blur: maps that attempt to model her environment and maps that represent her own experiences of places.

The narrator begins the exploration of Edberg by paying close attention to physical location, which is indicated primarily through the use of numerous prepositions:

A welt in the parkland on the raise between Dried Meat Lake and Meeting Creek, just off the Donalda/Duhamel trail: snagged between clumps of poplar and willow, the steady infusion of a prairie vapour from the everywhere tenacious low-growing rose bushes. (13)

There might have been a trail passed here, that cart trail through this region partly wooded and with scattered trees and coppice (J.B. Tyrell, 1887) once, a trail that angled across the sections and quarter-sections without the ninety-degree angles of the survey crews ... a trail that led between communities, between schools, between stopping places and boarding houses (with their lice and good company), between general stores, between horse-barns. (13–14)

She provides a detailed account of various locations and their spatial relation to each other in order to assess whether they still exist. Her map thus becomes a map of place and time, a map with its own chronotope. The narrator examines public places, the cart trail, the creamery, the cafés, the town pump, the blacksmith shop, the hotel, the post office, and many more to find out which sites are gone and which have changed or remained: "disappearing locations of appearances: sites of seeing" (29). The other map is one of personal experiences; it notes "allowances" and "forbiddences" (24–9) as well as memories associated with the buildings, streets, and sites mapped before. As the narrator shows, her maps of Edberg always revolve around the presence of the mapmaker herself. Her maps cannot claim neutrality but are instead a form of personal and social knowledge that is determined by the coordinates of place, time, and her own subjectivity. Therefore, like these maps, Edberg cannot be a fixed place to which the narrator can easily return; it cannot be mapped. Edberg becomes for the narrator "a fiction of geography/geography of fiction ... Invented: textual: un/read: the hieroglyphic secrets of the past" (40).

Similarly, Edmonton is read as a city whose division by the Saskatchewan River into north and south parallels the narrator's own experience as an adult woman with a divided self. She feels cut off from her childhood, separated from Edberg, removed from home, struggling to "start a life in Edmonton" (45). She realizes that the place to which she comes is one with "its own nebulous prairie history: a fort(ress) to be stormed" (44). Edmonton, the old trading post of the Hudson's Bay Company, has already been mapped by others. She tries to get to know the place through her reading: "Edmonton is a reading, an act of text, an open book" (47); "through the maze of your books you try to read this place" (52); "you read, entext yourself a city of pages" (53). In spite of her efforts, she lacks agency in this city where the streets walk her rather than vice versa (54). She cannot escape the restrictions she associates with the chronotope of Edberg. The geographical division she sees around her and the division she experiences inside are disruptive and feel like stagnation (48).

In her next exploration the narrator finds herself trapped in a similar dilemma. The presence of maps and cartographic principles is even more pervasive in the section on Calgary. The narrator considers "Calgary as quadrant, the sweep of a long-armed compass quartering the city NW/NE/SE/SW, segmented" (70). She consults maps to locate places in the city (59, 69) and hopes that they will also help her to find herself: "How to find yourself: see map" (71). However, Calgary, with all its maps, does not fulfill these hopes. To express her feelings of entrapment, the narrator compares the city to Jericho (57–8, 62, 74), the ancient city whose massive walls are brought down by seven trumpet-blowing priests and that is taken over by the Israelites. Does Calgary have to be destroyed in a similar fashion for the narrator to be able to free herself? The materialist nature of the twentieth century seems overwhelming in Calgary, its "iconography of money" overpowering (65). The narrator is left confused, caught in "labyrinths" of buildings, light and stone (72, 74): "who can find you here, a clumsy bawling beast in the centre of a web of thread, a cat's cradle of encapturement?" (73). In this state of confusion and distress, her desire to belong and to find a home becomes paramount (61, 62, 66, 68, 69, 71).

This desire for a home seems to be the driving force behind van Herk's geografictione (Manera 1995, 88; van Herk 1996, 130). The narrator literally and metaphorically recedes from and moves towards home: she moves north, then south, then north again. As the spiral movement of the narrative suggests, home is not a fixed entity, not a product, but an eternal process: "home is a movement, a quick tug at itself and it packs up" (van Herk 1990, 69). Paradoxically, to be home you must move. No matter how hard the narrator tries to map her own places, to find her home – in Edberg, Edmonton, or Calgary – she cannot be satisfied. The desire to escape, to leave again, is always present: "is this [Edberg] a place from which to launch a world" (33); "how to get from this point [Edmonton] farther, how to reach the reaches of the world, and maybe Russia" (48); "to belong then. Leaving not here but from here" (61). Home itself becomes a shifting signifier that has to be invented (33). Every return will be a return to something new; every home will be provisional. The title of the first chapter, "Edberg: coppice of desire and return," captures this notion in its image of a coppice, a thicket of small trees that is repeatedly cut back only to be allowed to regrow. Similarly, Edberg as the place of childhood and home is a place that, metaphorically speaking, has to be repeatedly cut down and reconstructed. Instead of becoming a reified myth, home becomes the goal of a continuously desired and deferred return.

In *Places Far from Ellesmere* the desire to return home, the longing for permanence and essence, is connected with the narrator's interest in "engravement," graveyards, and plots (23, 61, 62, 140), which Kirkwood (1991, 29) refers to as van Herk's "death-fixation." As Goldman (1993, 31) points out, however, "physical engravement, i.e., burial in the landscape, has affinities with the engravement or emplotting of fictions." The narrator contemplates: "To dare to stay here to die, to dare to stay after death, to implant yourself firmly and say, 'Here I stay, let those who would look for a record come here'" (van Herk 1990, 61). If home signifies safety, then the plot, in both senses, should promise refuge and protection. However, the familiar plots of novels promise women refuge only in marriage, insanity, or death. Her explorations of the three cities and her futile attempt to follow cartographic principles lead the narrator to a drastic measure: she moves away from the urban centres and pre-written maps and fictions to Ellesmere, the extreme north. Ellesmere Island does not figure as a place of permanent residence but as a destination for a camping trip with her partner Bob. This trip takes place in July, the brief summer weeks in the north. The narrator comes to Ellesmere from the south. For her, as for many others, the north is "a place to visit, not a land in which to stay" (Grace 1991, 250). Nevertheless, or perhaps therefore, she is driven by her hope for revelation, for the impossible: "At last, again, you think you've found a home. You search out possible sites for your future grave" (van Herk 1990, 140). Can she find a home/a plot on Ellesmere

Island? In the end her search is frustrated: "You are destined to become ashes. Ashes alone. There are murderers at large. You have imagined again and again places for your ashes to be scattered to the high winds" (141). She cannot find or select a safe place because there are no safe places, no safe plots – neither graves nor fictions – for women.

Unlike van Herk's geografictione, in which four chronotopes are dialogically related through the perspective of one character, Daphne Marlatt's *Ana Historic* juxtaposes and dialogically relates the perspectives of three women: Annie, Mrs Richards, and Ina. Their narratives are not divided into separate sections; instead, the text shifts rapidly between these (and other) perspectives. The result of this strategy is a non-linear and disrupted novel that resists and subverts notions of cohesion and master plot (Banting 1991, 125; Tostevin 1989, 38). While it may seem as if "Marlatt lets the story lie there, apparently in pieces," a closer examination reveals its intricate structure (Dragland 1991, 182) – what Keith Green and Jill LeBihan (1994, 434) have described as a "structured polyphony" rather than a cacophony.

Annie is married to her former college history professor, Richard, for whom she often does archival research in the library; they live in Vancouver with their two children, Mickey and Ange. Annie is trying to cope with the recent loss of her mother, Ina, whose death has created a threshold situation – a crisis and a break in her life – that results in Annie's own writing. Through her own memories of childhood, Annie tries to retrace the life of her mother Ina, a "proper" British lady, who, after leaving Malaysia, comes with her family to Vancouver where she suffers from loneliness and isolation. Ina's distraught behaviour is diagnosed as hysteria and treated with electric shock, which leaves her permanently disoriented. As Annie conducts research for her husband, she discovers a reference to a woman called Mrs Richards. Official historical documents tell her that Mrs Richards arrived in Vancouver in 1873 and worked as the second school teacher at Hastings Mill School. When she married Ben Springer the following year, she disappeared from the public record. Disappointed by the lack of information about her, Annie invents a history for Mrs Richards with the help of the latter's journal, which she finds stored in the archives of Vancouver.[6]

The similarity of sound and appearance of the three names suggests several interrelations.[7] Not only are the first names strikingly similar – Annie/Ana, Annie/Ina, Ana/Ina – but Mrs Richards becomes Ana Richards in the writings of Richard's Annie. As Lowry (1991, 94) has pointed out, the names "interrelate, rhyme and echo through the reading." Unlike other critics who read these characters as flowing and blending into each other (Tostevin 1989, 37; Chan 1992, 68), I would argue that their perspectives remain distinct while being interrelated through many parallels and conflicts. All three women are immigrants, wives, and writers. Annie writes a novel (Marlatt 1988, 140); Mrs Richards keeps a journal (29); and Ina writes family stories in a notebook (20). While they influence, relativize, and illuminate each other, they nevertheless remain separate characters who, in themselves, are not unitary but "heterogeneous subjects composed of multiple discourses" (Jones 1993, 143; see also Dragland 1991, 178). Marlatt (1989, 101) herself has referred to the stories of Annie and Ana, for instance, as analogies, twins, off-rhymes, and stories that echo each other.

When Annie comes across the references to Mrs Richards in the archives, she immediately realizes that "there is a story here" (Marlatt 1988, 14), a story she wants to pursue. The story of her mother's life is more difficult for Annie to write: "I-na, I-no-longer, i can't turn you into a story. there is this absence here, where the words stop" (11). In a way, she imagines for Mrs Richards what her mother could not imagine for herself and what she could not imagine for her mother (Grisé 1993, 92): "Ana/Ina whose story is this" (Marlatt 1988, 67). It is through her own memories of her childhood and the imagined conversations with her mother that she rewrites her life story. Once driven by the desire to "efface" her mother (50), to become "another (the other) woman in the house" (50), Annie is now disturbed by her absence. Without Ina, the "plotline" that Annie's life once followed is no longer clear to her (17). Ina used to keep her "on track," guiding her past digressions, alternatives, holes, and absences (17). The many asides ("you said") in Annie's writing attest to her mother's lasting influence as her guide and teacher as well as her constant critic who challenges her notions of history, fiction, and truth: "you go on living in me, catching me out" (141); "i feel myself in you, irritated at the edges where we overlap" (17).

In the case of Mrs Richards, Annie relies on the woman's journal, which helps her to reconstruct her actions as well as her thoughts. Her concern is not so much that she get the story right but that she explore the space of fictional possibilities, "the gap between two versions" (106). Annie compares the stories of official history to pictures that are framed and static:

framed by a phrase that judges ... sized-up in a glance, objectified. that's what history offers, that's its allure, its pretence. "history says of her ..." but when you're so framed, caught in the act, the (f) stop of act, fact – what recourse? step inside the picture and open it up. (56)

As Annie opens up the picture of Mrs Richards provided by the official documents, she challenges its selectivity and framing. In turn, the story Annie imagines for Mrs Richards opens up the picture of her own life. When Annie wonders about Mrs Richards's first name – "what is her first name? she must have one – so far she has only the name of a dead man, someone somewhere else" (37) – she chooses "Ana" without further explanation, a choice that hints at the connection between their life stories (39). Moreover, the name comments on Annie's endeavour of imagining her story: "ana / that's her name: back, backward, reversed / again, anew" (43). Ana is a palindrome that literally enacts what the prefix suggests. Annie/Ana is writing back to and writing anew the official history that does not recognize her actions.

Wondering why Mrs Richards disappeared from the records after her marriage (134, 146), Annie reflects on her own married life, asking herself whether there were other possibilities. Shocked at first by Zoe's suggestion of a relationship between Mrs Richards and Birdie Stewart, she does imagine how they could have become close, what they would have said to each other (138–9). Mrs Richards's story thus becomes "a historical leak for the possibility of lesbian life in Victorian British Columbia" (Marlatt 1990b, 15); it acts as a rehearsal for Annie and enables her to express her desire for Zoe so that their relationship becomes a contemporary rewriting of the imagined encounter between Ana and Birdie. In the exploration of these relationships, Annie refuses to pretend that she is a disinterested, objective observer or chronicler of history. On the contrary, she foregrounds her struggle to inscribe her own subjectivity. Annie's voice becomes the means for the reader to envision strategies of resistance, project them into the past, and continue their development in the present and future (Grisé 1993, 96–7). Annie realizes her implication in the stories of Ina, Ana, and herself and also her implication in the process of producing and maintaining gendered female bodies.

While the reader is well aware that Annie attempts to reconstruct Mrs Richards's and Ina's stories, the novel's fragmentary style succeeds in telling their stories without seeming to, without establishing a narrative authority. The dialogic relations between stories seem to undermine any consistent structure of embedding. Ana, Ina, Annie, and Ange become a "continuum of life stories" in discontinuous form (Grisé 1993, 92). *Ana Historic* gives voice to these previously silenced women by dialogically writing them into the gap between history and fiction. Marlatt's "genealogy for lost women" reinscribes these women as speaking subjects who can participate in the creation of their own worlds (Goldman 1992, 33; see also Lowry 1991, 84). However, the main interest of the novel is in the process itself rather than in the conclusions to the individual stories. It is no surprise, therefore, that Annie experiences particular difficulties with the beginnings and endings of the stories she reinscribes.

To suggest the notion of connectedness and continuum between these perspectives, Marlatt (1988, 129) skilfully shifts pronouns to blur the edges of these stories:

> she who is you
> or me
>   'i'
> address this to

Marlatt's shifting pronouns refuse the possibility of stable references. Rather than indicating that the self is unstable or unnameable, these shifting references resist the cultural inscriptions of women's bodies that Ana, Ina, and Annie have experienced. Thus, Marlatt "forces the reader to confront the degree to which the concept of the individual is dependent upon, and constructed by, discursive practices" (Chalykoff 1994, 5). If the reader engages with these practices, then the concept of woman can be reinscribed. Not only does Marlatt move beyond the subject-object paradigm to include the shifting "she," but she also uses the second person pronoun "you" to reinforce a sense of connection between the audiences in the novel; it brings together and heralds a culture centred on women who share lives and histories (Chan 1992, 69): "o the cultural labyrinth of our inheritance, mother to daughter to mother ..." (Marlatt 1988, 24). As Marlatt (1989, 100) has said in an interview, "that 'you' shifts around quite a lot, because sometimes it's 'you,' Mrs. Richards, a lot of the time it's 'you,' Ina – and sometimes it's 'you' reflexive, anywoman's you." The reader herself thus becomes part of the shared experience and has to take responsibility for the performance of the text; she is left unable to escape this address (Hutcheon 1988c, 19).[8]

The second person singular pronoun is also a crucial feature of van Herk's geografictione. Like Marlatt's pronouns, van Herk's "you" shifts frequently, especially between the reader of *Places Far from Ellesmere* and its narrator, who often seems to be addressing herself. The inclusive pronoun "you" that moves outward to include the reader reinforces the narrator's implication that all women are Annas who "have suffered from the rigid frame imposed by the representation of women as Woman" (Goldman 1993, 36). At the same time, the narrator here seems to be engaged in a conversation with herself, with the result that the "you" actually refers back to herself (Manera 1995, 89). While Thomas (1991, 69) has criticized this strategy as "alienating," as "a defense against self-disclosure," I see the technique as successfully suggesting that in every reading of herself the narrator's subjectivity is constructed through discursive practices.

Thus, the narrator foregrounds herself as a living text, a character being read.

Dialogic play not only occurs between Marlatt's life stories of three women and van Herk's chronotopes but also between these narratives and a variety of quoted documents. Both texts provide bibliographies that list many of the writers' immediate sources. They thus foreground the recognition, in van Herk's words, that "writing is an act of appropriation" (1990, n.p.). Marlatt's (1988, 81) Annie contemplates the dialogic quality of all discourse: "echoing your words, Ina – another quotation, except i quote myself (and what if our heads are full of other people's words? nothing *without* quotation marks.)" None of the documents quoted in these texts supports women's desire to write their own stories; each document has reduced women to Woman and has silenced them. All discourses are informed by power relations; however, as the narrators reread these documents and pry open the monologic economy of discourses from positions of difference and resistance, Marlatt and van Herk suggest that no discourse is exempt from being dialogized, opened up, and challenged. By examining how these discourses operate, the nature of their tactics and power relations, these authors question any postulate of causality and claim to monologic truth. Dialogic relations institute a strategy for inscribing voices previously unheard, and this strategy deprivileges dominant discourses of patriarchy and compulsory heterosexuality as well as the hegemonies they support.

I want to take a closer look first at van Herk's page of quotations, which follows the table of contents in *Places Far from Ellesmere*. Here the reader finds excerpts from Claude Lévi-Strauss's *Tristes Tropiques*, Michel Foucault's *The Archaeology of Knowledge*, and Albert Camus's "The Minotaur or the Stop in Oran." These quotes are followed by two sentences that are indented like the preceding quotes but that are enclosed in square brackets and left unidentified: "[In the explorations of memory and place lie unsolved murders; in the multiple dissensions of distance and time, certain conditions prevail. The world admits deserts and islands but no women.]" (van Herk 1990, n.p.). The speaker first quotes three renowned twentieth-century white, male, European philosophers and writers and then collates ideas and phrases from their quotations in order to create this new statement. As these phrases are recombined and brought into new contexts, they acquire different meanings and point to their own silences. The world, as written and constructed by men (in these quotations), includes deserts and islands but no women. Literally and metaphorically, women are neither acknowledged nor allowed into the text of the written wor(l)d. By adding the dialogic afterthought, the speaker admits herself into the world she has experienced as dominated and controlled by men, reclaiming the connection between desert, island, and woman: van Herk's entire text becomes an extension of this opening gesture of reinscription.

The most extensive quotations in *Places Far from Ellesmere* come from Leo Tolstoy's *Anna Karenin* (1875–77), which the narrator takes to Ellesmere Island with her "to solve a problem in how to think about love; to solve a problem in the (grave) differences between men's writing and women's writing: to solve a problem in sexual judgment" (van Herk 1990, 82). In her re-reading of Anna, she hopes to "un/read her, set her free" by providing a woman's reading of "a male reading of women" (82). The first three sections on Edberg, Edmonton, and Calgary already weave the thread of Tolstoy's novel into this geografictione (16, 33, 36, 48, 50, 64), but only when the narrator comes to Ellesmere does the actual un/reading take place.

Anna Karenin has traditionally been considered the prototype of nineteenth-century psychological realism. In the novel, Anna's adulterous passion for the young officer Vronsky in 1860s St Petersburg ultimately leads to her suicide. The narrator undertakes what both Pianos (1995, 98) and Goldman (1993, 35) have referred to as an exploratory strategy of a feminist reading of Tolstoy's novel: "reading is a new act here, not introverted and possessive but exploratory, the text a new body of the self, the self a new reading of place" (van Herk 1990, 113). Tolstoy is unable to deal with an independent woman who is not only sensual but who also reads (her own life). He has to destroy Anna for what he perceives to be a transgression of moral and social laws. Van Herk's narrator reads Anna out of her position of victimhood, and, in the process, Anna becomes a symbol for all women who are oppressed: "women are all Annas, caught or not" (82). If the narrator can un/read Anna, then women can find strategies of resistance to un/read themselves, to un/read the category of Woman that has stifled them.

To un/read Anna, the narrator quotes phrases and paragraphs from the novel and integrates them into her own text: "the words are stirred, mixed, like pieces of a jigsaw, broken up into their separate shapes and the whole picture lost, left to be reconstructed by another, a different hand" (113). The quotes no longer follow the chronology of Tolstoy's plot but become part of a new text that follows its own logic. Dialogic relations are created as the narrator compares her own situation and women's situations in general to Anna's; she highlights similarities and differences and thus exposes the ideologies that inform the narrative of Tolstoy's novel. The act of reading itself is significant:

Although her first desire is to read, she is distracted, perhaps because she is placed on that train by Tolstoy, and you know that he uses trains to displace her.

> At first she made no progress with her reading. For a while the bustle of people coming and going was disturbing ... she could not help listening to the noises ... all this distracted her attention.

Anna is travelling to Ellesmere; she needs to be transported there in order to read her English/Russian story. (133–4)

The narrator analyzes Tolstoy's desire to displace Anna, to unsettle her, to keep her from reading, but she turns his strategy against him by reading Anna's journey as bringing her to Ellesmere, where she will find the quiet and solitude necessary for her reading:

She will extinguish her lamp when she pleases.

> And the candle by which she had been reading the book filled with trouble and deceit, sorrow and evil, flared up with a brighter light, illuminating for her everything that before had been enshrouded in darkness, flickered, grew dim and went out for ever.

But not quite for ever. Here in the forever light of Ellesmere you are unreading the Anna that Tolstoy pretended to write. (138)

While Anna's reading light may go out in Tolstoy's novel, the narrator challenges this fact in the new context within which she performs the un/reading of the novel and Anna. In the constant light of Ellesmere, there is no reason for Anna's light to go out; it can be rekindled in the narrator's rereading. Anna's desire to read, together with the way she "trusts her reading and her body" (142), ensure her downfall in Tolstoy's novel, but the same qualities in van Herk's narrator can ensure Anna's freedom from Tolstoy's grasp.

Why does van Herk choose *Anna Karenin* as the novel for her narrator to un/read? The grief that van Herk (1996, 134–5) has identified as the main impetus for her writing of this geografictione is a grief for "the endless procession of female characters who were permitted no cartography of their own, tempted unto death by their malleable mappability, their killability." She has explained that her novels have focused on these women characters – Judith, Ja-el, Arachne, and here Anna Karenin – because of her desire to "question meaning, history, representation, to question our desires and duties, to question one another. And to re-write, inscribe differently, to re-verse the previously static and perpetually frozen" (van Herk 1991, 132). One of her strategies for inscribing a textual presence for women is to reclaim "lost, abandoned and misrepresented women's myths" (van Herk 1987, 12). By un/reading the story of Anna Karenin, for instance, van Herk has chosen one of the best known stories about women written by men in the Western world. In the spaces where her women characters enter forbidden territory and cross forbidden boundaries, van Herk's rewritings locate alternatives in order to "mime a fictional future" for women, to explore what is possible rather than what is probable (9). As the narrator frees the textual Anna, she also hopes to liberate women readers' desires (to imagine the liberation of other fictional women or themselves), and, by extension, the writer herself may be liberated from an oppressive textual tradition (Buss 1993, 201).

   Possibility is also a key notion in Marlatt's revisionist strategy of quotation, which enables Annie to project lives and texts for herself, her mother, and Ana out of the past and into the future. In this sense, *Ana Historic* becomes a reaction against a history in which women are a-historic (Dragland 1991, 180). Annie writes stories of who these women are and who they could be by providing an "analysis of the social context each of them inhabit [*sic*]" (Marlatt 1990b, 15). These social contexts are reconstructed through a wide range of texts that are mentioned, alluded to, or quoted from in the novel; eleven of these sources are acknowledged in the bibliography. They include historical studies and school textbooks about Vancouver and British Columbia, books of (clinical) psychiatry, the Bible, pop songs, novels, newspapers, and Hannah More's *Strictures* (1799). A rereading of the documents in *Ana Historic* shows that their discourses, which have supported official history and thereby silenced and objectified women, are not fixed; placed in a new context, they can be challenged and exposed as constructions. In the act of self-consciously reproducing monologic speech, the novel draws these discourses into a dialogic economy (Jones 1993, 142). In this process of dialogization, which Banting (1991, 125) has described as a form of translation, "the documentary language becomes denatured, provoked to yield its ideological biases. The language of history breaks down into its components, namely, the language of nominalization, categorization, hierarchization, domination, colonization, subordination, and control."[9] Annie is no longer interested in contributing to the books of "already-made" history that her husband writes by "looking for missing pieces ... missing facts" (Marlatt 1988, 98, 134). Nevertheless she realizes that she must engage in a different kind of history-making, "making fresh tracks my own way" (98), if she wants to participate in the creation of her world. Her dialogic encounters with the quoted documents become her strategy for deconstructing official history and opening up the still frames of historical facts to focus on the stories of people's lives, the "missing persons in all this rubble" (134).

Annie challenges the documents that speak of Mrs Richards not only because they lack information about her life but also because she questions the criteria that determine what constitutes history, especially the insistence on "cause and effect," the narrow focus on social status (48), and the Cartesian public-private split. The "historic voice (voice-over)" (48) retrospectively registers only public positions and familial status: Mrs Richards was a school and piano teacher; she came to Vancouver as a widow and the following year married Ben Springer. Marriage is equated with a retreat into the folds of family life, and, as a result, she becomes invisible to chroniclers of history. So selective and brief are the references to women, and in particular to Mrs Richards, in Alan Morley's *Vancouver: From Milltown to Metropolis* (1961), Major J.S. Matthews's *Early Vancouver* (1932), and A.M. Ross's "The Romance of Vancouver's Schools" (1971) that Annie can quote, read, and challenge them all (39, 47–8). What she misses in these texts is what she valorizes in her fictional rendering of Ana's life: her daily activities and reflections, her personality, and her friendships with other women in her community.

In some ways these absences of women in official history only reinforce what Annie learned in early life about the role and place of women in society. Her recognition triggers a quotation from M. Allerdale Grainger's *Woodsmen of the West* (1964):

a woman's place. safe. suspended out of the swift race of the world.

the monstrous lie of it: the lure of absence. self-effacing.

"Watch Carter when the 'donk' (his donkey!) has got up steam – its first steam; and when the rigging men (his rigging men!) drag out the wire rope to make a great circle through the woods. And when the circle is complete from one drum, round by where the cut logs are lying, back to the other drum; and when the active rigging slinger (his rigging slinger!) has hooked a log on to a point of the wire cable; and when the signaller (his signaller!) has pulled the wire telegraph and made the donkey toot ... just think of Carter's feelings as the engineer jams over levers, opens up the throttle, sets the thudding, whirring donkey winding up the cable, and drags the first log into sight; out from the forest down to the beach; bump, bump! Think what this mastery over huge, heavy logs means to a man who has been used to coax them to tiny movements by patience and a puny jack-screw..."

history the story, Carter's and all the others', of dominance. mastery. the bold line of it.

soon it will be getting dark, soon the kids will be coming in from outdoors. (Marlatt 1988, 24–5)

This quotation from Grainger powerfully asserts the presence of men in the world. Presence is defined in his novel by Carter's dominance and mastery over machines, nature, and women (through their very absence from history). This politics of power, together with "a language of possession" (Jones 1993, 151), ensures that history becomes, as Annie states, "the story ... of dominance. mastery" (Marlatt 1988, 25). This paragraph and other quotations from Grainger's novel in *Ana Historic* (63, 80) challenge what Ralph Andrews (1956, 12), who quotes extensively from Grainger's novel in his *Glory Days of Logging*, describes as "crystal clear word pictures of man and conditions of the time." Through her dialogic repositioning of quotations, Annie shows that these "word pictures" are specific to their socio-historical contexts and informed by patriarchal ideologies. Again, Annie engages with still frames, static pictures, which her rereadings begin to unsettle as she "think[s] what this mastery ... means to a man" (Marlatt 1988, 25).[10] She is determined to inscribe herself into her own history, her story; that is why she follows Grainger's quote with a description of her own domestic situation as she waits for her children to return home.

The connection between history, nature, and men is also challenged through the dialogic relativization of quotations from Lawson and Young's *A History and Geography of British Columbia: For Use in Public School* (1906):

tomboy, her mother said. tom, the male of the species plus boy. double masculine, as if girl were completely erased....

it wasn't tom, or boy, it wasn't hoyden, minx, baggage, but what lay below names – barely even touched by them.

"Douglas fir and red cedar are the principal trees. Of these, the former – named after David Douglas, a well-known botanist – is the staple timber of commerce. Average trees grow 150 feet high, clear of limbs, with a diameter of 5 to 6 feet. The wood has great strength and is largely used for shipbuilding, bridge work, fencing, railway ties, and furniture. As a pulp-making tree the fir is valuable. Its bark makes a good fuel."

clear of limbs? of extras, of asides. tree as a straight line, a stick. there for the taking.

Mrs. Richards, who stood as straight as any tree (o that Victorian sensibility – backbone, Madam, backbone!) wasn't there for the taking. (Marlatt 1988, 13–14)

In the description of the Douglas fir, its qualities for the economy are foregrounded: tall and wide, usable in a variety of industries – all of which serve the interest of man.[11] The act of naming, "Douglas fir," goes hand in hand with the patriarchal ideology of possession. In contrast, as a young girl Annie, through the use of a "double masculine," refuses to be named by her mother. She denies the act of naming its power and significance in a masculine economy and claims a part of herself as inaccessible to the language of men and history. As she dialogically engages with the quotation, she repeats parts of it with a difference, rephrasing it as a question: "clear of limbs?" (14). Annie exposes masculine values based on pragmatism and utilitarianism and supported by the same linguistic economy identified in Grainger's novel (Jones 1993, 149). When Annie uses the same terminology to describe Mrs Richards – "who stood as straight as any tree ... wasn't there for the taking ... imagining herself free of history" (Marlatt 1988, 14) – she not only mocks the quotation but reclaims the positive qualities of trees in her characterization of Mrs Richards and refuses the exploitation that comes with it in the masculine economy. Moreover, while Mrs Richards has been named by her husband through a marriage that operates within the same patriarchal discourse, she refuses to be controlled by it, refuses to be "there for the taking" in more than one sense.

Repeatedly, Annie places descriptions of the "important events in the world" that make up history ("the real story the city fathers tell" [28], such as the building of the CPR) side by side with those events from the women's realm ("not facts but skeletal bones of a suppressed body the story is" [29], such as the arrival of the first piano). Women's history values private events and is less concerned with pinpointing facts and figures of exploitation. In a particularly striking example, Annie imagines the counterpoint between the boat race that men write about and "the ships men ride into the pages of history" (121) and "women's work" (123) of giving birth to the first white child at Hastings Mill, which goes unrecorded in archival documents (113–27). Here the fun-filled, yet banal, leisure activities of men are regarded more highly than is the painful, life-giving labour of women. This example shows that the underlying criteria for men's and women's history are themselves highly contradictory and problematical. If a masculine discourse is indeed interested in productivity, would births not rate high on the scale?

When Annie attempts to tell her mother's story, to come to terms with her death and absence, she uses a similar strategy. She places the public, masculine discourse of the medical establishment, which diagnoses Ina as depressive and hysteric and subjects her to electroshock treatment, side by side her personal memories of her mother's emotional outbursts, anxiety attacks, and unhappiness in the family home. Four quotations are taken from Leonard Roy Frank's *The History of Shock Treatment* (1978), a compilation of conflicting perspectives on shock treatment collected from various documents. Although most of the sections Annie quotes endorse the treatment, her critical engagement with these quotations supports Frank's "demystifying message" (xiv). He seeks to expose the abuse of state-delegated power by psychiatrists who use shock treatment and furthermore "to arm psychiatric inmates with the knowledge and the will to resist assault by the psychiatric system" (xiv); Frank dedicates the book to "all those engaged in the struggle against psychiatric tyranny" (n.p.).

Annie's description of Ina's behaviour after returning from the hospital exposes the misleading rhetoric used to describe the treatment and identifies the side effects of amnesia as actual brain damage. The promise of health, of being herself again, is supported by the medical descriptions of the treatment but challenged by Annie's memories of the end result:

[Harald] came to my bedroom and we had long discussions about depression and what the psychiatrist said. you could go into hospital for only a few days, for treatment that would erase the thoughts that tormented you, and then you'd be yourself again in a week or two.

yourself again: who was that? i could barely remember the mother who'd laughed at "Hokey-Pokey," loved Abbott and Costello, read "The King asked the Queen and Queen asked the Dairy-Maid" in funny voices ...

"Glissando in Electric Shock Therapy is the method of applying the shock stimulus to the patient in a smooth, gradually increasing manner so that the severity of the initial onset is minimized." ...

when Harald brought you back from the hospital he brought back a stranger, a small round person collapsed in on herself. (Marlatt 1988, 144–5)

The woman who before was frightened and depressed, unsure of her identity, is left with no ability to feel or remember her identity at all. Given the severity of Ina's symptoms, Annie wonders whether the diagnosis of hysteria and the shock treatment are really designed to contain and silence women rather than to help them. Feminist critics of the medical establishment have pointed out that the medical discourse has relied upon such principles of domination for a long time.[12] As medical discourse connects behaviour to the body, it makes it into a scientific problem so that the body becomes an object for medical therapy. The result is, as Sherwin (1992, 85) points out, that "by medicating socially induced depression and anxiety, medicine helps to perpetuate women's oppression and deflects attention from the injustice of their situation." Haraway (1991, 14) supports this observation by arguing that "the biochemical and physiological basis of the therapeutic claims immensely strengthen[s] the legitimating power of scientific managers over women's lives."

Annie explores the history of hysteria in medical discourse, especially the long-held notion that hysteria was the result of uterine displacement and, therefore, a woman's disease.[13] A quotation from James Hillman's *The Myth of Analysis: Three Essays in Archetypal Psychology* (1972) indicates that one of the avenues pursued to "cure" women of hysteria was to remove their uteri (Hillman 1972, 255–6; Marlatt 1988, 89). Ina herself has suffered a hysterectomy as well as other invasive procedures (Marlatt 1988, 88). By comparing her own experiences of her mother's situation with the objectifying medical discourse, Annie exposes how diagnoses function as organizing mechanisms to support the principle of domination. Annie's reaccentuation of these quotations emphasizes that it is crucial to consider who speaks the name hysteria because, as Hillman warns (1972, 254), "where hysteria is diagnosed, misogyny is not far away." Through the authority to define what is normal or pathological, medicine often reinforces gender roles and existing power inequalities.

Annie's dialogic engagement with these and other quoted documents opens up the discursive fields in which they circulate. While *Ana Historic* acknowledges their existence and the extent to which they have constituted the subjectivity of women, Annie recontextualizes them to expose their ideological underpinnings. This process disrupts their monologic authority, challenges their logic, and leaves them in fragments, only to incorporate alternative tellings that occur in the cracks the re-readings have opened. Jones (1993, 142) reads Annie's assumption of the subordinate, supposedly non-authoritative, role of copyist in the novel as its most powerful subversive gesture. It allows her to explore the space between history and fiction, to challenge the binary opposition, and thereby to invent "a historical leak, a hole in the sieve of fact that let the shadow of a possibility leak through into full-blown life" (Marlatt 1990b, 15). In *Ana Historic* Marlatt insists that history can be changed because its own discourse is a fiction:

If history is a construction and language is also a construction—in fact, it actually constructs the reality we live and act in—then we can change it. We're not stuck in some authoritative version of the real, and for women that's extremely important, because until recently we always were—the patriarchal version was always *the* version, and now we know that's not true. We can throw out that powerful little article. When we change language, we change the building blocks by which we construct our reality or even our past 'reality,' history. (Marlatt 1993, 188)

Marlatt exposes the monologism of the male gaze and the historic voice-over in *Ana Historic*: indeed, she returns the gaze and replaces the voice-over with a polyphony of voices. Both strategies – performed through dialogic relations – are empowering possibilities for women to reclaim themselves as speaking subjects who participate in the creation of their own worlds.

In the worlds that women construct for themselves, they are no longer confined to the domestic space; they become aware of their own situatedness not only in language and the field of history but also in their natural environment. Both Marlatt's and van Herk's texts recognize that patriarchy has placed women and nature in the category of the absolute and alienated "other." Over the last two decades, the connections between the oppression of women and the oppression of nature have been explored within the context of ecofeminism.[14] Instead of insisting on the alienation of human beings from nature, ecofeminists consider the interdependent relations in human-human and human-nature interaction. Dialogism, with its focus on multiplicity and interrelatedness, reinforces the ecofeminist recognition of the necessity for diversity, interdependence, and reciprocity in these relations. Bakhtin himself never extended his ideas about dialogism to the relationship between human and non-human nature. For him, only speaking subjects seem to have agency. While non-speaking subjects can be participants in dialogue as the objects of utterances, they remain in the role of object. As Murphy (1991b, 48) has suggested, however, by bringing together dialogism with feminism and ecology, it is possible to break dialogism out of the anthropocentrism within which Bakhtin performs it. From such an ecofeminist perspective, I would now like to take a closer look at how *Ana Historic* and *Places Far from Ellesmere* develop the possibly dialogic relationships between women and nature.

In Annie's early memories in *Ana Historic*, nature, or, more specifically, the woods, are part of male territory, where men work on powerlines or clear land (Marlatt 1988, 12). Similarly, even the boys of the neighbourhood have already claimed "the Green Wood" as theirs, a place with a "fort," "slingshots," and "air gun" (12). Only a small section of the forest, "that part directly behind the garden, that part she and her sisters called the Old Wood," is left to the girls (12). Too close to the domestic, feminine space of the house, it is of no interest to the boys. To the girls, however, "the Old Wood" suggests safety, comfort, and familiarity: "moulted and softened with years of needle drift, tea brown, and the cedar stump hollow in the middle where they nestled in a womb ... sniffing the odour of tree matter become a stain upon their hands like dried blood" (12). Even this familiarity is overshadowed by the fear of those who, according to what Annie has been taught, truly control nature: "but what if the boys ... what if the men tried to bulldoze their woods? so what could *we* do? her little sister shrugged" (12). Annie internalizes this notion of separate spheres, which is endorsed by her mother who continually reminds her of the dangers of the woods in which men and bears may hide (18).

And yet, unlike her mother, who is afraid of the bush, Annie secretly trusts the land. The woods become her escape "from the world of men" (18). In the anonymous, undisturbed environment of the forest (18, 19, 46), she feels "in communion" with the trees and animals around her, "native" in the world of nature (18). Annie's attempt to write herself into history – partly through her own writing of a novel, partly through exploring her mother's and Ana's stories – finds a parallel in her desire to reclaim her familiarity with nature as well as her sense of belonging and connection. Both nature and women have been silenced by and have suffered from patriarchal culture:

Ana's fascination:

the silence of trees
the silence of women

if they could speak
an unconditional language
what would they say? (75)

Nature and women have been overwritten by the desires, bodies, and histories of men, fathers, and husbands; in order for Annie to liberate herself as a woman and to reclaim her positive relationship with nature, she needs to reinscribe women's desires, bodies, and histories and, with them, respect for the land.

In *Ana Historic* the most respectful and harmonious relationships with nature are associated with the presence of women, women's bodies, and love between women: Ana joins the two women she sees sitting in a pool in the woods beckoning her to join them (86); Annie finds two women kissing in a car that is parked in the woods (106–7); the birth of Jeannie Alexander's son takes place inside the house, but the nature of birth and women's bodies are closely paralleled with the natural setting outside, the trees, the rain forest, and the scarlet maples so that the country of the land becomes the country of the woman's body (127). Moreover, as Jeannie gives birth to her son and to the new Ana whose consciousness has been raised by her witnessing of the birth, Zoe metaphorically gives birth to a new Annie (Kelly 1995, 84). And finally, when Annie goes to visit Zoe at her house, she compares the community of the women to her early memories of nature: "i wanted to listen, as i used to listen in the woods to the quiet interplay of wind, trees, rain, creeping things under the leaves – this world of connection" (Marlatt 1988, 151). If nature's elements relate to each other dialogically, and if women relate to each other in the same way, then women and nature can also share, listen, respond, and connect with each other. In other words, they can relate dialogically.

In this context, it is not surprising that Marlatt's epigraph – "'The assemblage of facts in a tangle of hair'" (n.p.) – is a quotation from what has become one of the touchstone texts for ecofeminists: Susan Griffin's *Woman and Nature: The Roaring Inside Her* (1978). When Griffin (1982, 82) introduces a selection from this text in her later collection, *Made from This Earth*, she explains that, "though the book contains analytic ideas, it moves by the force of echoes and choruses, counterpoints and harmonies. In one way, the book is an extended dialogue between two voices (each set in different type face), one the chorus of women and nature, an emotional, animal, embodied voice, and the other a solo part, cool, professorial, pretending to objectivity, carrying the weight of cultural authority." In *Woman and Nature*, Griffin suggests that man has been alienated from both woman and nature in the patriarchal systems of the Western world, while woman and nature are seen as connected. Thus, both are established as proper subjects for domination; however, their connection can also become the source for women's strengths and a way to deconstruct patriarchy's discourse of domination.

Marlatt's specific quotation is taken from Book Four of Griffin's *Woman and Nature*, entitled "Her Vision." Here the speaker rereads a woman's body as a source of knowledge and history:

Fine light hairs down our backbones. Soft hair over our forearms. Our upper lips. Each hair a precise fact. (He has never permitted her to exercise her inalienable right to franchise. He has compelled her to submit to laws, in the formation of which she had no choice.) *Hair tickling our legs.* The fact of hair against skin. The hand stroking the hair, the skin. Each hair. Each cell. (He has made her, if married, in the eye of the law, civilly dead.) *Our hair lying against our cheeks.* The assemblage of facts in a tangle of hair. (He has taken from her all right to property, even to the wages she earns. He has denied her the facilities for obtaining a thorough education, all colleges being closed against her.) (Griffin 1978, 209–10)

For Griffin, and by analogy for Marlatt, facts of history are not derived solely from public events and are not dissociated from live bodies and personal experience; the body itself is a textbook of history, with Ina the most obvious and disturbing example. In an interesting way, the context of Marlatt's epigraph foreshadows the problematics of women, especially of Mrs Richards, in *Ana Historic*. Through marriage a woman like Ana fades into the background, disappears from public records altogether, becomes a housewife like Ina (whose emotional behaviour is controlled by a masculine medical establishment through shock treatment), or runs the household and supports her husband by doing research (like Annie). The absence of these women from official history drives Annie to explore their stories. It is the lives of all three women that Annie needs to write back into history; it is also their bodies, which have been controlled by men, and their connection to nature that need to be reclaimed. However, it is not only the theme of Griffin's *Woman and Nature* that resonates in *Ana Historic*; like Griffin, Marlatt employs dialogic relations between stories, voices, documents, woman, and nature. These texts challenge the monologism of patriarchy through a double-voiced discourse that critiques what it observes. Both texts posit a strategically monologic ending that concludes with the voices of a community of women.

Commentary on *Ana Historic* has often focused on the novel's utopian ending and the essentialism that has been said to ground Marlatt's reinscription of women, lesbianism, and the notion of origin. Does Marlatt indeed reinstate the old binary of nature versus culture as Davey (1993, 196) suggests? Is the literal and literary climax at the end "unexpectedly conventional in its utopian vision" and, therefore, unsatisfactory to some readers as Lola Lemire Tostevin (1989, 38) has claimed? Such readings of *Ana Historic* are, I believe, reductive because they remain within the hierarchical thinking of patriarchal discourse and ignore the more complex dialogic manoeuvres of the novel. Indeed, Marlatt (1991a, 104) anticipated such readings in an interview with Brenda Carr: "As soon as you try to write from the margin versus the centre, so that the margin is seen from the centre of its own values, then you're open to the attack that you're simply trying to reverse the hierarchy and make this *the* centre. This is a trap of binary thinking, which is always hierarchical. It says there has to be an either/or and it can't get to that place of both/and." *Ana Historic* obviously exposes a wide range of binaries crucial to Western patriarchal structures, but none remains in place. Through the exploration of a lesbian relationship with Zoe, Annie has not simply reversed her place within the male/female binary by privileging women or claiming the male prerogative of desiring women as Davey suggests (1993, 209); rather, their relationship suggests a different position that opens up the familiar binary, that deconstructs it in order to find a new space that is not determined by patriarchal discourse. As has been pointed out before, Annie explains early on that "when you're so framed, caught in the act, the (f) stop of act, fact – what recourse? step inside the picture and open it up" (Marlatt 1988, 56). However, only if the reader deems the exploration of this possibility worthwhile will she engage favourably with the ending of the novel.

Is it possible to imagine women in an altogether "unconditioned language" outside of patriarchal reference (75)? Annie certainly takes steps in this direction; she renames herself and, as Annie Torrent, begins to speak her own desire: "you. i want you. *and* me. together" (152). Her act of renaming becomes a disruption of the paternal genealogy in which women cannot speak or write (Goldman 1992, 37), but Marlatt pushes this disruption further when she shifts into a more lyrical mode in the final section of the novel. Here she seems to indicate a contextual shift into a lesbian culture that posits different terms of reference and form. Significantly, this last page of the novel remains unnumbered and is followed by another white page. The space of Annie and Zoe's relationship is located outside of the linearity of the novelistic genre, which is itself part of a patriarchal tradition.

It seems to me that the possibility of an "unconditioned language" is not really what is at stake at the end of *Ana Historic*. The point is not that this is an impossible moment (Davey 1993, 205). The point is not, as Goldman (1997b, 131–2) rightfully points out, that the close female relationships are based on an essentially feminine quality. What is crucial at the end of *Ana Historic* is the fact that the voices of women, of lesbian women, too long denied and marginalized, are not subordinated, appropriated, or normalized by the dominant discourse of a patriarchal, heterosexist society. Perhaps many readers' discomfort (or disappointment) with *Ana Historic* derives from this final gesture of resistance. And yet the conclusion is by no means closed or finished, nor is it the *inevitable* result of a hostile patriarchal environment (Green and LeBihan 1994, 441); on the last page Marlatt (1988, 90) is literally "writing the period that arrives at no full stop." The tensions explored through the dialogic narrative have not been resolved. The centrifugal and centripetal forces present in the text ensure a means of countering totalization so that any monologic imagination, such as Annie's alternative, serves a strategic function in the dialogic play of the text. The desire that feeds the relationship between Annie and Zoe also sustains the ongoing process that may and must include the reader ("you"), who will read the characters "into the page ahead" (n.p.). This movement towards the future suggests that the utopian element at the end of the novel does not indicate an idealist evasion into lesbianism or the nostalgic expectation of return to a long-gone, better past; rather, the working of lesbian desire here implies a counter-hegemonic impulse that needs to be linked to a transformative politics.

In *Places Far from Ellesmere*, the narrator finally escapes to Ellesmere to continue her search for a home, a future grave. She refers to Ellesmere most frequently as an island and a desert, both of which carry exclusively positive connotations for her. Ellesmere is "a happy island" (van Herk 1990, 105), an "island paradise" (113). While the isolation and wilderness of islands in the north may be associated with loneliness and danger, the narrator cherishes her sense of exile and the island's self-sufficiency (104, 125). In her "exquisite desert" (104) she does not bemoan the lack of population or the lack of rain that stifles vegetation. On the contrary, to her Ellesmere is a "fecund island" (77). She experiences a "northern desert of desire" in which the process of desiring and striving is more important than the achievement of goals (105).[15] Ellesmere is presented as different and set apart by the narrator, who has "cut all connexion to all places far from Ellesmere" (77). Ellesmere is absence, awayness, remoteness, and inaccessibility (77, 89, 105). This literal removal in spatial terms is also a relocation to a dream-like place of suspended time ("white nights"), a place with "no judgements exerting themselves" (110), a place that teaches "the pleasure of oblivion" (130) and is free of "the graspings of most of [ ]man's impositions, his history or fiction or implacable des/scribement" (113). Through its "extremity of north" (131), Ellesmere Island functions as a threshold chronotope for the narrator. The threshold of the north allows her to explore what is otherwise impossible. Here the narrator can attempt to escape the rules of southern patriarchal discourse and un/read *Anna Karenin*'s story of oppression, murder, and victimization. Here she can be "only a body" (77), desiring to be uninscribed by phallocentric discourse, pretending that she is suspended from the world of books, telephones, and newspapers. If her own suspension is possible on Ellesmere Island, then the island may become a refuge from the overdetermined, masculine representations of women (Goldman 1993, 32). In such a place they can explore a new discourse, new ways of seeing in which the illusion of absence becomes presence, the invisible becomes visible, and silence becomes a language, a form of transgression.[16]

As I read the narrator reading the text of Ellesmere in van Herk's geografictione, I am troubled, just as is Goldman (1997a), by the tension the narrator creates between her idea of the north as a "tabula rasa" (van Herk 1990, 77), an "undiscovered place" (113), and her explicit acknowledgment of and dialogic engagement with a tradition of Canada's north as defined by a history of male adventurers, explorers, and exploiters. Early on the narrator contemplates the question: "what justifies place?" (20). Does a place become a place through its land, rivers, animals, vegetation, and indigenous populations or through its discovery by white explorers and its opening up by the railway? Her response to these questions seems straightforward:

Henday (1754): Thompson (1787): Fidler (1792): Henry (1810): their wandering bivouacs. The flats of Dried Meat Lake "studded with groves of ash-leaved maples many of which are a foot in diameter" (Macoun, 1879); "the fertility of the Battle River district" (Deville, 1883); "partly wooded and with scattered trees and coppice" (Tyrrell, 1887). (20)

The narrator cites those who have written about the Canadian northwest before her: the first white, male explorers who surveyed, charted, and mapped the new land in the late eighteenth and nineteenth centuries. She also alludes to the crucial role played in this process by powerful institutions such as the Hudson's Bay Company, for which both Thompson and Fidler worked, and the Geological Survey of Canada, to which Tyrrell and Macoun were appointed. These references accomplish two things. By citing official history, the narrator sets up what she seeks to undermine; at the same time she shows that the concept of the north, or northwest – the Canadian frontier – is a construction that has shifted with every new exploration undertaken, every new area that was surveyed. The narrator thus questions any unitary definition of place and creates a space for herself to engage with dominant history in order to reinscribe a different narrative. Her own justification of place is based on personal memory. The sources and citations cannot replace the process of individual construction: "dream yourself a place: Edberg" (20).

I see another excellent example of this strategy of dialogically engaging with previous history in the narrator's attempt to chronicle the history of Ellesmere. A comparison of the entry for "Ellesmere Island" in the *Canadian Encyclopedia* with the narrator's commentary in *Places Far from Ellesmere* is instructive:

The island was sighted by William Baffin in 1616, but was not explored until the 19th century. John Ross discovered parts of the coastline in 1818 and the

island was named for the earl of Ellesmere during the Ingelfield expedition of
1852. Sir George Nares carried out extensive observations in 1875. (*Canadian
Encyclopedia* 1988, 687)

Ellesmere ... Hard to configure as an *island* at first, *sighted by William Baffin*
(how: from the shore/with a telescope/from his ship?) *in 1616, but not
explored until the nineteenth century.* The nineteenth century island: the nineteenth century novel. But *John Ross discovered parts of the coastline in 1818*
(too much symmetry), and *in 1852 the island was named, during the Inglefield
expedition, for the Earl of Ellesmere.* Why? Had he given them money? What
did they read on those ice-bound shores that suggested the island should be
named for him? And was their reading correct? Is it an Ellesmere, or something
else, some other name that other beings spoke? There must be another name,
somewhere, if one only had the eyes to read it. *Sir George Nares* led an expedition of the Royal Navy (*extensive* exploration) *in 1875* and 1876. (van Herk
1990, 97, emphasis mine)

The narrator not only challenges the prerogative of white men in the
explorations of the north but also questions the way that their expeditions have become history – that is, written history, deemed official and
authoritative, as exemplified by the entry in the *Canadian Encyclopedia.* The narrator creates a double-voiced discourse by reaccentuating
phrases and sentences from the encyclopedia – which I have italicized
– and questioning what they do not account for (asking for reasons and
practical considerations) and suggesting parallels important to her (for
example, between the nineteenth-century island and the nineteenth-
century novel). This form of dialogism shows that Ellesmere Island is
no "undiscovered place" (113) because history has documented its
exploration (Neuman 1996, 225). What the narrator points out, however, is that the expeditions of these men excluded women: "these
names, every mapped configuration male/lineated" (van Herk 1990,
88). The narrator intends to intervene, to undermine this familiar discourse of exploration with its masculine biases, in order to be able "to
read through, past this male historiographical fiction" (84) and, it is
hoped, to map "the impossible geographies of dream and passion"
(van Herk 1996, 133). What she inadvertently shows, of course, is that
Ellesmere Island is *not* an "undiscovered place," a "tabula rasa."
    Moreover, in the process of reinvention, as the narrator explores
Ellesmere Island from a woman's point of view, she silences those
whom she herself can "other" and displace, the "other beings" who
actually discovered the island, who gave it their own name (van Herk
1990, 97): "Forty-two hundred years ago hunting bands roamed
beside the inlets and fjords of Hazen Plateau. They had a name for

Ellesmere, you are sure of that" (98). Only a few brief references (20, 97, 98) speak of the presence of First Nations peoples in the north and their encounters with white explorers, which are alluded to by the references to Anthony Henday and Alexander Henry. While Shirley Neuman (1996, 225) emphasizes the fact that van Herk's "contestation is specifically of the misogyny of European fiction and its derivatives in settler cultures," Goldman (1997a, 157) argues that *"Places Far from Ellesmere* does not address the political and imperial agendas that continue to determine the fate of the Arctic." I believe that van Herk's own discourse of resistance becomes complicit with the oppressive masculine discourses she seeks to disrupt. Only this erasure and complicity allow her to think of Ellesmere as a "tabula rasa" (77), a place where she can be alone with Anna Karenin.[17] This approach is even more surprising considering van Herk's (1991, 1–11) fascinating examination of her journey to Grise Fiord on Ellesmere Island with her Inuit guide Pijamini in her crypto-friction "In Visible Ink."

By creating a double-voiced discourse, the narrator reads the palimpsest of the north for the woman's story that has been inaccessible and unacceptable until now, concealed by a masculine historiography and geography. In turn, she superimposes this story of woman on the official historical and geographical constructions to which we have grown accustomed. What she does not do is move outside of this opposition in order to see other layers of this palimpsest. In "Stealing Inside after Dark," van Herk (1991, 139) reflects on the role of palimpsests: "[The book] encloses: pages, words, ideas; it can, for a period of time, enclose the reader, although only when it is itself opened. That paradox speaks to the presence of book(s) in life, to the writing (palimpsestic) of books, their reading (palimpsestic), and their textual suggestiveness (palimpsestic) as audience, as substitute and subterfuge, as illusion and artifact." Only our own palimpsestic reading of this geografictione can reinscribe what van Herk leaves unconsidered.

A similar strategy, I would argue, can be detected in Scott Barham's cover illustration. The grey and white map of British Columbia and Alberta, which shows the area of Edberg, Edmonton, and Calgary, serves as the ground upon which a coloured insert is placed. This insert looks like a collage of a map of the Arctic archipelago, a picture of an island, presumably Ellesmere Island, in the shape of a woman's (Anna's) body, and a grid of Calgary that is superimposed on the northwest coast of Greenland, separated from Ellesmere Island by the Kennedy Channel. In this collage, the womanly shape of Ellesmere Island is superimposed on all the existing maps and becomes the centre of the cover page and van Herk's geografictione, erasing geographical distinctions and differences in the process and making possible "a whole new cartography of women as subjects" (Neuman 1996, 228). But what is "real" in this cover? What is the original text that has been obscured and overwritten by masculine readings? Is it Ellesmere as woman, Ellesmere as the mother of women, and north as feminine? While the dominant narratives of the north are gendered masculine because of masculine traditions of exploration, mapmaking, and historiography, the land of the north is at the same time configured as feminine, exotic, the "other." Van Herk's geografictione suggests that only this reclamation of the north as feminine enables the narrator to un/read and thus free Anna from Tolstoy's plot. But is not her inscription of Ellesmere as woman in danger of being complicit with and co-opted by a discourse that has always written the island in terms of such familiar tropes as the virgin land to be conquered? Isn't it complicit with a discourse in which the frontier of the north has been, in Grace's (1997, 172) words, "equated with Woman, but denied to women"? Isn't it also complicit with a long tradition of maps being figured on or out of female bodies (Howells 1996, 120–1)? I am hesitant to argue here for a successful strategic move in *Places Far from Ellesmere* because I see little desire on the narrator's part to deconstruct the monologic approach she presents in essentializing the north.

In reclaiming Ellesmere from official history and reinscribing it as feminine, the narrator frequently relies on anthropomorphic descriptions of the island: "a northern body" (van Herk 1990, 131), "thinly naked" (90), "fat with the flesh of heated snow" (96), a body with head, ears, and palm (124, 142). This body is explicitly gendered: "female desert island with secret reasons and desires" (130), "the landscape of a woman" (131), "no one's mistress" (139), "islanded woman" (142). Again, I sense a tension between the narrator's personification and sex-typing of Ellesmere and her desire to reconstruct the narrative of Tolstoy's Anna. With Murphy (1988, 155) and other ecofeminists, I would ask whether her strategy opposes the patriarchal ideology of domination or whether it inadvertently reinforces elements of that ideology and thereby limits its own effectiveness in subverting the system it opposes. While it may be worthwhile to treasure the land and women in a culture in which both are exploited, anthropomorphic and gendered descriptions of Ellesmere as woman cannot be used without evoking the patriarchal framework within which these descriptions have supported the oppression of women and nature. To think of the island as a woman's body maintains the male/female dualism that hierarchically divides. *Places Far from Ellesmere* shows few traces of a dialogic challenge to these dichotomies or of a struggle to deconstruct the old paradigm that rests on "humanity's false egotism fed by anthropocentrism" (162). In spite of the narrator's reverent revaluation of northern space as feminine, she seems only to invert traditional gender valuation and ultimately to reinscribe the patriarchal sex-typing she wants to undermine. To claim a natural rather than a constructed alliance between woman and the land, I believe, only binds her ever more tightly to the narrative of domination in which Anna Karenin, for instance, finds herself.

In her reinscription of Ellesmere as woman, the narrator initially seems to rewrite both land and woman with agency. The narrator frees the women, "reader and Anna and Ellesmere" (van Herk 1990, 139), who are "watched, judged, condemned" (126), so that they can read Ellesmere themselves (139). However, the narrator depends on Ellesmere to make this possible because "only the north can teach what reading means" (132).[18] In spite of this interdependency, the narrator does not see herself as part of the land. She remains an observer, albeit a meticulous one; only occasionally does she wish to become part of the land, "to become Ellesmere" (121), by submerging herself in the rivers (100, 121). In her descriptions of the environment – harebells, poppies, muskoxen, glaciers – the narrator shows a fascination with objects, but she does not pay much attention to how elements of the environment interact or to what role she plays in this interaction. Rather than becoming part of the landscape, she takes control of it in order to un/read Anna.

Ultimately, however, Ellesmere Island – "the islanded woman" – and Anna remain passive: "Ellesmere, this high sun-shadowed plateau left holding Lake Hazen in its palm, this islanded woman waiting to be read a justice or a future" (142–3). This final shift into the passive – "waiting to be read" – removes the agency, freedom, and self-sufficiency the narrator earlier read for both Ellesmere and Anna. Another look at the cover shows that the picture of Ellesmere in the shape of a woman also shows a passive, and rather seductive, body, the body of someone who may be sleeping or dead. With one hand at her side and one tucked between her legs, her knees slightly pulled up, her large breast exposed, and her hair floating toward the North Pole, this woman is not about to take action. And Anna Karenin, of course, is killed in the end, with the narrator knowing all along that she is "dead before she begins, the end already read. You know where she is going, have pre/read that destination" (van Herk 1990, 83). Unable to read their own futures, are both Ellesmere and Anna left helpless at the end, still dependent on the discursive practices of a patriarchal system? The ending remains ambivalent. Is the final sigh, "Oh Anna" (143), an expression of pity and sorrow over the inescapability of the dominant discourse – of the Canadian north, of Tolstoy, of the literary tradition? Does it declare the solidarity of the speaker with Anna, women, the reader, and a feminine north?

Van Herk's geografictione employs dialogic strategies to map its own text. The narrator engages dialogically with many of the earlier readings and histories of Ellesmere Island, the north, and nature. When it comes time to un/read Anna, however, the space in which that is possible becomes one very much controlled by the narrator. Her trip to Ellesmere Island and her reinscription of the island as woman is monologic in that it subordinates every other context and history to this perspective. This gesture, like the narrator's relocation to the north, does not perform the kind of paradigm shift that leads to actual practice for change. Her anthropomorphic and gendered reinscription of the north risks being undercut and co-opted by an essentialism that easily plays into patriarchy's oppression of women and nature.

The processes of un/reading in Marlatt's *Ana Historic* and van Herk's *Places Far from Ellesmere* always signify more than a one-directional reversal of action; they never simply express negation. Instead, they need to be understood as double movements in which every un/reading becomes a new reading, every untelling a new telling. Every reading also means being read, every deconstruction implies a reconstruction, and every act of undocumenting implies another act of documenting. In both texts dialogism functions as the central strategy to perform these double movements. In this chapter I have focused my attention on the dialogic interrelations of chronotopes and women's life stories, the dialogic play with genre conventions, and the dialogic incorporation of quotations from other texts.

Each of the subjects, or still frames, to use Marlatt's metaphor, is placed into a new context so that it is no longer static and self-sufficient but takes on new meaning and begins to shift. As chronotopes, stories, genre conventions, and quotations begin to sound differently in their new contexts, they are defamiliarized, rehistoricized, and re-energized. In both *Ana Historic* and *Places Far from Ellesmere*, these dialogic relations attempt to break down the familiar rules of formation, the dualisms and hierarchies, upon which patriarchal discourses of history, fiction, literature, and geography have rested. Through dialogism, these binaries are not merely reversed; instead, their structure is undermined, and the hegemony they support is unsettled in order to explore the spaces between, the alternative sites and concepts. As Jones (1993, 160) has argued in her discussion of *Ana Historic*, "This economy of un-thinking at the expense of the given is neither outside history (a-historic) nor assimilated to it, but ana-historic: it redefines an intertextual space in which the writings that map out 'woman's place' are forced to 'finance their own subversion'."

Because un/reading is ultimately a reconstructive practice, *Places Far from Ellesmere* can be driven by van Herk's (1991, 132) desire "to invent a women's world," and *Ana Historic* can be seen as Marlatt's (1989, 98) attempt "to do a woman's version of history." These processes of reinscribing women's histories, of literally putting their bodies on the map (in the case of van Herk), and of "mapping the unmappable" (van Herk 1996, 134), do not necessarily lead to a narrative authority for women or stability and unity of their subject positions. At the end of Marlatt's novel, for example, Annie's subjectivity is still in process. Although she engages in a relationship with Zoe, their coming together points into the future of other contexts, other struggles. I believe that a strong argument can be made to support such a gesture of strategic monologism because it serves to resist normalization by the dominant discourse and ultimately seeks to deconstruct its monologic spaces. What Fuss (1989, 20) has so convincingly argued in the context of the essentialism debate may be a helpful reminder here: "the radicality or conservatism of essentialism [monologism] depends, to a significant degree, on *who* is utilizing it, *how* it is employed, and *where* its effects are concentrated." These questions of who, how, and where also have to be asked when we challenge van Herk's and Marlatt's texts, as I think we should, for not reflecting on their own exclusionary processes – especially in terms of race and class – in their construction of new histories.

My reading of van Herk's strategy of reinscribing Ellesmere Island and the north as feminine has been skeptical. The narrator's dialogic engagement with chronotopes and quoted documents increasingly becomes a means of control in her attempt to revision the north and Anna Karenin. Although the narrator initially seems to resist any unitary definition of place, the essentialism that informs her authoritative construction of Ellesmere Island undermines and counteracts the dialogic strategies she employs. While van Herk's un/reading stalls at the end of *Places Far from Ellesmere*, Marlatt's un/reading moves beyond the last page of *Ana Historic* as it projects a transformed social world for which we need a transformative political practice.

5 Critiquing the Choice That Is Not One: Jeannette Armstrong's *Slash* and Thomas King's *Green Grass, Running Water*

The counter-discourses developed in Jeannette Armstrong's *Slash* (1985) and Thomas King's *Green Grass, Running Water* (1993) challenge the internal colonization suffered by Aboriginal peoples in Canada and signal a contestatory politics of representation in content as well as in narrative structures.[1] Both *Slash* and *Green Grass, Running Water* respond to the choice Aboriginal peoples have long faced in both their literary representations and their social contexts in Canada: assimilation or extermination. The novels reject this simplistic binary antagonism, which ultimately leaves Aboriginal peoples no choice because both options are forms of (self-) annihilation. Until not too long ago, assimilation was the official government policy towards Aboriginal peoples, but even today this assimilationism is a powerful implicit agenda directed towards the social, economic, and political recognition of Aboriginals in society.

The history of assimilation begins with early colonization and includes the British North America Act, 1867; the Indian Act, 1876; the Indian Act's amendment in 1951; the struggle over the federal White Paper in 1969; and finally the official policy of multiculturalism (1971), which has functioned "to decentre the historically and culturally specific claims of Aboriginal peoples ... submerging them in a vast, abstract, undifferentiated, multicultural mosaic" (Kulchyski 1995, 63). These policies have separated Aboriginals from white society and have often alienated them from their own communities (Dickinson and Wotherspoon 1992, 406). More recently, we have seen some public recognition of the damaging effects of such assimilation practices on

Aboriginal communities and their relationships with non-Aboriginals. The *Report of the Royal Commission on Aboriginal Peoples*, initiated in 1991 and released in 1996, identifies many of the difficulties facing Aboriginal peoples in Canada today; it accounts for these difficulties historically and recommends specific goals and steps to bring about change. The following year, with the Delgamuuk ruling, the Supreme Court of Canada acknowledged the existence of Aboriginal title and recognized that rights and title may be established through oral history evidence. What remains central on the political agenda is the question of whether and how self-determination and land claims can be negotiated within a Canadian nation-state.

Slash and *Green Grass, Running Water* insist on discourses of culturally specific, rather than universal, rights that expose the totalizing power of the choice that is not one and that voice an alternative third position, which is realized not only in the novels' character portrayals and plots but also in their narrative structures. This alternative has been described as a return to traditional approaches, or simply the "Indian way" (Currie 1990, 150) or as "liberation through self-determination" (Horne 1995, 263). While Slash, the protagonist of the novel by the same name, for example, supports the right to individual positions at the end, he does not, as Margery Fee (1990, 175) points out, endorse the pluralism of a liberal multiculturalism; instead, he emphasizes the need to recognize difference in opinion and aims for solidarity: "Each position is important and each has the right to try for it. We should all back each other up" (Armstrong 1985, 235). Moreover, the novel suggests that the reductive "choice" between white assimilation and Aboriginal tradition also allows for a position of disidentification, in which otherness does not have to imply subordination but can become "anotherness" (Godard 1990b, 217).

A similar binary has been perpetuated in representations of Aboriginals in non-Aboriginal institutions and media. Stereotypes of the Noble Savage, the Mystic Shaman, or "the children of nature" have idealized and romanticized Aboriginal peoples while images of the drunken, lazy savage have demonized them.[2] Within these fixed categories, Aboriginals are rarely depicted as individuals. Both Armstrong and King expose these representations of Aboriginal peoples as interested constructions, rejecting what Marilyn Dumont (1993, 48, 49) has called "colonial images" that portray monolithic images of "nativeness." The novels show a range and multiplicity of Aboriginal experiences, in rural, traditional, and reserve environments as well as in urban settings. Part of Slash's struggle is to reject images of himself and his people as either *"too Indian or not Indian enough"* (Dumont 1993, 47) and to find enough confidence to demand to be seen as different, but not inferior, even in the face of discrimination (Armstrong 1985, 86). Similarly, the characters in *Green Grass, Running Water* challenge the criticisms of white culture that they are no longer "real Indians" (King 1993, 141, 187), at the same time exploring how to "become what [each of them] had always been. An Indian" (262). The need for new self-representations that leave behind the signs of internal colonialism is one of the driving forces of these two novels.

The desire for new representations is closely connected with Armstrong's and King's attempts to defy another false choice, that is, the opposition of Western literary traditions and Aboriginal oral storytelling. Both texts make extensive use of direct speech, for instance, incorporating speech patterns of the vernacular through their choice of words, speech rhythms, and sentence structures. Often direct speech is used to create a sense of oral narration as stories are retold within the novels. *Slash* and *Green Grass, Running Water* perform a critical recuperation of these stories and the methods of storytelling that white Western culture has often devalued as naive and simplistic. The novels refuse to posit speech and writing as absolute opposites and, instead, examine their complex interrelations. The result is a novelistic hybridity that explores the notion of "orality in literacy" rather than orality and/or literacy (Calinescu 1993; Dickinson 1994, 321). As Peter Dickinson (1994, 320) explains, through storytelling, novels can "give voice to Indigenous memory systems long silenced by the history of imperialism, and transform the usually solitary reading experience into a more cooperative and responsive act of listening."

What are the strategies employed by Armstrong and King to encourage such a responsive act of listening in their readers? I believe that it is primarily the dialogism of these texts that counts on readers to be active in the process of locating choices beyond familiar binaries and recognizing opportunities for Aboriginal self-determination. When Armstrong and King explore generic hybridity, orality in literacy, or double-voiced discourse, they expect more of their readers than what Bakhtin (1986, 69; 1981, 282) calls "passive understanding," which suggests that readers only duplicate the novels' ideas in their minds; rather, these strategies encourage readers to enter into a relation – to be sympathetic, resistant, ironic, appreciative, or mocking (to name only a few options) in their "actively responsive understanding" (1986, 68).

Armstrong's novel may be seen as more "polemical" than King's, to borrow King's own terminology, because it chronicles the imposition of non-Aboriginal expectations on Aboriginal peoples and the methods of resistance employed by the latter to maintain their communities (King 1990a, 13). King's "associational" novel, on the other hand, focuses on an Aboriginal community and the daily activities and ordinariness of its members rather than on the conflict between two cultures (14).[3] The historical circumstances for the writing of *Slash* help to explain this difference. Involved in the Okanagan Indian Curriculum Project that began in 1979, Armstrong (1991, 14) was trying to develop material for the school system: "we wanted a tool to use in education, to give not just the historical documentation of that time but, beyond that, the feeling of what happened just prior to the American Indian Movement, and what happened during that militancy period." As a result, the need to document the problems of assimilation for both Aboriginal and non-Aboriginal readers drives Armstrong's *Slash*. It seemed appropriate that the novel be published by Theytus Books, the first Aboriginal-owned and -operated Canadian publisher.[4] However, the novel's obvious educational purpose has made many academic critics uncomfortable, and Helen Hoy (2001, 41) has problematized her experience of "disjunctive readings" in the classroom (e.g., when students see *Slash*'s foremost value as lying in its historical "raw material" and consequently dismiss its novelistic qualities). Manina Jones (2000) has made a good argument for recognizing the centrality of the novel's didacticism in our understanding of *Slash*. I am less interested in the information retrieval that the novel invites than in the narrative strategies that dialogize the text and their didactic effects. Compared to *Slash*, King's *Green Grass, Running Water* seems less openly didactic and more playful, albeit no less serious. Although critics seem to agree that the novel is hilarious and witty, they do not usually account for or explain how humour works in this text. Here I explore how the techniques King uses to dialogize the novel, such as multiple perspectives and parody, and his reliance on the reader's participation, contribute to what I call the "serious humour" of *Green Grass, Running Water*.

Armstrong uses Tommy Kelasket, a young Okanagan man later nicknamed Slash, as the homodiegetic narrator who also functions as the primary focalizer in the novel. Slash describes his own experiences; he tells his own story of what it means to be Aboriginal without being despised or silenced by non-Aboriginals. As Fee (1990, 172) emphasizes, "This [a first-person voice] may not be a subversive tactic in the classic realist text or in the popular novel, but it is within the literary discourse of Canada. Aboriginal readers finally will find what white Canadians take for granted – a first-person voice that does not implicitly exclude them." To foreground the voice of the Aboriginal narrator and focalizer is to refuse to allow the dominant discourse to reabsorb or normalize the voice of Aboriginal resistance and difference. The use

of a homodiegetic narrator does not suggest, however, that Slash establishes a unified or autonomous subjectivity. On the contrary, the novel
carefully inscribes Slash's identity as a process of struggle rather than
as a ready-made product, as a community-based rather than as a self-
sufficient project. The novel traces Slash's development from the sixth
grade to early adulthood, from an undisturbed life on the reserve
through his involvement in Aboriginal activism in Canada and the
United States in the 1960s and 1970s to his return to life on the reserve
with his young family. This focus on Slash's perspective does not result
in a monologic narrative, however. On the contrary, Armstrong internally dialogizes Slash's perspective to show his development by reveal-
ing and staging the kaleidoscope of voices and stories that have made
him who he is.

The seemingly unmediated representation of Slash's perspective (suggested by colloquialisms, fragments, grammar errors, etc.) often disguises the double-voiced quality of his own discourse. Sometimes fragments of the discourses of those with whom he collides are
incorporated into his own speech. Mostly, Slash distances himself from
the discourses that try to shape his life and intrude into his language
through stylization or the use of quotation marks. However, these
strategies of distancing differ only in degree, and the lines between
marked quotations, imitation (which directly appropriates someone
else's discourse and merges with it), stylization (which recognizes the
word as belonging to someone else's discourse), and hidden polemic
(which does not include but is determined by another's discourse) are
easily blurred (Bakhtin 1984a, 198–200). In his rendering of the events
at Wounded Knee, for example, Slash clearly marks the discourse of
white authorities as questionable and suspicious:

A couple of senators arrived to "talk" and they went in with that same attitude. However, they came out saying that the "hostages" didn't want to leave
... That sure put a crimp in the actions being contemplated by National Guard
forces. The "hostages" were necessary to lay some charges against their "captors" to justify the massive military-like presence which was escalating rapidly
towards a confrontation. What good were "hostages" if they wanted to stay
and support the Indians? (Armstrong 1985, 116)

The quotation marks explicitly draw attention to the words "talk,"
"hostages," and "captors," clearly defining them as borrowed terms.
They are part of someone else's language. What the senators may
describe as "talk," a neutral term suggesting a conversation between
equals, is seen by the Aboriginals as a euphemism for a one-sided

order. Who qualifies as a "hostage" and a "hostage taker" similarly depends on the position of the speaker. Through the use of quotation marks, Slash dissociates himself from the position of the authorities.

Towards the end of the novel, Slash discusses with a friend the recognition of Aboriginal rights in the Constitution:

Why do you think there was a moratorium called on uranium explorations? Why do you think Berger recommended a ten year stop to any further development until land claims was settled? It's what they are doing right now. Settling it. They will buy out the land and the billions of dollars worth of resources on it for as little as they can. Then after that they will "give" you rights in some areas of it within provincial regulations for conservation ... They'll continue to "negotiate" on rights until that is done. Then they'll give us whatever they choose because our greatest weapon will be in their hands. (241)

The opening questions are phrased in the language of bureaucrats, but then Slash marks his own position by using quotation marks to emphasize the hypocrisy of the word "give" and "negotiated" as employed by the government (because the rights that Aboriginals claim are theirs already and do not need to be given or negotiated). The second use of the verb "give" is no longer marked, however, and it becomes more difficult here to hear the voice of anyone other than Slash. Such blurring of different voices signals the (inevitable?) complicity of Slash's discourse with the hegemonic discourses he opposes.

While quotation marks unmistakably indicate distance, imitation and stylization, which are the other two frequently used forms of double-voiced discourse in the text, often rely more heavily on what may be called intonational quotation marks. Consider the following example:

Talks happened on the reserve, too. Especially after an *action committee* was formed. Chiefs from other reserves were meeting with our Chiefs of the Okanagan, to talk about *changing the Indian Act* and things like that. I never went to them meetings much. (53, emphasis mine)

The phrases I have italicized stand out in this short paragraph. Their diction suggests that they are taken from the context of political activism and legal matters, which separates them from the casual tone ("talks happened," "and things like that") and the ungrammatical phrases ("them meetings") of Tommy's description. Similarly, when Slash summarizes reports and events, he often borrows the language of such texts and contexts without marking them: "In B.C., the Kelly

Report recommended that the government enter into negotiations with the Indians on land claims questions. In South Dakota, the Sioux battled for the validity of an 1868 treaty guaranteeing their sovereignty" (159); "The leaders had been trying to convince the government that they should be included as equal partners in the talks over whether or not to bring the constitution into Canada's parliament rather than leave it as an act of the British parliament" (232); "In B.C. the government announced a seven year moratorium on explorations and mining of uranium" (235).

In addition to these strategies of double-voicing, Armstrong dialogizes Slash's narrative through his own direct speech in conversation and the direct or reported speech of numerous others. When Slash reproduces his own direct speech, it is usually part of a significant conversation with someone important to him, such as Jimmy (43–5, 220–4, 234–5), Uncle Joe (55–6), Elise (96–8), Chuck (140–1), Sam (148–9), his mother (164–6), Maeg (225–8), Dave (241–3), and his son (250). One particular form of direct speech Slash repeatedly employs is the reproduction or retelling of "mini-stories," for example of his older cousin Joe (17), his Uncle Joe (39), and especially his grandfather Pracwa (19), all of whom are described as gifted storytellers. These mini-stories greatly contribute to the dialogization of the narrative and the construction of a community (Emberley 1993, 137).

At times, it seems that Slash remembers and recounts events in his story not so much for their own sake as to allow characters to talk and interact. While he may be the narrator of his own story, as Frank Davey (1993, 61) has pointed out, the long quotations of direct speech emphasize scenic presentation, thereby reducing, albeit not avoiding, the readers' awareness of his role as narrator. In his narrative he restages the political debate; such debate is sometimes represented quite literally, as when he describes the events of a band meeting (Armstrong 1985, 133–6). While summarizing parts of the discussion ("Some suggested that we should plug up the courts with cases. Others said that we should use this case to set an aboriginal rights precedent" [133]), Slash directly quotes a "visiting Chief," "an Elder" (134), "one woman," and "another man" (135) at length. He is always listening to other points of view, other voices around him, without ever finding a tidy solution to this multiplicity of voices (Petrone 1990, 141). Rather than offering a synthesis at the end, *Slash* emphasizes throughout how different voices have mutually influenced each other, in particular how they have contributed to the formation of Slash's character. That significant maturation and self-awareness occur in Slash's character is emphasized by the fact that he follows many of his (in)direct quotations in the last chapter with phrases such as "I understood then" (Armstrong 1985, 203, 211,

212), "I realized then" (203, 210), "I had learned" (208), "I saw then" (218), "I could see" (212), and "It was clear then" (218). Not only are we reminded repeatedly that Slash has grown into a confident Aboriginal man, but we also learn that constructive interaction, in the form of discussion, conferences, and ceremonies – not violence or escape – is what got him there.

While the use of extensive quotations emphasizes that Aboriginal culture is highly oral (Davey 1993, 61), its effects are more complex than that. As Julia Emberley (1993, 132) argues, the shift to the mode of speech and storytelling destabilizes – although it may not be able to escape – a simplistic generic categorization because it provides a textual space to consider an alternative inscription of the history of Aboriginal political argument. Emberley further suggests that Jacques Derrida's heterogeneous concept of writing helps us understand the alternative position Armstrong's novel inscribes through storytelling (144–7). In *Of Grammatology*, Derrida (1976, 11, 14) deconstructs what he sees as the principal opposition of the Western metaphysical tradition: voice, which is considered natural and immediate, and writing, which is perceived as derivative and representative. He attempts to show how speech and writing share the same features when it comes to signification: the intelligibility of any sign depends on the differential network of signifiers so that no mode of language, spoken or written, can claim an unmediated embodiment of meaning.[5] Orality and literacy are then no longer categorical opposites but, rather, find themselves in differential relation.

The dichotomy between speech and writing has been the basis for universalist evolutionary theories, such as Walter Ong's in *Orality and Literacy* (1982), which posit a linear progression from a primitive oral to a superior literate consciousness. These deterministic models have often informed the paternalistic attitudes of Western critics towards the literary accomplishments of Aboriginal peoples. Because Aboriginal writings do not fit the conventions of Western literary traditions, they have been regarded as obscure or unsophisticated. However, critics of the orality/literacy divide have argued that orality and literacy should be understood as concrete social practices within specific contexts and not as being in developmental or hierarchical relation (Calinescu 1993, 177; Finnegan 1988, 160–1).

Although Bakhtin has identified the incorporation of multiple speech genres as a way of creating heteroglossia in the novel, his distinction among genres proves problematic in a discussion of *Slash*. Bakhtin (1986, 62) acknowledges the heterogeneity of both oral and written speech genres, as well as their socio-historical specificity, but he also distinguishes between primary and secondary genres, explaining that primary genres are simple while secondary (complex) speech genres "arise in more complex and comparatively highly developed and organized cultural communication (primarily written) that is artistic, scientific, sociopolitical, and so on." While secondary genres are not exclusively literary genres, his classification of the oral story as a less complex or developed genre betrays his own ideological bias (i.e., the Western literary tradition). His narrow Eurocentric perspective extends to his characterization of the storyteller. For Bakhtin (1984a, 192), the storyteller "is not a literary person"; he/she belongs in most cases to "the lower social strata, to the common people" who bring with them oral speech. Bakhtin's distinction between speech genres itself may be valid, but the implication of a hierarchical relationship reinforces Western aesthetic conventions that attribute inferior qualities to Aboriginal writing. In reading Aboriginal literature, non-Aboriginal readers and literary critics need to recognize different sets of cultural assumptions.[6] So while it is important to recognize the predominance of storytelling in *Slash*, its significance and contribution to the dialogics of the text may be different from what Bakhtin's observations suggest. Lee Maracle (1992a, 87) eloquently summarizes the importance of (oral) stories for Aboriginal cultures: "Words are not objects to be wasted. They represent the accumulated knowledge, cultural values, the vision of an entire people or peoples. We believe the proof of a thing or idea is in the doing. Doing requires some form of social interaction and thus, *story* is the most persuasive and sensible way to present the accumulated thoughts and values of a people."

The role of the reader/listener is probably the aspect of storytelling that non-Aboriginal critics have taken to most easily. Storytelling foregrounds the notion of addressivity, which Bakhtin (1986, 95, 99), in fact, recognizes as a constitutive feature of all utterances. Because a story has to be told to someone, without whom it would not exist, the role of the listener is of great importance. In the oral performative context of the story, cooperation between storyteller and listener is critical. As Ron and Suzanne Scollon (1984, 179) suggest in their study of Northern Athabaskan oral traditions, the oral tradition, as represented by narrative performance, relies on "mutual respect between storyteller and listener in a one-to-one situation, the mutual negotiation of position that never assumes that one side should be allowed to make its own sense of the situation 'stick.'" What, then, is required of the reader of *Slash*? Listen and hear, we may want to answer, because Slash reminds the audience over and over again that he listens to those around him and thus hears about what is going on.[7] Hoy (2001, 35) suggests that the novel's insistence on these activities should be read as "a metafictional commentary on the challenge [the novel] offers its readers." In other words, to achieve the responsive understanding I referred to earlier, readers do what Slash models for them in the text: they hear the perspectives represented in the novel and put them in relation to each other and to themselves, thus activating the dialogic relations of the text. Slash's own maturation, which I described earlier as characteristic of the last chapter, is the result of years of listening and hearing. Through this kind of active understanding, readers ultimately become speakers themselves; they will respond in some way even if such a response is delayed (Bakhtin 1986, 68–9). Through the narrative techniques that include stories and encourage dialogic relations between them, Armstrong thus dramatizes the process of "actively responsive understanding."

The novel, moreover, draws attention to its own staging of the narrative as oral performance through the self-reflexive prologue and epilogue, two parts of the book that, so far, have not received any critical attention. The prologue begins with a focus on the act of narrating: "as I begin to write this story, I think back" (Armstrong 1985, 13). Right from the beginning then, we know that what follows is a retrospective telling, but it is a telling in written form. The decision to write has prompted the narrator to revisit his past in order to understand the links between his present and past selves: "I look at that child and find him a stranger and yet he is nearer to me, as I am now, than when I became a young man full of a destructive compulsion to make change happen" (13). In fact, the two words repeated most often in the prologue, aside from the first-person pronouns, are "understand" and "change." Slash is preoccupied with identifying the reasons for his change. Introductory phrases such as "I must examine" and "I must understand" foreground the reflective and critical quality of the narrative as well as the need for and urgency of its telling. In other words, the narrator prepares his audience for an autobiographical story that will chronicle his growing sense of self-awareness, culminating in the final chapter.

In the prologue, however, Slash also explains that this story about himself is at the same time a story about his people: an easy slippage between the first-person singular and plural pronouns highlights this interdependence. The recognition of this dependence is really the outcome of the story he is about to tell. Although Slash is involved with various political groups and movements throughout his life, he comes to realize that his feelings of worthlessness and powerlessness are the result of his missing connections with his Aboriginal (Okanagan) community, its traditions, and his family.[8] Once Slash realizes that, as an Aboriginal, he is "important as one person but more important as a part of everything else" (203), his life takes on a new meaning. He can no longer justify being selfish or indifferent about what happens, for example, to his health because his illness or death would be an irreplaceable loss to his community. As Slash speaks of "our descendants" and "how their world shall be affected," he connects his present time of writing with his past, which will come under consideration in the story.

But the prologue does not end here. It continues with a disclaimer: "The characters in this novel are fictitious." If these are not Armstrong's preliminary words but, rather, are part of Slash's introduction, then we are left with a double disclaimer. Armstrong has written a novel in which her protagonist sets up his autobiographical story as fictional. Does a double insistence on fiction make it non-fiction? Probably not, but Slash's words here seem out of place, especially given his explanation in the epilogue that he decided to tell his story for his son (253). What would be the point of passing on to his son a fictional autobiography?

The epilogue, which is not listed in the table of contents, returns to the present time of narration established in the prologue: "Tonight, I sit here up at the Flint Rock and look down to the thousands of lights spread out in the distance" (253). The narrator's tone is relaxed and contemplative; he seems at ease as he surveys the scene in front of him. His description of the sun, clouds, and grass emphasizes the senses, especially sight, touch, and sound. He seems to have a new awareness of nature unparalleled in the prologue and the chapters themselves. His observations that he "feel[s] old," has "seen many things for a young person," and has "chosen [his] path" underline this sense of maturation, as does his sense of destiny as a teacher (253). As he identifies his son as his reason for telling his story, Slash returns to his focus on the future that he already established in the prologue. As one of his people, he feels a responsibility especially for the next generation. This orientation towards the future becomes more and more pronounced in the final chapter as well. Just before Slash learns of his wife Maeg's death, he tells his infant son: "If I keep to the Indian path and protect your rights the way Pra-cwa explained, you will be the generation to help them white men change because you won't be filled with hate ... You are the part of me that extends in a line up toward the future" (250).[9]

The epilogue closes with a poem presumably addressed to Slash's son: "Let Me / kiss your footprints / in the grass." This first body movement of bending down to kiss the ground suggests not only love but also humility and admiration, and these are directed at the two things most precious to Slash at this point: his son and nature. Once self-identified as "a warrior," he is no longer the fighter who spoke in the prologue of "destructive compulsion"; rather, he asks for permission ("let me") to kiss, pray, and open his "way / among grasses." And yet, the only surrender Slash acknowledges is the one to nature as he ends the poem: "The wind will wipe out / little traces of you."

The final shift into the poetic mode is one of many challenges to generic codes in *Slash*. The novel's hybrid form incorporates elements of European historical fiction, the "Native confessional mode developed in the Indian Movement," the oral anecdote, and self-reflexive narrative strategies (Godard 1990b, 214). The genres of the *Bildungsroman*, the romance quest, and the picaresque novel have also been discussed in relation to the novel (Davey 1993, 57). Such hybridity, however, may only present a difficulty for readers who recognize these Western literary genres and expect generic stability. To Aboriginal readers, the novel may not be "Aboriginal enough" because of its play with orality and literacy. By employing multiple narrative conventions, *Slash* succeeds in resisting Western literary discourses that have tended to frame the Aboriginal in terms of binary stereotypes; moreover, it rejects the notion of an essential aspect of Aboriginal writing and thereby displaces the fetishization of Aboriginal tradition (Godard 1990b, 220). The novel manages to situate itself simultaneously in a position of resistance and complicity. The double-voiced generic discourse that emerges from this position is echoed in Slash's double-voiced speech throughout the novel. The frequent back and forth movement between oppositional discourses, categories, perspectives, and conventions challenges readers to stay vigilant throughout. What to many critics is a naïve or didactic, and therefore simplistic, text asks readers to put into relation what, in the novel, is separate. Through its documentation of Aboriginal resistance and its narrative structures, *Slash* recognizes social conflict and political process within Aboriginal cultures and between Aboriginal and non-Aboriginal societies as crucial. Thus, as the third option, self-definition together with political analysis and activism can become "the foundation for pro-action rather than re-action" (Currie 1990, 150).

Not unlike *Slash*, but in an even more pronounced way, King's *Green Grass, Running Water* achieves the "blending of oral literature and written literature" that is characteristic of what King (1990a, 13) has called "interfusional" writing. He incorporates elements of the oral tradition and invader-settler narratives into a creative hybrid, "an intricate collage of multiple 'vignettes'" (Horne 1995, 260), and, in the process, makes storytelling itself a topic. The result is what King (1994, 5) himself has called "a very flat book," a book not driven by climaxes but by the characters' activities.[10] Aware of generic expectations of European-North American writing, King observes that oral stories shifted his attention to repetition, cadences, and the characters' "little movements," which "tickle" him (5). As a result, *Green Grass, Running Water* unfolds as a "complex polyphonic discourse" (Goldman 1999, 25), a relational text that foregrounds its many characters and perspectives and the relations between them. It is in these relations – between perspectives, parody and parodied texts, and novel and readers – that we discover humour as one of King's most powerful strategies. The humour, however, is not there for its own sake: it is there to inform, to expose, to challenge and change, a notion captured by critics when they speak of King's "humorous subversiveness" and "subversive humour" (Wyile 1999, 111; Fee and Flick 1999, 134; J. Andrews 2002, 113). The goal of King's humour is not always to be subversive though (i.e., to undermine an existing concept or system); sometimes King's humour is there to observe and to urge readers to concentrate and to take responsibility for understanding what they read. To suggest such a broad notion of humour and to emphasize its complexity, I prefer to speak of King's serious humour.

Since critics have accounted for the humour of King's novel primarily by examining the inversion of some of the ideological pillars of Western thought (such as Christianity, history, progress), I want to shift the attention first to the novel's narrative structure. Little is straightforward about King's use of narrators and focalizers. In fact, part of the novel's wit – and readers' confusion – derives from the difficulty of identifying a consistent narrative voice and keeping track of the frequent shifts between what at first appear to be many separate stories: There is the story of the storyteller and Coyote; the one involving the four Blackfoot Indians; the ones about Alberta, Babo, Latisha, Norma, Charlie, Lionel, Eli, Portland, and Dr Hovaugh; and a number of creation stories. How exactly do these stories relate to each other? On the first page of *Green Grass, Running Water*, we encounter a homodiegetic narrator who refers to himself as "I" and who is in conversation with Coyote in the fictional present of the narrated world. This narrator remains unnamed and ungendered throughout the novel; we have no access to his/her inside views, nor does s/he present any descriptions that would reveal biases or previous experiences. What we know we know from the conversations with Coyote. This lack of details has led critics to the two extreme positions of either thinking of this "I" as a "universal narrator" (Peters 1999, 73) or conflating the narrator with the author (Chester 1999, 49); most critics have had little to say about the narrator's role.

The narrative act itself is the main event, the constitutive element, of the story involving the narrator and Coyote. The narrator is clearly limited to the narrative present and to one (albeit unspecified) place.

However, the narrator points out that more than one story is unfolding simultaneously, for s/he refers repeatedly "to the other story" (King 1993, 237). It appears that, at the beginning, the narrator also tells this other story, the creation story with which the novel begins; the novel suggests that the first person pronoun of "I can tell you that" in the creation story (1) refers to the same narrator as the one in "I says" in conversation with Coyote on the same page. Later the narrator suggests that Coyote may eventually be able to tell this story (269), and Coyote agrees (329), making his first unsuccessful attempts (348–9, 431). Part of the humour in the story of the narrator and Coyote derives from the unpredictability of when their conversations may interrupt other stories in the novel, but it is probably the nature of their conversations that makes readers laugh. Most of their conversations read like a commentary on the events unfolding in the creation stories; usually, Coyote will make the first observation about anything from food and water (41, 69, 104) to specific events such as Changing Woman leaning over the edge of the world (105, also 145, 196, 224, 232, 294), concepts Coyote does not understand (146–7), and the quality of the story ("This is beginning to get boring" [295]).[11] Often Coyote's comments deal with details and trivialities that will amuse readers because they seem unimportant to the big picture. Other times his comments are completely unrelated to the story, for instance, when he comments on his favourite month (195) or on not being ticklish (329). In these situations the narrator tries to keep Coyote on track, admonishing him, telling him what to do (his favourite phrase being "pay attention" – 38, 100, 104, 195, 394);[12] clearly, the narrator has superior knowledge of the story to be told and tries to keep Coyote in check. When challenged, Coyote has excuses:

> Say, they [those rangers] says, Who killed these dead
> rangers? Who killed our friends?
> Beats me, says First Woman. Maybe it was Coyote.

> "Ah, excuse me," says Coyote. "I was asleep at the time."
> "What time was that?" I says.
> "When were the rangers killed?" says Coyote. (70)

In this example, Coyote interrupts the creation story because he disagrees with something being said about him. When the narrator challenges him to be more specific, Coyote cannot provide an answer – presumably because he made up his excuse – so instead he sheepishly answers with a question that would provide him with the information to back up his excuse. As readers, we are amused not only by Coyote's attempt to excuse himself but also by how open he is about his own manipulation of the truth. The narrator ends up exasperated, reminding Coyote over and over again that they have things to do, a story to tell (40–1, 323). When Coyote struggles to work out whether he is "an Indian" or "a White," the conversation with the narrator appears humorous to the reader because of Coyote's repeated attempts at logical deduction (392–3). What his attempts ultimately reveal is, of course, that characteristics such as having a keen sense of smell or being compassionate are insufficient to define one's identity and that identity labels fall short of lived reality.

But there are more stories in the novel than the narrator talking to Coyote and the story of creation. In the sections that tell the stories of the Four Indians and the other characters, both told in the past tense, we find a heterodiegetic narrator who is not part of the narrated world and about whom we learn very little. Most readers seem to assume that the unnamed homodiegetic narrator of the fictional present becomes the heterodiegetic covert narrator of the other parts of the book. If that is so, then the narrator has gained omniscience about the thoughts, motivations, and feelings of the other characters and is no longer restricted by space and time constraints. And yet, as Patricia Linton (1999, 233) has pointed out, such omniscience is the very "stuff of humour" in *Green Grass, Running Water*. While the narrator has superior knowledge about the creation stories (their content and sequencing), history, terminology, and much more, and admonishes Coyote to be more attentive and cooperative, s/he is nevertheless unreliable and unsure about his/her ability to tell the "right" story (232). In fact, the Four Indians also question whether such omniscience and independence is possible (49), even though they, too, have a strong sense of proper beginnings, sequence, and content.

In the stories about the Four Indians, they themselves try to become narrators. That is what the phrase "this according to" promises at the beginning of each of the four sections of the book, for it mimics the title of each of the gospels in the New Testament, foregrounding the fact that, with each teller, the telling, too, will change. However, it seems too simplistic to say that the Indians simply take turns narrating the story. For example, in the first part of *Green Grass, Running Water*, the heading "THIS ACCORDING TO THE LONE RANGER" is followed by a conversation between the Four Indians with inquit phrases referring to the latter in the third-person. When the Lone Ranger begins the story (11), it is still within quotation marks. Not until the second part of the book is the introductory phrase "THIS ACCORDING TO ISHMAEL" immediately followed by the actual creation story, presumably then told by Ishmael. Robinson Crusoe and Hawkeye pick up in parts three and four, where the previous Indian left off (231 and 328). Moreover, in no part are we given any indication of how much is narrated by each Indian. I suggest their narration is limited to the creation story since they would not narrate themselves in the third person, nor are they omniscient with regard to the characters. They are, however, the ones who make the most explicit metanarrative comments in *Green Grass, Running Water*. They comment on omniscience (49), but, when they refer to a specific page number in order to avoid repetition, they also show that they are aware of being characters in a book (234). They make it impossible for readers to suspend their disbelief for too long and get caught up in the more realistic sections in the novel.

These more realistic sections are the ones about the central Aboriginal characters who live in Blossom, Alberta. King presents them through contrapuntal, quick glimpses. Although these characters do not function as narrators, they act as focalizers for large sections. When the focus of the story shifts, the focalizer changes as well, and we learn more about that character's perspective. Marlene Goldman (1999, 35) describes these frequent shifts as the "carnivalesque rotation among focalizers" and suggests that it "parallels the multi-faceted structure of the Sun Dance," where different points of view have a kaleidoscopic effect. While I find the notion of the circular structure helpful, I am more hesitant to invoke the carnivalesque. The shifts between focalizers do not in themselves produce carnival. We never know where the next narrative section will take us and how that new perspective will affect the overall picture, but "carnivaleque" is not the same as unpredictable and arbitrary. Actually, the many narrative section are usually linked through simultaneous events, locations, characters' relations, or exact repetition of words. These strategies create a kaleidoscope rather than carnival.

Let me take a closer look at how the different character perspectives relate to each other. King's character portrayals reject the binaries of the white "imaginary Indian," displacing the familiar stereotypes of Aboriginals as unemployed rural folk with alcohol and drug problems; Aboriginal characters in *Green Grass, Running Water* are neither demonized nor idealized. Alberta Frank teaches history at the university in Calgary from an Aboriginal perspective; she is involved with two men, Charlie and Lionel, but despite her desire to have a child, she would prefer to be independent of both. Latisha runs the Dead Dog Café in Blossom and raises her children by herself; she is recovering from an abusive relationship with her former spouse George Morningstar, who later abuses his access to Aboriginal ceremonies to take pictures for a white magazine. Norma is Eli's sister and Lionel's aunt and highly values Aboriginal culture and community; she is critical of her family members who have denied their Aboriginal heritage. These Aboriginal women are presented as agents of their own lives; they are strong women who nevertheless have their share of problems.

When it comes to the male characters, King's characterizations are less positive. Portland, in order to become a B-movie star in Hollywood, denies his roots and transforms himself into the "imaginary Indian" that white society expects him to be. Eli is the Aboriginal gone white, "the Indian who couldn't go home" (King 1993, 286). Once he has left for Toronto, where he becomes a professor of English at the University of Toronto and marries Karen, a white woman, Eli no longer returns to the reserve. Charlie was employed as a token Aboriginal lawyer by Duplessis International Associates, the company that is building the Grand Baleen Dam and that needs to convince, or force, Eli to leave his cabin so that they can open the sluice gates: "they hired him because he was a Blackfoot and Eli was Blackfoot and the combination played well in the newspapers" (116). And Lionel, after working for the Department of Indian Affairs, gets stuck with a job at Bursum's store, giving up on his potential and dreams. These men, whom Horne (1995, 268) has described as "mimic men," change, however: Eli retires to his mother's cabin after her death, fiercely fighting the construction of the dam for ten years; Portland becomes the victorious chief in the "fixed" movie at Bursum's store; Charlie loses his job but reunites with his father; and Lionel leaves his job at Bursum's, returns to the Sun Dance, and defends his Aboriginal values against the intruder George. Thus, even the more problematic male characters defy simple stereotypes, which allows King to show that the idea of the Aboriginal is always a construction: it was in the past, and it is in the present. "As times change," King (1994, 3) insists, "those constructions change." As he creates characters who determine their own self-images and make their own decisions, King is able to show a broad range of characters rather than a reductive and false binary.

The narrative provides the reader with brief glimpses into the lives of these Aboriginal characters, but the relationships of their stories to each other and to their Aboriginal culture suggest that their individuality is possible only through their sense of community. All of the characters experience the tensions between their desire for independence and community. However, a self-determined identity and a sense of belonging to a community seem to depend on each other. Only when the characters return, literally or metaphorically, to their Aboriginal community do they experience peace of mind and a sense of wholeness. Yet, with the strength that belonging provides come the responsibility and obligation to mend and keep up the community (King 1990b, 67).

But how? Maria Campbell (1995, 89) believes that "the together remembering of the bits and pieces can, and will, realize our community and rebuild our nation," "Realizing community for my people is *Meena kah tip aim sooyak*. To own ourselves again. In other words, self-government" (86). In *Green Grass, Running Water*, the Sun Dance provides a good example of community responsibility and renewal. The re-emergence of Sun Dances in Aboriginal communities after they were banned in both the United States and Canada when government regulations and Christian missions were established on reserves/reservations in the nineteenth century signals such an act of self-determination (Hirschfelder and Molin 1991, 284; Gill and Sullivan 1992, 291). Alberta actually remembers an incident in her teens when her family wanted to attend a dance in Browning; they were harassed at the American border, and their outfits were confiscated (King 1993, 256–7). The novel does not have to describe the sacred events of the Sun Dance for the dance to become a focus of the narrative as the characters prepare for it. Latisha and Norma continue a long tradition of their foremothers by attending the dance, but Alberta, Eli, and Lionel mark a return and a new beginning by joining the community festivities.

So what is the point of these many narrative perspectives and of the complex narrative structure that seems to be impossible to pin down? The multiple narratives decentre any authoritative perspective in the novel. The fragmented narrative structure gives authority to the voices of all characters involved in the novel, refusing a monologic voice, a strategy that Kim Blaeser has singled out as a characteristic of contemporary Aboriginal literature (quoted in Young-Ing 1993, 184). However, the novel only becomes more than a collage of many separate pieces if the reader considers all stories, all perspectives in relation to each other. The task at hand is not to find out which story is accurate but to explore how they differ from and relate to each other. In the words of the storyteller, "'There are no truths, Coyote,'" I says. 'Only stories'" (King 1993, 391). As King (1990, 65) said in an interview with Constance Rooke, talking about *Medicine River*, he doesn't "try to make these layers and linkages line up perfectly." Highlighting the gaps between narrative sections, King exposes the interstices of his narratives as sites where meaning can be negotiated.

However, the novel does not so much sustain neat separations between stories and perspectives as attempt to keep those boundaries from solidifying. Coyote, for example, is able to move between the present of the narrator and the past of the Four Indians (King 1993, 230, 273, 293, 316, 327, 357, 416, 431), but the Indians, too, begin to interact with two of the characters, Lionel (383) and Babo (427).

Moreover, First Woman, who is part of the creation story told by the narrator, dons the black mask of the Lone Ranger (71) and then passes as white. Shortly after, once she has taken off her mask, she is arrested for being Indian (72). Later, in Fort Marion, she once again passes as the Lone Ranger and walks out of the prison (100). Is First Woman then the Lone Ranger whom we have already encountered on page nine, or are there two Lone Rangers in the novel? All of these characters are trickster figures. The Indians show qualities of the trickster as they appropriate the identities of the four settlers to escape from Fort Marion (417–19) and change names and gender identities, although only Babo Jones seems to know that they are women (53). While tricksters are often quite literally known for their trickery and crude behaviour, the Four Indians function as creators, culture heroes, and teachers (Gill and Sullivan 1992, 308). They frequently play a role in the process of creation: they try to tell the right story, to do it right (14). These trickster-transformers function as culture heroes who assist the Creator with the world and the storyteller with the word (M.L. Ricketts in Bright 1993, 21; Hirschfelder and Molin 1991, 58).

Coyote, one of the most common trickster figures in Plains and West Coast cultures, participates in the creation stories but also has a more destructive side. S/he is responsible for the earthquake and the ensuing flood that destroys the dam and kills Eli (King 1993, 415). S/he is brave and cowardly, conservative and open-minded, wise and stupid, mischievous and sincere (Bright 1993, xi). S/he cannot help tampering with the world. Coyote, like the Four Indians, seems to be able to change gender identities. He seems responsible, however, for impregnating both Mary (King 1993, 269–72) and Alberta: "'But I was helpful, too,' says Coyote. 'That woman who wanted a baby. Now, that was helpful.' 'Helpful!' said Robinson Crusoe. 'You remember the last time you did that?' ... 'We haven't straightened out *that* mess yet,' said Hawkeye" (416). In spite of, or maybe because of, the contradictions s/he represents and the confusion s/he causes, s/he is a paradoxical figure important for his/her role in change, criticism, and self-reflection. King (1994, 6) explains his use of Coyote in *Green Grass, Running Water*: "What I needed in this particular novel was a sacred clown. Someone who could point out the fallacies in situations and arguments and who made sure that nothing stayed done."[13] Although the Four Indians and Coyote are helpers of the creator in his project of fixing the world, some things always get "messed up" along the way (King 1993, 416, 427). While the novel may come to an end, the reader has learned that the trickster figures will eventually return and retell the story to fix it – again, and yet again.

When the readers encounter the storyteller, Coyote, and the Four

Indians, they learn immediately that this is only one of many times that the stories of the creation of the world have been told. Significantly, the novel begins with Aboriginal creation stories told by the storyteller and Coyote as well as the Four Indians;[14] the monologism of Christianity is not only displaced but mocked in the initial play on dog and god/God as a backward dog or a lesser coyote. The Lone Ranger is chastised when he begins with fairy tales and the story of Genesis: "'That's the wrong story,' said Ishmael. 'That story comes later.' 'But it's my turn,' said the Lone Ranger. 'But you have to get it right,' said Hawkeye. 'And,' said Robinson Crusoe, 'you can't tell it all by yourself'" (14). The intersections of the cyclical nature of these retellings and repetitions with the developing narratives show that linearity is not an inherent trait of the lives of the characters but a fiction created in the process of reading. Their life stories are part of a larger story reenacted by the storyteller and the trickster figures. One of the events that the Four Indians repeatedly re-enact is the incarceration of Aboriginals at Fort Marion in 1874. Just as Alberta retells the story over and over again in her history classes (18–21), the Indians re-enact it and escape every time by assuming other identities, such as those of the four settlers. As Horne (1995, 268) has pointed out: "this frequent retelling is also a way of ensuring that this history of oppression not be forgotten."[15] Given the repetitive and recursive qualities of these stories, there can be no closure, no final word in this novel.

The role of the reader in the performance of the text is crucial not only for intratextual relations between perspectives but also for the many intertextual references in *Green Grass, Running Water*. As I said earlier, King subverts the expectations of a white invader-settler culture by reinscribing or parodying many of its central icons: Christianity (especially the Bible), notions of progress, literary canons, history, and stereotypes of Aboriginals. However, as Donaldson (1995, 34) has rightfully pointed out, King does not simply subjugate or obliterate these myths through the intertextual process. By resisting and satirizing these "ideological pillars," which exposes them as "fraudulent and destructive" (Horne 1995, 259), King puts Aboriginal traditions and self-determination in their place. The naming of characters relies heavily on intertextual references,[16] so do allusions to novels.[17] Many of these references function as jokes or games; they work only if the reader is able to pick up on them.

One particular technique of King's "contestatory intertextuality" (Donaldson 1995, 40) is parody. More specifically, it is parody that goes beyond mere imitation and relies on double-voicing; this kind of parody uses the other discourse and puts it to new uses by making specific changes at the level of diction or tone, or by changing its speaker or context. The result are two voices that are opposed in this internally dialogized discourse (Bakhtin 1981, 324; 1984a, 193–4;). King (1999, 70) explains his desire to explore such double-voicing in an interview with Peter Gzowski: "I wanted to ... drag that myth [of creation stories] through Christianity, through Western literature and Western history, and see what I came up with." The clash of voices he ends up with will often strike readers as humorous because of their level of incongruity, but once again this is not humour for its own sake; rather, King incorporates what Bakhtin (1981, 55) has called "the permanent corrective of laughter" through his use of parody.

Two specific examples will suffice to illustrate this point.[18] Consider the novel's title: *Green Grass, Running Water*. It is a shortened version of the common phrase used in treaties between government and First Nations to signal the government's sincerity: as long as the grass is green and the waters run (i.e., supposedly forever). In retrospect, we know that many of these treaties were not honoured, that Aboriginal lands and natural resources were appropriated, that government promises were broken. Acknowledging this history, in contemporary contexts speakers have inverted the meaning of the expression (Linton 1999, 218). Now it means "not forever." Each time the expression is used in the novel, it "resonates throughout the narrative as a code for betrayal, but betrayal compounded so many times that it has become predictable" (218). The first time it is used by a chief in the TV movie that Charlie and Alberta are watching (King 1993, 208): "'My darling,' the [White] woman on the television was saying, 'I don't ever want to leave your side.' 'As long as the grass is green and the waters run,' said the chief, holding her in his arms" (208). If we do not know anything about the history of treaties (and we can assume that is the case with the white woman in the movie), we may read the chief's words as a proclamation of his never-ending love. If we do know the history, however, and are aware of the contemporary use of the phrase, then the chief's words become a prediction, if not a promise, of betrayal. Two characteristics of this situation heighten the humour of King's parody in this example. One is the fact that the historical roles are reversed in this scenario (i.e., the Aboriginal betrays the white); the second is the fact that the promise and betrayal are gender-coded, possibly exposing the stereotypes of Aboriginal men that inform contemporary gender relations.

The second time the expression is used in the novel it is once again spoken by an Aboriginal man (Eli), but this time the latter is in conversation with a white landowner who suggests to him that he should move his cabin so that the dam project can proceed as planned. On the surface, Eli seems to contradict Bursum's statement, "Can't stay there forever" (267). But, as the narrator is quick to explain, it is just a "nice phrase" that "didn't mean anything. It was a metaphor" (267). In other words, the expression stands in for something else – in this case, the exact opposite. Eli speaks the words fully aware that, regardless of his own intentions and sincerity, he won't be able to continue living in his cabin. Either he will have to move the cabin out of the water's way or he will have to die in it.

The third repetition of the phrase is part of the creation narrative. A.A. Gabriel asks Thought Woman to sign a paper for identification purposes: "As long as the grass is green and the waters run, says that White Paper in a nice, deep voice. Oops, says A.A. Gabriel, and he shoves that White Paper back into the briefcase. Wrong paper, he says. That one is for later" (271). How does the parody work in this example? While a white paper is, generally speaking, a government document outlining policy and future action on a specific issue, the White Paper the novel alludes to is most likely the Trudeau government's 1969 White Paper, which proposed the removal of the special status of Aboriginals and resulted in strong Aboriginal opposition (Flick 1999, 160). Once again, what sounds like a marker of government sincerity will in the end turn out to lead to appropriation and disregard of Aboriginal rights. This scene is particularly funny because Gabriel realizes that this White Paper does not belong in the creation story; he already has foreknowledge of what will happen in history, that treaties will be disregarded and that the White Paper will once again try to do away with Aboriginal rights.

How, we are left to wonder, are we supposed to read the novel's title then? To have the phrase borrowed from the language of treaties appear in the title immediately highlights the fact that we are dealing with relations in this novel – relations between governments and communities, between people, between Aboriginals and non-Aboriginals. It also suggests that stories are part of historical contexts; the meaning of the expression depends on its context (in the treaties, in today's usage), but it also depends on the speaker. It functions as parody exactly when it is spoken by an Aboriginal person because, in appropriating the speaking position of the non-Aboriginal person, the Aboriginal speaker reverses the meaning of the expression. In this way, the title also alludes to promises made and broken and to the importance of power differentials that decide who can make and break such promises. Moreover, the title functions as a metacommentary on the novel itself: what exactly is "not forever" in the novel? I am inclined to read what is depicted in its narratives and the way these narratives are put together as a moment of taking stock. Neither content nor form are going to be the most pressing issues, the most suitable techniques, forever.

In the same exchange between A.A. Gabriel and Thought Woman, King (1993, 270) incorporates another parody, this one of the words of the Canadian National Anthem:

And that Card begins to sing.
Hosanna da.
That's what it sings. Hosanna da, hosanna da, hoanna da.

"I know that song," says Coyote. "Hosanna da, in-in the highest, hosanna da forever..."
"You got the wrong song," I says. "This song goes 'Hosanna da, our home on Natives' land.'"
"Oh," says Coyote. "That song."

Gabriel's card, which is described as "very white" with "gold lettering" and "A.A. Gabriel's picture on it" (270), seems to stand in for Canada, but Coyote and the narrator recognize different songs in its "Hosanna da." Coyote thinks of the liturgies of the Church, particularly the phrase "Hosanna in excelsis" ("Hosanna in the highest") said during the Sanctus and Benedictus, which are sung during High Mass as well as in the procession on Palm Sunday. The word "Hosanna" is also what, according to the New Testament, the crowd shouted when Jesus entered Jerusalem for the last time (Matt. 4:9; Mark xi:9, 10; John xii:13). These words of praise and rejoicing would reinforce Christianity as one of the main ideological belief systems in (white) Canada. At the same time, Coyote's recognition of the phrase may evoke the underlying Hebrew "hosha'na," which is a request for salvation and part of the Jewish oral tradition. Even Coyote's reading of the card's song is thus potentially double-voiced, struggling between triumph and need.

The narrator, on the other hand, recognizes the opening lines of the national anthem – with two small but significant changes: Instead of "O Canada!" the narrator remembers "Hosanna da"; both have the same number of syllables, the single-letter injection "o" has become "ho," and the "c" of "Canada" has shifted to "s." Instead of "Our home and native land!" the narrator remembers "our home on Natives' land." The two phrases sound remarkably similar, but the small changes (conjunction turned preposition, adjective turned plural possessive form) result in significantly changed meaning. The narrator's parody, his change of the original words and, thus, their intention, uses the term "native" to refer to the indigenous inhabitants of Canada, not those born in Canada regardless of racial and ethnic background. This parodic strategy exposes the history of European colonialism that led to the exploitation of Aboriginal lands. The humour lies not only in the change of wording and its new meaning, however, but also in the difference the speaker makes. It would be unimaginable that a national anthem, an outward sign of national identity, and those who sing it would pride themselves on their own history of dominance and injustice.

The issues King addresses through his complex narrative structure and use of parody are no doubt serious, but the reader's pleasure in making sense of these techniques and the laughter of recognition soften what Jennifer Andrews (2002, 92–3) refers to as "the biting critique that is part of the text's wit." Laughter certainly reduces distance and hierarchy and can make difficult topics accessible. As Bakhtin (1981, 23) explains in "Epic and Novel":

Laughter has the remarkable power of making an object come up close, of drawing it into a zone of crude contact where one can finger it familiarly on all sides, turn it upside down, inside out, peer at it from above and below, break open its external shell, look into its center, doubt it, take it apart, dismember it, lay it bare and expose it, examine it freely and experiment with it. Laughter demolishes fear and piety before an object, before a world, making of it an object of familiar contact and thus clearing the ground for an absolutely free investigation of it.

King's serious humour offers readers both "a buffer zone of sorts" in this close-up of colonialism (J. Andrews 2002, 112) and the opportunity to understand better the history and power relations that inform the narratives of *Green Grass, Running Water*.

King obviously takes his humour quite seriously. Not everything that is funny on the surface should be taken lightly. By getting readers to laugh at themselves, by blurring familiar divisions and categories – whether between reality and fiction in his character constructions or between history and gossip – King enjoys "putting the reader on the skids" (1994, 5). It is no wonder then that his humour is unsettling, no wonder that he uses trickster figures that will constantly keep the world moving, who won't tolerate complacent stasis. This sort of cross-referencing and interrelating is demanding for the reader. Reading *Green Grass, Running Water* is not an easy task. In order to make sense of the novel, readers need to connect stories, perspectives, intra- and intertextual references; they also need to become listeners and make the novel into a story or an oratory so that they will notice the puns and the shifting voices. It is not important that the readers understand all the jokes or connections King makes, but it is important that they begin to negotiate meanings in the many in-between spaces of the narrative. Whether the audience consists of Aboriginal or non-Aboriginal readers,[19] the novel teaches them to listen, to connect, and to negotiate rather than to speak.

Although I read King's novel as dialogic in terms of its multiple perspectives and use of parody, I hesitate to speak of it as carnivalesque.[20] Even though carnival, in Bakhtin's (1984b, 15) understanding, is about the drive towards liberation and subversion through displays of opposition, degradation, darkness, the grotesque, and death, it is nevertheless "a *temporary* suspension of all hierarchic distinctions and barriers ... and of certain norms and prohibitions of usual life" (emphasis mine). The aim of carnival may be renewal, but in the end it is an authorized transgression of norms that will affirm the status quo without bringing about actual liberation. *Green Grass, Running Water*, however, advocates more change, not change limited to the street theatre of carnival.

Both *Green Grass, Running Water* and *Slash* strive for discourses of critique rather than discourses of negation. As Godard (1990b, 221) has pointed out, their transformative practices come out of the analysis and critique of binary discourses on Aboriginals. These novels create spaces for a critique of the choice that is not one; they open up sites where counter-hegemonic positions can be constructed (Emberley 1993, 136). In the process of such inscriptions, self-determination allows Aboriginals to redefine the knowledge that invader-settler cultures have imposed – knowledge that has silenced, annihilated, or marginalized Aboriginals in settler histories of discovery. In these novels, knowledge is reclaimed as interpretation through storytelling (Emberley 1993, 150). The novels' textual politics support the notion of orality in literacy through their incorporation of oral features, embedded narratives, and dialogic interpellations of stories within written texts. By interrelating multiple voices and listening to stories, the reader re-enacts the characters' experiences of performatively constituting their identities. Their narrative strategies unfold an epistemological process as a way of knowing through telling and reading.

The "Aboriginal pedagogy" that Armstrong's and King's novels display teaches readers that they cannot look to these texts and their incorporated stories as "evidence" of the past (Fee and Flick 1999, 138). As Julie Cruikshank (1990, 14) points out, oral tradition should be understood as "a window on ways the past is culturally constituted and discussed." It is important not only *that* we read these stories but *how* we read them. In her introduction to *Sojourner's Truth*, Lee Maracle (1990, 11–12) explains how Aboriginal stories differ from those within the European tradition:

Most of our stories don't have orthodox "conclusions"; that is left to the listeners, who we trust will draw useful lessons from the story – not necessarily the lessons we wish them to draw, but all conclusions are considered valid. The listeners are drawn into the dilemma and are expected at some point in their lives to actively work themselves out of it.

In *Green Grass, Running Water*, Eli similarly introduces his words to Lionel: "'Can't just tell you that straight out. Wouldn't make any sense. Wouldn't be much of a story'" (King 1993, 361). As readers/listeners, we are not provided with solutions in these novels; instead, it is our responsibility to engage with the stories and novels and to make sense of them.

If we engage with the "dilemma," Maracle (1990, 13) suggests, we can become tricksters, "the architect[s] of great social transformation." Although Maracle may thus be granting the reader permission to engage more playfully with texts, to abandon traditional categories and hierarchies, Susie O'Brien (1995, 82) reminds us of the contradictory inscription of the *white* trickster. While the notion of the trickster can be liberating, Maracle's categorical definition of the other as white and European simultaneously limits "the freedom of the white Trickster to transcend difference and den[ies] the reader's freedom to assert a multivalent identity" (O'Brien 1995, 83). As a non-Aboriginal reader, I feel simultaneously accommodated and alienated by my readings of *Slash* and *Green Grass, Running Water*. This tension reinforces my belief that dialogic relations and storytelling do not signify only play in these novels; readers need to take seriously the contradictions and conflicts the texts reveal. The performative element in Armstrong's and King's novels keeps categories and positions, including the reader's, from solidifying: it keeps conflicts alive. By participating in these performances, we can affirm possibilities of intervention.

6 Is Difficulty Impolite? The Performative in Margaret Sweatman's *Fox*

In his exploration of nation as narration, Homi K. Bhabha (1994, 145) questions the homogeneity and authority of a nationalist pedagogy in which people function as a priori historical objects. The performative, Bhabha suggests, is a counter-hegemonic strategy that constructs people as subjects in the present; it does not just negate the accumulative history of the pedagogical, but, through repetition, it destabilizes and subverts the claims of the pedagogical to transcendent authority. "The liminality of the people," Bhabha explains, that is, "their double-inscription as pedagogical objects and performative subjects – demands a 'time' of narrative that is disavowed in the discourse of historicism" (151). Margaret Sweatman's *Fox* (1991) creates that temporality of the in-between and shows how the performative can operate through a narrative restaging of the Winnipeg General Strike. The novel presents a collage of multiple perspectives, leaving the reader with the often difficult task of relating them to each other. Many readers, Sweatman (1993, 163) suspects, will find such difficulty impolite because "it is a rejection of the discursive pact with the reader which insists on a prescribed message." Discarding the criterion of politeness, Sweatman uses the performative in *Fox*, both in a literal and a metaphoric sense, to challenge the authority of the prescribed message of the past and to show readers that the present informs that past and is therefore full of possibilities. In this chapter I show how the novel foregrounds the performative through its narrative structure, especially through Sweatman's use of double-voiced discourse; I also focus on the relations between specific perspectives, especially those of the two central female characters.

The Winnipeg General Strike is probably the single most studied event in Canadian labour history.[1] The principle of collective bargaining was the central issue during the strike, combined with the demand for a living wage and a general improvement of working conditions. Labour and socialist politics have been examined through the strike and the formation of the One Big Union, and state policies have been analyzed through the NWMP action during the days of unrest. Traditionally, historians have sought to contextualize and explain the labour confrontation through political and economic analysis, disregarding, for example, the role of language and discourse in the reconstruction of strike issues (Reimer 1993). Either the strike has been seen as part of Western radicalism (Bercuson 1990), or, in revisionist readings that develop a "labor revolt thesis," the strike has been treated as part of a nation-wide ideological challenge that was connected to international changes (G. Kealey 1984). In the first critical analysis of the role of women in the Winnipeg General Strike of 1919, one that Sweatman acknowledges in the novel's bibliography, Mary Horodyski (1986, 28) wonders: "For all that has been written on women's actions during the Winnipeg general sympathetic strike of 1919, it could be concluded easily that females were not there at all, that they passed the six weeks holidaying at Lake Winnipeg. The historiography of the strike has been male-centred, and like all of history which refuses to include women and renders them invisible, it has been severely biased and incomplete." To foreground these biases and to aim for a wider representation of perspectives on the strike seems to be the driving force of Sweatman's novel; *Fox* thus becomes a rewriting of the events surrounding the Winnipeg General Strike, or, better, a radical revising of the events as historiography has told us about them (Ellis 1991, 71; Fischlin 1995, 57).

Sweatman's novel is by no means the first text to use the Winnipeg Strike as its historical setting. Douglas Durkin's 1923 novel *The Magpie*, republished in 1974, is set around the same time. The protagonist Craig Forrester, nicknamed Magpie, has just returned from the war and is full of hope for a new age in which all the promises of reform made during the war will come true. However, his expectations are frustrated. He finds himself opposing Lasker Blount, the strike-breaking expert brought in to deal with the Winnipeg workers, as well as his upper-class wife Marion Nason, whose superficiality and greed become unbearable to him. In the end, neither strikers nor capitalists allow the protagonist to live a satisfying life. Forrester returns to the countryside where he grew up and is reunited with his childhood sweetheart Martha Lane. While in *Magpie* the strike provides background and motivation for some of the characters' actions, Sweatman's approach works the other way round: she seems to explore her characters' perspectives in order to understand the strike. The focus is somewhat different in Ann Henry's play *Lulu Street* (1975), first performed in Winnipeg in 1967. Here two working-class women, Elly and Mrs One, whose father and husband are involved in the strike, take centre stage. Mrs One's hopes that "everything will go back to normal" once the strike is over (Henry 1975, 110) are shattered when her husband is killed during the riots of "Bloody Saturday" and Elly's father leaves to escape arrest. However, the play says very little about the strike itself, and the women remain in the kitchen of their rooming house. Sweatman's *Fox* reinscribes a wider range of women into the narratives of the strike: women who went on strike, women who marched and were jailed, women who organized the food kitchen at the Oxford Hotel, women who were only marginally inconvenienced by the strike and regarded demonstrations as entertaining spectacles, women who substituted for workers, and women who tried to feed families when food supplies were quickly diminishing.

Fox follows the chronology of events between 22 December 1918 and 21 June 1919, also known as "Bloody Saturday."[2] Sweatman combines public events, which have constituted the nationalist pedagogy, with private ones, which perform disruptions of this homogeneous narrative. Readers recognize the following central events: the crucial assembly in the Walker Theater on 22 December 1918, the first strike announcements on 1 May 1919, the General Strike vote on 14 May, the establishment of the Citizens' Committee of 1,000 on 16 May, the forty-minute legislation passed on 6 June, the arrests of 16 and 17 June, and Bloody Saturday on 21 June. Similarly, the reader can identify a range of historical persons, for example, six of the strike leaders arrested on 16 and 17 June (George Armstrong, R.B. Russell, A.A. Heaps, R.E. Bray, William Ivens, John Queen), as they interact with fictional ones such as MacDougal and the messenger boy, Stevie. Reinhold Kramer (1999, 53) argues that these and other strategies "tie *Fox* to the older tradition of the historical novel" without making it a historical novel in any unproblematic sense of presenting "true history." Its self-conscious blurring of the line between fact and fiction, its use of collage, and its anti-mimetic techniques (which emphasize the performative) instead make *Fox* another example of historiographic metafiction.

Frequently, the chronological progression of events seems to pause by counterpointing activities that occur at the same time or by focusing on one event seen from the perspectives of different characters. The latter is foregrounded, for instance, when Sweatman (1991) ends several prose sections with her characters' reflections on the future:

Drinkwater "looks into the stark early spring night and he sees *the future*" (78); "MacDougal sees the night's lush wing descend. He sees *the future*" (80); "Mary breathes deeply ... [her] hands stroking, caressing, wakening, *the future*. And she sees, that it is *good*" (81); the Canon suggests that "they could use me and I will do as I can by them. For the new. For change ... For the new" (82); "And Eleanor sees the future. *And it is missing*" (84). By creating such parallelism at the end of these consecutive sections, Sweatman invites the reader to relate the perspectives of these characters to one another without having the characters themselves interact. All five seem driven by the prospect of their future, except for Eleanor, whose lack of direction and sense of self translate into a lack of vision for the future.

By contrasting events that occur at the same time, Sweatman creates a different sense of interconnectedness. For example, while Eleanor is entertaining friends at a toboggan party (1–5), "The Unlawful Assembly" takes place at the Walker Theatre (6–8), a mass meeting co-sponsored by the Winnipeg Trades and Labour Council and the Socialist Party of Canada. Many prominent speakers express their views on the controversial policies of the present Union government (for example, the Orders in Council passed under the War Measures Act, the military intervention in Russia, and the incarceration of political prisoners) and call on the workers to "unite and overthrow the capitalist system" (8). Similarly, while Eleanor and her friend Grace are talking about Eleanor's brother Tony, who died in the war (30–2), a meeting is being held at the Labour Church, the church for workers organized in Winnipeg by W. Ivens (32). Later, while Eleanor is concerned about making a confession to MacDougal, he is at the mission teaching immigrants (67–71). And while Mary's wedding to Drinkwater is under way on 17 June (182), the strike leaders are arrested (184–9), which significantly weakens the strike efforts. The opposition that is set up through these narrative counterpoints is one of private versus public, middle class versus working class, women versus men, and anti-strike versus pro-strike positions. On the one hand, these multiple counterpoints expose the banality of the lives of middle-class women, such as Eleanor's and Mary's, who in the face of social unrest continue to focus their attention on entertaining friends and ensuring their own well-being. On the other hand, the strategy emphasizes that the mundane activities/concerns of these women are nevertheless political acts. While working-class women were redefining the political in terms of family and community rather than through institutions (L. Kealey 1989, 136), the novel reminds us that middle-class women were complicit with the politics of the strike through their non-involvement. In addition to its insistence on multiple ideological positions, the strategy of counterpoints also conveys a sense of simultaneity; the novel thus not only moves forward but also broadens its scope by embracing multiple viewpoints and thus expanding laterally.

Multiplicity and the dialogic relations that the reader is encouraged to establish (such as the recognition of counterpoint through correspondence and contrast relations) in fact characterize the overall organization of *Fox*. The book is an intricate collage of roughly 100 sections that vary in length from just a few lines to up to six pages. Some of these sections have titles (which sometimes function as ironic commentary); others are separated by dividing marks on the page; and some are dated while others are not. The text incorporates sections of prose fiction, quotations from the mainstream and labour presses,[3] advertisements, letters, a telegram, song lyrics, entries from the canon's diary, extracts from Rev. John Maclean's diary, inscriptions of signs and banners, quotations from public speeches (e.g., from F.J. Dixon and William Ivens) as well as quotations from Karl Marx and immediate commentators such as J.S. Woodsworth and so on. Sometimes sources and authors are identified, sometimes they are not. This multiplicity of perspectives cannot be reduced to a binary opposition between middle and working classes, as is common in critical studies of the strike. The novel's multiplicity is more multifaceted and complex than the strategy of counterpoint alone may suggest: each perspective represented in the text (whether in a character description or a quoted document) brings with it not only its specific language but also the socio-historical context from which it emerged. Sweatman (1993, 159) explains that her reading of Bakhtin's "Discourse in the Novel" informed the way she approached writing *Fox*:

I chose to write a polyphonic, overtly dialogic novel because that seems to me to be the most appropriate way to write about a small-scale civil war, the General Strike in Winnipeg in 1919, where intellectuals were jailed for "sedition" – which is not only the use of inflammatory language, but is the use of such language in an environment, a cultural, and economic, and therefore, political context which will hear, receive, enact that language. The Marxist language (in combination with the Social Gospel, Methodist and millennial language) was dynamite just after the first war. That is dialogism.

Bakhtin's notion of language as dialogic, as always having both speaker and listener, which Sweatman highlights in this comment, also applies to the novel as a whole. Sweatman seems acutely aware of the role of readers who will "hear, receive, enact that language" in a context more than eighty years removed from the events of the novel.

Sweatman's collage of documents and discourses emphasizes that understanding and retelling the strike involves processes that are not linear and continuous but, rather, highly fragmented. The novel, in Sweatman's (personal communication, 1 May 1995) words, becomes a forum, an argument, in which different contributions are placed side by side and are to be negotiated. Readers perform such negotiation by drawing, what Bakhtin (1984, 91) calls, "a dotted line" between each perspective "to the point of their dialogic intersection." The novel, however, refuses to offer transitions or explanations to facilitate this process. Creating cohesion or cause-and-effect relationships is left up to the readers.

Around three crucial events the text appears most fragmented: the Forty-Minute Legislation (Sweatman 1991, 170–2), "Strikers' Tuesday" (174–6), and Bloody Saturday (193–6). If we look more closely at the part dealing with the forty-minute legislation, then we can see how a reader may establish dialogic relations between the sections placed side by side. The highly fragmented nature of this part insists on the simultaneity of the perspectives presented; it also creates a sense of urgency (and possibly confusion) that mirrors the events around the passing of the legislation. There is no heading for this section, which opens instead with four italicized lines, flush-right on the page, that look like a poem:

The history
of all hitherto existing society
is the history
of class struggles

HERE. HAVE A CIGAR. Today's a day for the History Books, yessir. Here. I'll light it for you. Yessireesir, and it's about time too, we showed those Reds who's running this country, them or Constituted Authority. By God we know how to pull together for the sake of the Dominion, bless her heart. (Sweatman 1991, 170)

The opening lines come from the first part of Karl Marx's *Manifesto of the Communist Party* and are followed by five lines of prose, which, with their opening deictic "here" and the offer of a cigar, are obviously taken from a speech, although they are not marked by quotation marks. The speaker, presumably a man, maybe a member of the Committee of One Hundred, identifies himself as part of a larger "we" that represents the "Constituted Authority" at work in the interest of the Dominion against "them," "those Reds" who have to be gotten rid of, as the Queen says in the joke that follows in the next indented section.

Right from the beginning Marx's "class struggles" are restaged in these opening two sections – one italicized and relined, the other not – and further emphasized by the opposition between King/Queen and the dairymaid in the joke. Moreover, the repetition of "history" in "History Books" immediately links the first two sections, inviting readers to contemplate the different perspectives from which history is viewed in these two instances.

The next section, consisting of two incomplete sentences, shows no such obvious connecting points:

Like a bullet, like a bomb dropped from the sky in the night. Three readings in the House of Commons, three readings in the Senate, and the unqualified approval of the Governor-General. (170)

If we know enough about the strike, then it will be clear that this prose section refers to the forty-minute legislation; otherwise, we will not learn about the occasion for the speaker's words until we get to the capitalized headline on the next page: "FORTY-MINUTE LEGISLATION." The opening similes, "like a bullet, like a bomb," which convey the speed, the forcefulness, and surprise effect of the legislation, make it unlikely that these words are part of the earlier speech; in fact, later on (171), the speaker explicitly refers to the approval of the governor general, which is also mentioned here. However, through their reference to means of destruction, the similes connect with "the ruins / of feudal society" in the next unidentified and relined quotation from Marx's *Manifesto*:

> *modern bourgeois society*
> *that has sprouted*
> *from the ruins*
> *of feudal society*
> *has not done away with*

Gentlemen. It is late and we are all tired. We have worked hard tonight. (170)

Marx's quote remains incomplete ("class antagonisms" is missing at the end); the italicized quote runs into the next section of direct speech so that the salutation "gentlemen" becomes the object missing from Marx's sentence: "modern bourgeois society ... has not done away with gentlemen." Sweatman forces a connection here between Marx's quote and the bourgeois speaker by means of syntax, but she continues to develop the tension between the two by once again interrupting the

speech with the indented and capitalized words FORTY-MINUTE LEGIS-
LATION. What labour, with some disdain, called the forty-minute legislation (Bumsted 1994, 48) is referred to by the speaker in neutral terms
as "the amendment to the Immigration Act." The next section, a single italicized sentence, reads like a quote from that very act. Those considered revolutionary and born outside of Canada, who were previously protected by their status as Canadian citizens (through their
British birth or naturalization), could now be deported as easily as
immigrants from other countries. This amendment promised to have a
devastating impact on many of the strike leaders. These serious implications are thrown into even starker relief by the speaker's celebratory
words following: "May I propose a toast." The next indented and capitalized line, "DEPORT THE ENEMY ALIEN!" is probably the speaker's
toast, followed by a narrative section that describes the reactions of
members of the audience. At the same time, the placement of the toast
on the page and its capitalization connects it with the previous reference to the "FORTY-MINUTE LEGISLATION." The toast spells out in the
language of the strike opposition – that is, the upper classes – the message that the forty-minute legislation, a labour term, ultimately conveys.

Once again, another italicized, unidentified, and flush-right section
turns out to be a quote from Marx's *Manifesto*, and, once again, the
words run into the following narrative prose.

> *the bourgeoisie*
> *has drowned*
> *heavenly ecstasies of religious*
> *fervour,*
> *in the icy water*
> *of egotistical*
> *calculation. It has*
> *resolved personal worth*

into exchange value. In a used bookstore in Winnipeg, a man is chewing on an
unlit pipe and reading, late, late into the night, into the small hours of the
morning. (Sweatman, 1991 171)

Not only is *"exchange value"* immediately linked with the reference to
the bookstore in the next sentence, but the suggestion may also be that
the man, whom we can identify as MacDougal, is reading the same
words of Marx that we have been reading and has been doing so while,
in another part of town, politicians have been celebrating the passing
of the amendment to the Immigration Act. This part of the book ends
with another quotation from Marx, in the same format as the previous

ones, followed by a snapshot of what is going on "outside the book-store" (172). Someone is watching MacDougal's bookstore, and the narrator invites the reader to take a closer look: "See his lean face under his hat" (172).

Even though Sweatman provides a list of sources at the beginning of the novel, she does not always provide sources for her quotations in the text itself; this part on the forty-minute legislation provides a good example of this inconsistency. Readers may feel invited to do some detective work of their own, to immerse themselves in the events and discourses of the strike to track down origins. Some quotations, such as those from Karl Marx, may seem so obvious that they do not require acknowledgment; however, it is also possible that, in some instances, the source does not matter because the language clearly positions the quote ideologically. Ultimately, Sweatman is mirroring our daily realities, within which we are confronted with and borrow from so many perspectives that often we can no longer identify their sources. Or, for that matter, vouch for the accuracy of our quotations. In his discussion of *Fox*, Kramer (1999) points out that Sweatman repeatedly changes the documents she incorporates into the text. While he argues that these changes "make the narrative slightly less reliable" (57), he sees them primarily as showing "the intrusion of the present upon the past" (53). The latter point suggests that every quotation (and every retelling of past events) will be changed by the new context within which it is placed or by the perspective from which it is narrated. It is therefore always double-voiced, "serv[ing] two speakers at the same time and express[ing] simultaneously two different intentions" (Bakhtin 1981, 324). If, as a result, double-voicing becomes a condition of every retelling, then accuracy becomes increasingly problematic as a criterion for evaluation since it assumes a fixed point of reference, an origin that we may no longer be able to determine.

Sweatman conveys different views of the legislation in this part not only by counterpointing the actions of politicians and workers but also, and even more poignantly, by putting in front of us, by means of the incorporated genres, the different languages they use to express themselves. Discourse plays a crucial role as communities in Winnipeg enact exclusion and inclusion; it becomes highly charged in a society that attempts to censor public speech and literature. "Alien," "red," "Bolshevik," "socialist," and "revolutionary" are the words most commonly used in *Fox* to show how a language of exclusion operates to ostracize strike supporters. As Benstock, the "Dominion Censor" who accuses MacDougal of selling seditious literature, points out to him: "'things must be in harmony, in pleasing agreement with the Dominion'" (Sweatman 1991, 24). With the support of censorship

laws, charges of seditious conspiracy or libel are used to make potentially revolutionary literature inaccessible and to muzzle public criticism. In the later trials of the strike leaders, in particular in the case of
Robert B. Russell, sedition was defined by Judge Metcalfe as intending
"to excite discontent or dissatisfaction; to excite ill-will between different classes or the King's subjects; to create public disturbances"
(quoted in Bumsted 1994, 67). Free discussion was acceptable as long
as it did not take place *"under circumstances likely to incite tumult"*
(118). Sweatman's novel powerfully asserts that discourses are social
struggles, that books are not just words on a page, as MacDougal sar-
donically tries to convince Benstock (Sweatman 1991, 23). In the novel
the discourses of inclusion and exclusion have material effects on those
supporting and opposing the strike efforts in Winnipeg in 1919, that
is, in concrete socio-historical contexts.

One particularly effective strategy Sweatman employs to reaccentu-
ate incorporated genres is their translation from prose into poetry,
what Kramer (1999, 53) describes as the relining of prose documents.
The sentences from Marx's *Manifesto*, which I quoted earlier in this
chapter, serve as good examples of this process of dialogizing through
generic translation. I agree with Kramer that the shift to poetry in
many instances recovers "the fervency of socialism in 1919" (54);
however, at the same time, Sweatman also displaces and hybridizes
generic conventions. By defamiliaring quoted texts, she draws the readers' attention not only to the language used but also to its generic form.
For Bakhtin (1986, 86), speech genres are "relatively stable typical
forms of construction of the whole"; these forms are found in typical
situations, use typical themes, and establish particular relations
between words and reality under typical circumstances (87). In other
words, each genre "has its method and means of seeing and conceptualizing reality" (Bakhtin 1978, 133). When Sweatman relines a section
from a prose document such as Marx's *Manifesto* – that is, when she
turns parts of it into poems – she forces the reader to pay attention.
Marx's words may be familiar, but their presentation is not. What
changes, we are asked, when the form changes? When the context
changes? Sweatman's double-voicing thus becomes multilayered: the
first double-voicing occurs in the quotation itself as the quote begins to
operate in a new context, taking on new meaning; the second occurs in
the generic shift from prose to poetry, presenting readers with a new
way of seeing Marx's words and his reality.

For the most part, no overt narrator seems to orchestrate or control
the multiple perspectives and incorporated documents in the novel.
The fragmented, paratactic narrative attempts to remain free of hierarchies, although Sweatman (personal communication, 1 May 1995)

acknowledges that these can never be avoided completely, that she cannot, for example, escape the role of writer as imperialist (personal communication, 2 May 1995). At times, the narrator moves into the foreground – for example, through the foreshadowing of MacDougal's arrest (Sweatman 1991, 46) and Mary's marriage to Drinkwater (179–80), and the frequent evaluations that inform his/her descriptions (especially as the ironic critic of Mary but also as the bemused observer of Eleanor). In these cases, the narrator functions as focalizer, but focalization often shifts to other characters as well, especially to Mary and Eleanor. In these sections, the narrative quickly, and often unexpectedly, moves back and forth between psychonarration, free indirect discourse, and interior monologue.[4] The following is a frequently used pattern in which the narrative moves from description to interior monologue within the same sentence and from one sentence to the next:

Eleanor has dreamed a long dream about MacDougal, dammit the man's become an obsession, I need a trip out of town, go to Uncle Rodney's cottage at Kenora, go to Chicago, go downtown today anyway, have lunch with somebody. She opens her eyes. Today is my birthday. The lonely dream recedes, echoing. She studies the mole on her right arm. (83)

To capture the uniqueness of individual characters through free indirect discourse and interior monologue, Sweatman often uses the vernacular and oral storytelling, but she also relies on syntax to set her characters apart.

Two of the main characters in the novel are the middle-class women Eleanor and her cousin Mary, both of whom live in Crescentwood, a wealthy, residential area in South Winnipeg. Eleanor is the first character to be introduced in the novel:

Eleanor is tall, taller than most men, and her face is long, her thin nose long as a lake-edging highway, her long face and her eyes like almonds, almost, a very strange long woman. She likes her own almond eyes, actually. She says to hell with those fat and innocent faces, my bones, my damn cheekbones anyway, will be fine on my face when it's old ... She looks like a big bird, a hawk, a prairie falcon ... Her hands are too big, her fingers splayed, she flings her hands about when she speaks. Her feet are long ... she's too awkward, she has long since outgrown herself. (1)

Eleanor not only fails to meet the expectations of feminine beauty exemplified by Mary's "perfect narrow eyes blue and clear" (2) and the "young faces round as biscuits" (3), but her unusual appearance correlates with different interests as well. She would rather stay in "her dark room where she lives and listens" (2) than entertain her friends at a toboggan party; she joins the men in the library where they retreat to smoke and enjoy "a bit of manly company" (4); she reads papers, such as the *Winnipeg Tribune*, and would rather learn more about "the Alien and the Bolsheviki threat" than go out to listen to a band play in town (5).

In contrast, Mary is the "perfect" woman; she is twenty-one years old, petite and pretty, reads Henry James, suffers from a "nervous disorder" (116, 63), and looks for a man who will take care of her. She is engaged to be married to Drinkwater, the up-and-coming businessman who emulates and seeks advice from Mary's father, Sir Rodney. Mary's hopes for the future are bright: "forever after life will be a calm ocean crossed in the luxuryliner of joint fortunes and Drinkwater will carry a walkingstick and he will place one hand in the pocket of his evening coat, just so" (73). Although Mary is appreciated for her faultless appearance, the narrator frequently exposes her innocence, ignorance, and simplicity: "Mary ... feeling every inch a slender young thing, is performing a function quite new to her. She is *thinking*" (61). As a woman whose "lips are Nearly Rose," whose "cheeks are Tender Peach," whose "skin is Linen and Cream," and whose "eyes are Royal Blue" (26), Mary defines herself – as the narrator facetiously and ironically suggests – through the language and values of fashion and beauty ads. Mary is interested in contemporary social issues such as the struggles of the workers only in so far as they affect her lifestyle. Her main goal is to ensure her status in the class environment in which she has been raised.

Through her marriage to Drinkwater, Mary will remain safely within the boundaries of their community, which Sir Rodney has taken care of by buying a house across the street from his own place. However, her safe and comfortable lifestyle does not provide her with the excitement she desires; Mary has to take matters into her own hands to create a sense of danger and temptation. The novel exposes her occasional transgressions of rules and boundaries, which consist of sneaking out of the house without her father's permission to attend a parade with Drinkwater (162–6), premarital sex (179), and, most interestingly, her "B & E" (123–5). From the sketchy narrative it becomes clear that Mary frequently walks the dog as an excuse to "visit" houses that have been deserted by their neighbours for summer vacations: her father "doesn't realize she's going out so late, again, tonight" (124). Anticipating her excursion, Mary "knows exactly which house she'll hit tonight. The Squib-Avonhersts' on Harvard" (124). Walking through the house, inspecting the owner's interior decorations, she is humming the Hebrew Benediction, which "reminds her of a christen-ing" (124). Is Mary sanctioning her own actions, providing her own blessing here? This scene can be read, I believe, as an example of her arrogance as well as of her thoughtlessness. Eventually, she sits down in a chair. In these brief moments of her "break and enter," Mary has suspended all social rules and laws of property, but these transgression do not ultimately upset her place in the world of the middle class. As long as she is not caught, they are only temporary transgressions that actually confirm her social status because she is in control of their out-come and does not have to fear any repercussions.

Eleanor looks and behaves differently; therefore, she does not truly belong. She struggles to understand the situation in which she finds herself: "what is this transformation?" (13). She tries to appreciate the world around her by reading articles in the papers, but she has to rec-ognize her own limitations and her limited world view: "has she ever met a poor person"; "Her brother is dead. She hadn't had the wits to blame anybody, and it's her fault, she is so stupid!" (13). Eleanor tries to break free from her middle-class environment by moving out of her father's house and beginning to read: "MacDougal isn't even sarcastic with her, he doesn't seem to expect her to know anything, why should he expect anything, when he knows she runs on a short leash in this goddam suffocating city" (68). MacDougal, the socialist friend of Eleanor's father, is her guide and love interest, and seems to guarantee her entrance into working-class circles. She no longer feels a part of her father's world and "has slipped out of his vocabulary" (90):

But whereas tapestries, a desk with pigeon-holes for papers thin with the neces-sities of a big business, paintings and vases above and upon a grand piano, whereas all these things once gave Eleanor a *name*, the secure feet-on-the-ground knowledge of herself as *Eleanor*, daughter of, sister of, niece of, cousin of, member of – but owner of nothing, not really, it all belongs to Father. (68)

Compelled by the Social Gospel, which sought to apply Christian principles to a variety of social problems engendered by industrializa-tion,[5] Eleanor tries to get involved in the workers' activities, goes to meetings with MacDougal, and joins the food kitchen (167–9). She tries to dissociate herself from the community she was born into and seeks other communities in which she can define herself, which she can join by her own decision, seeking "revolutionary enthusiasm" (14). She finds it difficult, however, to leave her familiar world behind, the clothes, the luxury, the lavish furniture, the food, the manners. She is still an observer and remains passive when she should be helping Mac-Dougal: "And only later ... as she folds herself into her reading-chair, does it occur to Eleanor that she might have helped MacDougal with the boys at the Mission pool ... She might have joined MacDougal in his care of the children" (161); "Eleanor stands beside him [MacDougal] ... MacDougal with the dead boy in his arms. Eleanor standing beside them, her empty arms waving, waving, waving" (197–8). Unlike Mary, Eleanor does not seek temporary transgressions within her own community but a permanent reorientation that challenges the foundations of her life. At the end of the novel, Eleanor still lives in two worlds at once: she may have become resistant to, but she is still complicit with, the middle class. When she goes to MacDougal's bookstore still unaware of his arrest, we learn from a police officer who functions as focalizer that he "has been instructed to leave her alone ... She must be rich to get special attention like that. She sure looks rich" (190). In addition to her treatment by others, she reflects on her own participation in Mary's wedding: "MacDougal I love you and today I am being driven to Westminster Church in a baby-blue Packard. It's a conspiracy, MacDougal, but I am just a spy ... and she sees in the mirror that she is her own double agent" (185).

As a result, Eleanor lives in the space in-between, in "double-time," to borrow Bhabha's (1994, 145) term; she no longer belongs to her father's world, but she does not belong to the world of MacDougal either. In fact, at a Labour Church meeting she realizes that she "is happy. She doesn't belong here; she's perfectly at home, orphaned at last. Anything can happen. Now! my life is rich. No one looks at her, or if they do, something is different. She's part of something here, they expect her to take part. Damn right, she says, damn right I will" (Sweatman 1991, 94).[6] Uncomfortable with her "impossible self" (117), feeling "stricken and embarrassed and disconnected from herself at every juncture" (39), Eleanor is not yet able to define herself in any new terms. Her immediate goal is to lose herself, to leave herself behind (154), which gives her comfort: "she opens the window and stands there for a long time, breathing, her breathing marking the time, numbering the voices, her father, and her brother, her relations falling from her, the voices departing from her, leaving her alone at the window looking out" (91). Eleanor's personal transformation suggests that social change can become more than a visceral experience for the women of the middle class. Her challenge to community and class boundaries functions as a crucial strategy of the novel's performative discourse that disturbs, displaces, and disrupts the homogeneity of the pedagogical.

Language plays a crucial role in Eleanor's attempt to become her own woman. She realizes that her own perspective and her own discourse are valid:

She has recently discovered (and maybe this discovery has given her freedom) that she can indeed listen in a fragmentary way ... And another thing: it doesn't matter anymore that her patterns of translation differ from MacDougal's or her father's. The men speak their public language, and it is a marvel, their absolute sentences, and Eleanor, living under and between, always outside, has a place she can furnish according to her own design. She has decided this is good. (120)

I read Eleanor's "patterns of translation" and their valorization as a metacommentary on the alternative tellings of history in the novel. Just as they enable her to see how her perspective and language differ from those of men, *Fox* encourages the reader to engage seriously with a fragmentary, revisionist reading of the Winnipeg Strike as an alternative to the masculine historiography that has projected an accumulative public history. Through its restaging of events, *Fox* simultaneously evokes and erases the boundaries that have supported the pedagogical.

When the novel provides glimpses into the lives of working-class women, the focus is no longer on love interests, mood changes, and luxuries but on material necessities such as food, rent, and a minimum wage. The reader learns about the effects of the strike on these women and about their coping strategies. In anticipation of diminishing food supplies, women fill up wagons to stock up on food: sugar, turnips, and carrots (92–3). Moreover, on 24 May, women begin to set up a food kitchen that is initiated and maintained primarily by Helen Armstrong and the Women's Labor League. The example of the food kitchen shows how many women were on strike at the time, but it also stresses the sense of solidarity among women. The kitchen was a service provided by women mainly for the support of other women.[7] It provides Eleanor with an opportunity to become part of the women's community by getting involved with their work (167–9). However, food is not the only problem faced by the working-class characters in *Fox*. The women on strike also find it difficult to pay rent without an income. The Relief Committee helped to fund cash donations, and special appeals were made to help the women in need because society feared that working women may turn to prostitution for economic support (Tranfield 1989, 34). The novel picks up on these unspoken concerns and makes them explicit in its description of Aileen, who works as a sales clerk at Eaton's and turns to prostitution so she can pay her rent and afford the clothes she is expected to wear at work (35–7).

The novel also depicts working-class women who organize for militant purposes. The women attack two delivery-truck drivers whose scab work undermines the struggles of the workers on strike (141–3).

Again, the narrative emphasizes the sense of community among women: "One of the ideas is they stick together because they're all alike, the women, but what happens is, they're together because of their differences. It makes them quiet" (141). Moreover, it also shows how the women are perceived in the press. The statement of a detective, which was printed in the *Winnipeg Tribune* on 21 June, is quoted at the end of the section, attesting to the dangerous and defiant nature of the striking women (143). Throughout the novel, tension builds between the descriptions of working-class women and the sections that focus on Eleanor and Mary. Once the reader begins to relate these perspectives dialogically, the stories of the working-class women openly challenge the complacency of the middle class and the stereotypes of women's roles in society.

In spite of the labour turmoil of 1919 and earlier years, gender roles were firmly inscribed in Canadian society. Indeed, as L. Kealey (1989, 141) points out, class and gender expectations were intertwined: "respectable middle class or upper class women would not participate in such unseemly behaviour." Moreover, women deserved special protection during the strike. The Strike Committee tried very hard to prevent violence and reminded the strikers repeatedly to adhere to "fair play" in the struggle (Bumsted 1994, 33–4). The methods of the authorities were labelled ungentlemanly and secretive, and the strikers were instructed that their own behaviour should be that of "decent men" who "treat women by the rules of decent society, even in the midst of a bitter struggle" (Reimer 1993, 230). Women who stepped outside accepted gender roles would lose their protection as women.[8] *Fox*, however, does not discipline these female characters for their transgressions; rather, it highlights and re-evaluates their militancy during the strike in order to emphasize their solidarity. In other words, it presents their actions as a form of mutual support rather than as a display of meaningless aggression.

Issues of ethnicity and race further complicated how gender and class were connected in establishing communities and rules of conduct during the strike. As Horodyski (1986, 34) has noted, whenever possible the women involved in riot actions were referred to as foreigners. That women were involved in militant action was unsettling, but if they were designated as immigrants, then the problem could be contained. Similarly, the behaviour of immigrant men was often described as cowardly and furtive and was contrasted with the manly and forceful characteristics of the British men; through these comparisons, non-British men were implicitly depicted as feminine (Avery 1976, 219). The role of "foreigners," or "aliens," as they were variably referred to, was paramount during the Winnipeg Strike.[9] At the beginning of the strike, Winnipeg was already geographically segregated in terms of class and race: the working-class consisted mainly of "new immigrants" (mostly Slavic and Jewish) who resided in the north part of town, while the primarily British middle and upper classes lived in the south and west end. Anti-immigration sentiments were strong in the late 1910s (as the conscription crisis, calls for disenfranchisement, and the Orders in Council of 1918 suggest), and immigrants were increasingly singled out by the business community, especially by the Citizens' Committee, as the instigators of political and industrial unrest. As Benstock explains to MacDougal: "'we intend to focus that blame away from the Government, we choose to lay the blame elsewhere, the foreign element will do nicely'" (Sweatman 1991, 24). The strikers, however, asserted that it was class not race that really mattered in their fight. Indeed, the *Western Labour News* charged the capitalists as the "real aliens" who served only themselves and not the community (Reimer 1993, 232; Avery 1976, 217).

The returned soldiers further complicated this situation because most of them were hostile to immigrants. As the headlines in *Fox* show, newspapers such as the *Winnipeg Tribune* used the opposition soldier/"alien" in their rhetoric (Sweatman 1991, 116, 126), and anti-labour loyalist veterans used it on their strike banners (165). That the category of "enemy alien" was a convenient and flexible construct is shown in Sweatman's section on the forty-minute legislation of 6 June, which amended section 41 of the Immigration Act to allow for the deportation of British subjects under the conditions of undesirability (170–2). In other words, in *Fox* all of these interconnected references to class, ethnicity, and gender challenge a definition of "Canadian" that depends upon the construction of an "other" that must be excluded; this exclusion is not only directed at strikers, and sometimes at unruly women, but is also predicated on the figure of the "alien."

Sweatman's interest in the interconnections between questions of gender, ethnicity, and class in her rewriting of the strike have not saved her, however, from criticism regarding the absence or silence of working-class and immigrant characters (Ellis 1991, 73; Sweatman, personal communication, 1 May 1995). What readers learn about the working-class women, they tend to learn from the outside looking in. Occasionally, working-class characters function as focalizers but not to the same extent as do Eleanor and Mary. As Sweatman (personal communication, 2 May 1995) has explained, reciprocity of the gaze is important if one is to achieve respectful representation. Worried that her own positioning would lead to the sentimentalizing or patronizing treatment of working-class characters, she decided to evoke their presence through ellipses and gaps, through the dialogic relations actualized in the novel's collage (Sweatman, personal communication, 1 May 1995).

Stevie Macovitch, the young messenger boy, is the only immigrant character given a voice in *Fox*. He seems to appear everywhere, benefiting from the services he can render for people during the strike. Mac-Dougal takes particular interest in him after he learns that Stevie's mother is sick and cannot come to work (Sweatman 1991, 48–9). In the novel it is Stevie who is killed in the riots of Bloody Saturday: "He sees MacDougal waving to him, he goes to him ... Stevie, in the middle of the road, eager to receive a message from his friend this so-serious MacDougal. The bullet, the hot shell, in the boy's face, it shoots off the face, he falls" (197). By making the dying "alien" a young boy, the novel highlights the vulnerability of the immigrants during the strike. While the "other" is literally killed at the end of the novel, the boy's innocence exposes the senselessness and injustice of this construction of the "other" and of the violence directed against him. The sense of futility at the end of *Fox* seems to foreshadow the "profound dissolution within the working-class experience" that followed the strike in Winnipeg (B.D. Palmer 1983, 177).

The difficult question of representation is approached from a slightly different angle in the final "List of Illustrations" (199–200). The list may come as a surprise to readers because there are no illustrations or references in *Fox* with which this list could be linked. This last part consists of six prose sections, each given a heading ("Photograph #1" to "Photograph #6" [Sweatman 1991, 199–200]). As referential art, photos are often considered to testify to the "real" existence of what they show. By narrating rather than showing the photographic images, however, Sweatman challenges the notion of their referentiality and stasis. Because narration depends on a speaker and progresses in time, the photos-turned-narratives are exposed as subjective, dynamic constructions of a distinct narrator. At times, this narrator seems to describe specific images, possibly while sorting through a box of photos or flipping through an album, but at the same time the images become occasions for more general contemplations about the power and shortcomings of language and the process of writing. The first few photo descriptions depict women with children or children alone, while the last two refer to group shots – one of the parade passing the Legislature, the other of a confrontation on the streets, which "is the photograph on the front page today" (200). It is with the four private images of individuals that the narrator engages most, directly addressing the women (possibly the same woman) in photos 2 to 4. Sweatman's use of the second-person pronoun here emphasizes the connection between photographer/speaker and photo/narrative: every photo is taken by a photographer from a particular perspective, just as every narrative is told by a narrator with a particular perspective. Any objectifying gaze that the observer may direct at the photos is challenged by the narrative. Sweatman's strategy here resembles the techniques she employs throughout the novel to resituate and rewrite the events of the strike. Defying the objectifying gaze of historiography and nationalist pedagogy, *Fox* returns the gaze by inscribing a multiplicity of perspectives to tell the stories of people as subjects.

These perspectives are not simply added to the nationalist pedagogy though; they constantly have to be renegotiated in dialogic relations. As a result, *Fox* performs interventions, not containment. The polyvalency of voices and their relations is reminiscent of the "fox" in the novel's title. Only one character, Drinkwater, actually sees the fox (53). However, both Drinkwater and Mary show a fox-like appearance and behaviour: Drinkwater has a "fox-blond" body (40) and Mary "stops like a fox, gleaming and red" (2). The association of the fox with a sexually attractive woman applies to both Mary and Aileen (36). The fox is cunning and sly (Sir Rodney is referred to as an "old fox" [198]), out for his/her own best interest, unlikely to get caught. That the novel seems to privilege the telling of stories from an advantaged view could itself be read as "foxy," as Daniel Fischlin (1995, 62) has suggested, because that perspective is "given to dissembling and self-deception, and therefore a useful marker of the novel's exposition of the 'advantaged' as an inverted ethical signifier." The title may thus be a commentary on the subversive gesture of the novel itself. Through occasional (foxy) sightings and repeated performances, the novel can dislocate the homogeneous narrative of the pedagogical.

Sweatman dissolves the seamless historiographic narrative of the Winnipeg Strike in *Fox*, giving up the panopticon of an omniscient narrator (Fischlin 1995, 59). She incorporates voices of shifting contexts, public and private voices, family and community voices, creating a collage of distinct sections. Only by placing the numerous sections in dialogic relation with each other, by performing the text so to speak, can the reader make sense of the multiplicity of perspectives. Sweatman has commented on the problematics of the performative, explaining that to keep the reader interested the novel needs to balance old structures against fresh transgressions (Sweatman 1993, 161). These transgressions are not formalist projects but, rather, rewrite the ending of the historical record. The novel interrupts the pregiven, monumental narrative of the pedagogical by challenging its causality and monologism. In an open-ended, at times even careless, way the performative intervenes in the gaps, in the reaccentuations of incorporated genres, and speaks from in-between times and places. Its difficulty will seem impolite only to those who prefer to homogenize experiences; it will not seem so to those who desire to articulate resistance and alternatives.

7 Writing into the Page Ahead[1]

There is neither a first nor a last word and there are no limits to
the dialogic context (it extends into the boundless past and the
boundless future).

Mikhail Bakhtin

The novels I have discussed in the preceding chapters suggest that culture is not a homogeneous construction. They recognize, in Bennett's
(1993/94, 196–7) words, "that there is a collection of cultures within
the *idea* of English Canada, not so much a mosaic as a kaleidoscope,
an arrangement of fragments whose interrelationships, while ever
changing, nevertheless serve – by virtue of their container, we might say
– not only to influence what we see when we look through the glass,
but also to affect the placement of the other elements in the array." The
dialogic relations between voices in these texts neither inscribe utopian
negations of the dominant discourse nor seek a simple resolution by
privileging one discourse of resistance over another. Difference is their
point of departure and their continuing impetus for communication
and struggle.

The heterogeneity that these contemporary novels make visible is
not a happy rainbow coalition. By rejecting the notion of dialogism as
a normative liberal pluralism, the novels – and their readers – do not
have to presume equality between voices; instead, they can acknowledge that inequality is historically and socially constructed (San Juan
1992, 140). I disagree with the neo-conservative argument that the less
we say about inequalities and injustice, the less frequently they will
occur and the less likely they are to provoke a backlash from the
majority. On the contrary, I believe that we need to learn as much as
we can about forms of oppression in the past and the present, from
racism and sexism to homophobia, forced relocations, and genocide.[2]
Contemporary novels can contribute to this process of education if we

understand literature as a discourse that interrogates our ways of knowing. If we begin to see literature and social context as inextricably connected, then we can look to literature not only for its constructions of communities but also for the specific devices and strategies it uses to express and revise them. The cultural-narratological approach I have proposed seeks to examine, mediate, and critique cultural representations, both aesthetically and politically.

My exclusive focus on Canadian literature places this study in the ongoing debates about the relevance of national approaches in literary studies. In 1993 Davey argued that we already lived in a post-nationalist state and that contemporary novels "inhabit a post-national space, in which sites are as interchangeable as postcards, in which discourses are transnational, and in which political issues are constructed on non-national (and often ahistorical) ideological grounds" (259). I have considered some of the same texts that Davey examined in *Post-National Arguments*, but I have arrived at different conclusions. I believe that the question of the national is a central one in these contemporary novels as they seek to understand what exactly "Canada" stands for and how we can intervene in its construction. In this sense, a national approach, questions about nation construction, and an analysis of the relationship between nation and literature are still relevant at this time of increasing globalization. What we find, when we leave a nineteenth-century European notion of nation behind, is that the novels discussed here challenge a homogeneous and universalist understanding of Canada by exposing dominant constructions and interpellating silenced voices, oppositional or alternative positions. If, as Mukherjee (1995b, 441) suggests, we reject the idea that Canadian literature needs to follow "a" Canadian tradition, defined in Eurocentric terms, then we can develop "a new nationalism, a nationalism whose grounding premise will be Canada's heterogeneity," a nationalism that can be "an effective, multifaceted *strategy* for decolonization" (Kelly, quoted in Fee 1995, 689). The analysis of resistance literature contributes to the challenge of the familiar, dominant discourse, which continually "intensifies itself, maintaining in effect a closure" (Itwaru 1994, 2). The direction of a literary criticism that explores Canadian culture, including Canadian literature, as a site of struggle rather than as a homogeneous entity will give a new impetus to Canadian cultural history.

I have attempted to find a way of reading the selected novels critically, without simply sanctifying or sacralizing their discourses of resistance and thereby closing them off from critique. It would be too simplistic to suggest that polyphonic novels simply inscribe everything that disadvantaged voices are looking for. It is necessary to show the complexity of these particular novels, and of counter-hegemonic discourses in general, by exposing how discourses are always internally multi-layered and often ambivalent. In my discussions of Kogawa's humanist position, van Herk's essentializing of the feminine north, and Marlatt's strategic monologism, I have been suspicious of the moment when strategic positions solidify into positions of permanent complicity, when they ultimately affirm the hegemony they seem to de-privilege. I believe that such critical readings are necessary because I am concerned that an indiscriminate and a priori valorization of resistance discourses and polyphonic narratives would discourage the questions that might challenge generalizations. We need a self-conscious criticism that can help us understand contemporary inequalities in order to combat them, a criticism that explores the ideological signification of narrative structures in contextual studies.

The extent to which I consider cultural contexts in my readings differs from chapter to chapter and even within chapters. I believe it would be counter-productive to prescribe what constitutes the "right" amount of contextualization. Rey Chow (1993, 38) has warned us of the danger of supplying contexts for literary texts too readily: "The hasty supply of original 'contexts' and 'specificities' easily becomes complicitous with the dominant discourse, which achieves hegemony precisely by its capacity to convert, recode, make transparent, and thus represent even those experiences that resist it with a stubborn opacity."[3] I have been aware of the problematics of my colonizing the selected novels and their discourses of resistance by using Bakhtinian and narratological theories for my critical framework. In the process of writing, I have attempted to look over my own shoulder, so to speak, to detect such gestures of colonization and containment, but I cannot completely free myself of a certain degree of complicity. Moreover, regardless of my sympathy for resistance discourses, I realize that my attempt to explore these counter-hegemonic voices is always different from their own struggle, no matter how much I may feel tempted to gloss over that distinction.

What I have proposed here is a particular, cultural-narratological way of reading contemporary Canadian fiction; my selection of texts remains, however, limited. The chapter on Joy Kogawa and Sky Lee could have been expanded, for instance, by a discussion of Wayson Choy's *The Jade Peony* (1995). This novel consists of three parts, each narrated and focalized by another child of a Chinese family that has immigrated to Canada and settled in Vancouver's Chinatown during the 1930s. Its multiple perspectives are determined largely by the age and gender of each child and provide interesting refractions of each other's narratives. Hiromi Goto's *Chorus of Mushrooms* (1994) explores the dialogic relations and struggles between three generations of Japanese Canadian women and would be interesting to compare with Kogawa's *Obasan*. My discussion of *Obasan* could also have been followed by a reading of its sequel, *Itsuka* (1992), in which Naomi becomes involved in the Japanese Canadian redress movement and which ends on Settlement Day, 22 September 1988. For a more complete look at Kogawa's writings, I would have liked to counterpoint these two novels with *The Rain Ascends* (1995b), in which the narrator Millicent learns that her father abused young boys during the years he worked as a minister. I suspect that the narrative structures of these novels, which show less internal dialogization of the narrators' perspectives and little or no use of incorporated genres, further support Kogawa's humanist belief in the value of truth and positivism and her interest in "spiritual questions," especially about the existence of evil (Kogawa 1995a, 27).

To explore rewritings of northern narratives more extensively, I would have liked to have read van Herk's *Places Far from Ellesmere* with, or against, Mordecai Richler's *Solomon Gursky Was Here* (1989), Thomas Wharton's *Icefields* (1995), Rudy Wiebe's *A Discovery of Strangers* (1994), and Elizabeth Hay's *The Only Snow in Havana* (1992). Hay's text could be connected with van Herk's geografictione by focusing on their interrelation of multiple chronotopes, through which the narrators search for a displaced home, and their challenges to traditional generic boundaries of the novel. Hay's narrator explores alternative narratives to the masculine histories of the north, literally and metaphorically questioning its monolithic whiteness and meditating upon the connection between snow and fur. My reading of Richler's, Wharton's, and Wiebe's novels would have focused on their rewriting of Canadian history from distinct perspectives and their challenge to the fact/fiction opposition through the montage of documentary and fictional elements.

There are several novels that could have broadened my analysis of the performative in *Slash* and *Green Grass, Running Water*. King's *Medicine River* (1989) raises interesting questions about the dialogic relations between its eighteen individual chapters, which may be read as a short-story cycle rather than as a novel. In her second novel, *Whispering in Shadows* (2000), Jeannette Armstrong explores the perspective of Penny, the main character, by creating complex interrelations between a heterodiegetic narration that establishes Penny as object and some of Penny's letters and diary entries, in which the character writes her/self. The stories of Ruby Slipperjack's *Silent Words* (1992), Lee Maracle's *Sun Dogs* (1992b), and Eden Robinson's *Monkey Beach* (2000), on the other hand, are presented by homodiegetic narrators whose perspectives are internally dialogized, for example, through storytelling. Beatrice Culleton's *In Search of April Raintree* (1983) presents a fascinating counterpoint between the two voices of Cheryl and April, who respond in opposite ways to the choice between assimilation and oblivion. Such duality is also a central structuring device in Tomson Highway's *Kiss of the Fur Queen* (1998).

In this book, novels with multiple perspectives have been of particular interest to me. For example, it is worth querying whether multiple voices necessarily guarantee dialogic interaction. Margaret Atwood's *Life before Man* (1979) (focalized by Elizabeth, Nate, and Lesje) and Carole Corbeil's *Voice-Over* (1992) (focalized by Odette and her daughters Janine and Claudine) invite this kind of examination. While Atwood's novel also shows internal dialogization of the three individual perspectives, which emphasizes their interconnectedness, the interrelating of the multiple perspectives in *Voice Over* seems more superficial. However, Corbeil's novel creates increasing tension between the isolation of the three different perspectives and the strong family bonds between mother and daughters. At the same time, it traces Claudine's search for a voice of her own to replace the voice-over of the patriarchal and monolingual and monocultural environments in which she lives.

The framework of dialogism and cultural narratology presented here could also be used in a diachronic examination of Canadian fiction in order to explore whether it is accurate to say that "the more contemporary the text, the greater the degree of dialogism" (Grace 1987, 123) or whether Bakhtin's theories, based on the concept of otherness, are generally well suited for the study of Canadian literature. Cavell's (1987) work on James De Mille's *The Dodge Club* and Robin Howells's (1993) reading of Frances Brooke's *The History of Emily Montague* can serve as useful starting points. A broadened corpus should also include monologic texts that attempt to suppress the dialogic principle and thus the potential for discourses of resistance. In other words, to exclude monologic texts from the theorization of dialogism positions them as though they were unified, thereby enshrining the myth of a Canadian uniculture.

But why restrict the discussion of dialogism to novels? Bakhtin has been criticized repeatedly for his "peculiar pronovelistic generic chauvinism" (Parks 1991, 56), and I myself believe that dialogism may be a productive critical tool in reading other genres, such as poetry and drama.[4] While some specific aspects of the cultural-narratological framework would be irrelevant, I think the central idea of contextualized readings that recognize forms as ideologically charged could be helpful. For Bakhtin (1981, 399), both poetry and drama are monologic forms that lack the qualities of "novelness": "The language of the novel is structured in uninterrupted dialogic interaction with the languages that surround it ... But poetry, striving for maximal purity, works in its own language, *as if* that language were unitary, the only language, as if there were no heteroglossia outside it." The poet, according to Bakhtin, aspires to speak in a language free from dialogization over which s/he has full control. This is not to deny that poets and readers are aware of the heteroglot world around them but, rather, that heteroglossia is suspended "by convention" (285). Even the discourse of doubts must be presented in a language that will not be doubted in poetry (286). However, heteroglossia, the internal dialogism of one perspective, the messiness of daily life, and the contingencies of history suggest that an exploration of dialogic relations may be fruitful in texts such as Margaret Atwood's *The Journals of Susanna Moodie* (1970), Daphne Marlatt's *Steveston* (2001/1974), Marlene Nourbese Philip's *She Tries Her Tongue, Her Silence Softly Breaks* (1989), and George Elliott Clarke's *Whylah Falls* (2000/1990).

Similarly, Bakhtin (1981, 405) argues that "pure drama [classical forms of drama] strives toward a unitary language, one that is individualized merely through dramatic personae who speak it. Dramatic dialogue is determined by a collision between individuals who exist within the limits of a single world and a single unitary language." He recognizes, however, that contemporary realistic social drama may indeed be heteroglot (405). While Bakhtin (1984a, 34, 188) believes that drama is inherently "alien to genuine polyphony" because it is "almost always constructed out of represented, objectified discourses," he emphasizes repeatedly that a monologue is not necessarily monologic. Bakhtin's views on drama were obviously based on specific kinds of drama. It could be argued, of course, as Harvie and Knowles (1994, 157) have done, that contemporary Canadian drama has become "novelized" so that questions previously relevant to novelistic discourse are now relevant to drama as well.[5] Many contemporary Canadian plays focus on dialogic monologues; these are plays in which one actor performs multiple roles (these performances remain predominantly monologic), several actors play one character (a strategy that is potentially dialogic but often neutralized), or monologues "in which a single character engages in a dialogical accounting for a 'life' that is in some sense represented autobiographically" (141). Features of novelization are visible, for instance, in Guillermo Verdecchia's *Fronteras Americanas (American Borders)* (1993), Monique Mojica's *Princess Pocahontas and the Blue Spots* (1991), Sharon Pollock's *Getting It Straight* (1992) and *Blood Relations* (1981), and Wendy Lill's *The Occupation of Heather Rose* (1987). The single consciousness of the character is shown as a mosaic of many conflicting voices that may show a development or resolution of his/her life. The disruption of authoritarian discourses – patriarchal, ethnocentric, and so on – is enacted through structural means, a blending of performance styles, exaggeration, inversion, and (often) transformations.

Dialogism may also provide a particularly useful focus for studies of cross-generic texts such as Marlatt's *Salvage* (1991b), which combines poetry, fiction, and autobiography in five large sections. In each section Marlatt, as she explains in the foreword, rereads and rewrites some of her earlier writings in light of her own feminist reading of the late 1980s. She salvages not only what she considers her own "failed" poems but also the dominant discourses of gender, class, and sexual orientation by subverting their monologic claims and reshaping them to inscribe within them her own positions of difference. A similar desire for dialogic relations informs Marlatt's search for alternative ways of reading the self in her collection of essays *Readings from the Labyrinth* (1998). Uncomfortable with the idea of reprinting old essays, she uses journal entries and excerpts from letters written around the time of each piece to situate it, adding details about the specific occasion of its writing and including flyers of conference programs, handwritten notes, and photographs. Marlatt uses the dialogic relations between the texts incorporated to keep the essays from becoming static and single-voiced.

Another example of a hybrid text is Linda Griffiths's and Maria Campbell's *The Book of Jessica: A Theatrical Transformation* (1989), which endlessly repeats, as Joanne Tompkins (1995, 149) points out, the rehearsal procedure that characterized the initial production of the play *Jessica* at 25th Street House in Saskatoon as well as the transformations of the text and the relationship between the two women. The hybrid form of the text is the result of its three separate sections: "Spiritual Things" is Griffiths's retrospective narrative of events that led to the play and the book, framing numerous extracts from dialogues between the two women; "The Red Cloth" presents the carefully edited transcript of conversations between Griffiths and Campbell in 1988; and *Jessica* is the script of the actual play. In the presentation of the three sections, chronology is displaced and, with it, the notion of linear causality that could explain why or how things happened the way they did. Only if readers are willing to renegotiate and rehearse the relations among the different systems of signification presented in the text can they arrive at preliminary scripts of their own, although they will always ask for yet another post-script. A focus on dialogic relations in *The Book of Jessica* also allows the reader to explore Griffiths's own narrative authority and the extent to which her assertion of control supports the hierarchies of discourse and race that the project and the book presumably seek to undermine.

I combine the concept of dialogism and cultural narratology in order to read for ideological signification in narrative structures. This form of culturally oriented literary criticism rests on the belief that working for social justice and commitment to critical theory, including variants informed by poststructuralism, are not necessarily at odds with each other. An analysis of dialogic relations in novels, I argue, can expose the sites for interventions that novels seek out, the gaps in what used to appear like seamless constructions of Canada, its culture, and its literature. In these sites, the texts inscribe silenced voices, allow their characters to claim identification with their environment, expose false choices, and rewrite monologic history through an emphasis on fragmentation, the montage of documents, the challenge to generic boundaries, the reconsideration of the role of communities, and the foregrounding of the performative. By exploring these subversive strategies, critics can affirm the possibilities of intervention that contribute to alternative constructions.

For the title of this book, *Challenging Canada*, I chose the verb "challenge" in order (1) to highlight the fact that the discussed novels constitute resistance literature and (2) to identify "Canada" as the object of their resistance: they call into question Canada, the multiplicity of what they understand Canada to be, and, in the process, they assert that Canada is no fixed entity but, rather, something that is shaped in specific ways by specific interests in specific contexts. However, these novels do more than question or accuse. In their challenge, they ask for, in fact they demand, responsive action, which is why I prefer "challenging" to such oft-used verbs as "reimagining," "renegotiating," or "rethinking." I have used the participle form of the verb, which allows for two possible readings. Either it suggests that "challenging" is an adjective that characterizes Canada as demanding, difficult, and/or stimulating, or it is part of a progressive verb form that emphasizes the continuity of the challenge and its implied need for recognition. If the latter, the title remains grammatically incomplete because it lacks a finite verb. Moreover, it leaves the subject position empty and thus nicely accommodates the multiple positions of agency suggested by my discussion. Who, we may wonder, does the challenging?

Throughout *Challenging Canada* I have spoken about the novels and their authors as resisting images and constructions of Canada as an innocent or benign nation; I have also emphasized the important role that readers play in activating the dialogic relationships informing these texts. As critics, I believe that we have the opportunity to participate in this challenge by using a theoretical framework that allows us to foreground how texts use dialogism for the purpose of resistance. This is one kind of responsive action. As teachers, we can respond to the challenge of these novels in additional ways not only by including them on our reading lists but also by rethinking the ways that we approach them in the classroom and the ways that we can make those classrooms themselves into dialogic spaces.

Have I answered Bal's haunting question "what's the point?" – the question with which I started? I would like to believe that I have, but the very thought makes me uneasy. I am reminded of Gwendolyn MacEwen's (1989 [1974], 163) poem "The Discovery," which ends with the following lines: "I mean the moment when it seems most plain / is the moment when you must begin again." Maybe it is time to return to the very questions that have led to and shaped this project. Maybe it is time to take seriously what, in the context of counter-discourse, Wilson Harris (1985, 127) has called "complex rehearsal" – a process in which one continually needs to "consume" one's own biases while trying to expose the dominant discourse. Following MacEwen and Harris, I need to re-cite and re-site this project, so that my own discourse remains dynamic and the endlessly deferred product becomes secondary. In other words, the "last" word of this sentence can only be the "last" word of this book in so far as it is also the beginning of a new page and a new project.

Notes

1 Northrop Frye borrows the phrase "peaceable kingdom" from Edward Hicks's painting of the same name. In his "Conclusion to a Literary History of Canada," originally published in 1965, Frye (1971, 249) identifies the "quest for the peacable kingdom" as a distinct characteristic of the Canadian tradition. I have used the phrase here as a descriptive term for Canada itself, which is the way it circulates most widely today; see, for instance, Michael Ignatieff's (2000, 136) Massey Lectures.

2 Following Antonio Gramsci, I use the term "hegemony" to describe "the set of values and beliefs through which the ruling class exercises its power over the masses" (Cavell 1993, 344); it is a dynamic process with degrees of completion because the hegemonic group must continually make compromises in its attempt to incorporate ever more elements of society. Hegemony does not simply refer to visible class power but describes an intricate interlocking of coercion and consent embodied in social, political, and cultural forces. As a result, in practice hegemony can never be singular; its internal structures are highly complex and include concepts of counter-hegemony (Williams 1977, 112–13).

3 Mieke Bal and Inge E. Boer (1994, 7) used the question themselves when they organized a conference on "the possibilities of theory for the practice of cultural analysis, critique, and history." The collection of essays that resulted from the conference is appropriately entitled *The Point of Theory*. See also Culler's (1994) introduction to the volume.

4 See Helms, James, and Rodney (1996) for more detailed theoretical

thoughts on constructions. For useful introductions to the ideas of constructivism, see Watzlawick (1984); Herring (1985); Guba and Lincoln (1989); Schmidt (1992); and Schwandt (1994).

5 For useful distinctions between these concepts, see Bhabha (1990); Brennan (1989); Ashcroft, Griffiths, and Tiffen (1998); Kertzer (1998); and Ignatieff (1993).

6 See Foucault's (1978, 92–3) explanation of power as a complex strategical situation in a particular society:

power must be understood in the first instance as the multiplicity of force relations immanent in the sphere in which they operate and which constitute their own organization; as the process which, through ceaseless struggles and confrontations, transforms, strengthens, or reverses them; as the support which these force relations find in one another, thus forming a chain or a system, or on the contrary, the disjunctions and contradictions which isolate them from one another; and lastly, as the strategies in which they take effect, whose general design or institutional crystallization is embodied in the state apparatus, in the formulation of the law, in the various social hegemonies.

7 See also Scott (1986, 1988); Fuss (1989); Butler (1990); and Haraway (1991). On the notion of race, see in particular Gates, Jr (1985, 6), who describes it as an arbitrary construct; Goldberg (1993, 80–1), who speaks of a "fluid, fragile, and more or less vacuous concept"; and Gunew and Yeatman (1993, 9), who define race as a "social formation." See also the essays in Gregory and Sanjek (1994), which are informed by questions of race in non-essentialist understandings of identity. However, it should be clear that, in focusing on these dimensions, I am neglecting many others, such as age, religion, ablebodiedness, and so on, that also contribute to situating a subject. Butler (1990, 143) explores the political impetus that can be derived from "the exasperated 'etc.'" and the invariable failure to provide a complete representation of subject positions.

8 These categories have also been usefully described as "interlocking systems of oppression" (Bilson 1991, 53) or as "constructive social and cultural relations of ruling" (Bannerji 1993, xxii). See also Ng (1993, 188); Butler (1990, 10); and Gregory (1994, 27–8).

9 Ashcroft, Griffiths, and Tiffin (1989, 23) explain that the term "Third World literature" has been suggested as a politically and theoretically more appropriate term than "Commonwealth literature," but they see it as "limited and pejorative" (see also Tiffin 1983, 25). The term has been used to refer to the literatures of developing countries in Africa, Southeast Asia, and sometimes the Caribbean, which have experienced the effects of colonization (Slemon 1987, 10). It is most commonly used in opposition to such imperial cultures of the First World as Great Britain, Japan, and the United States, although critics disagree as to whether US

literatures should also be considered postcolonial. Alan Lawson (1995, 21) proposes using the term "Second World" to refer to "more or less that part of colonial space occupied by the postimperial, so-called settler colonies" that are otherwise left out of the First World/Third World opposition – an opposition within which notions of the Third World and the postcolonial often fold in upon one another. This category usually includes Australia, Canada, and New Zealand (Lawson 1991, 67). Aware of the political and discursive difficulties of the term, Lawson describes the Second World as "a polemical reading position that finds a peculiar power in the dynamic *relation between* those apparently antagonistic, static, aggressive, disjunctive – even dis/abling – binaries with which we have inscribed our cultural condition" (68).

10 In *Culture and Imperialism* Said (1993, 12–13), in an exemplary manner for cultural analyses, sets out to examine "how the processes of imperialism occurred beyond the level of economic laws and political decisions, and – by predisposition, by the authority of recognizable cultural formations, by continuing consolidation within education, literature, and the visual and musical arts – were manifested at another very significant level, that of the national culture, which we have tended to sanitize as a realm of unchanging intellectual monuments, free from worldly affiliations."

11 In the context of Canadian literature, note the work of Godard (1984/85, 1987, 1990a, 1990b); Grace (1987, 1990); Cavell (1987); Hutcheon (1988a, 1988b); Kuester (1992); Howells (1993); and van Toorn (1995). Although not dealing with Bakhtin's concept of dialogism, Irvine (1986) and Howells and Hunter (1991) focus on the connection between narrative strategies and socio-historical context. Evelyn Cobley's (1993) study of First World War narratives convincingly shows that modes of representation become bearers of ideological significance, but her analysis covers a wide range of (non-Canadian) texts and does not focus on specifically dialogic forms. See Jeanne Delbaere (1990) for essays that discuss multiplicity, polyphony, and dialogism in Canadian fiction; however, these essays do not provide much contextualization. In *Masculine Migrations: Reading the Postcolonial in "New Canadian" Narratives*, Daniel Coleman (1998, 17) accepts Bakhtin's claim that the novel is a site of "polyphony in contest" and suggests that "the dialogue between competing ideologies of gender and culture ... will be readily discernible in narratives by migrant writers." He also describes the "understanding of human subjectivity as diaologic" (9). His interesting discussions of novels do not, however, further employ Bakhtin's concept of dialogism.

12 I first proposed the methodological framework of cultural narratology in a presentation, entitled "When Dialogism and Narrative Theory Meet: Exploring a Paradigm for the Analysis of Multiple Voices in Fiction," I

delivered at the 1994 Narrative Conference in Vancouver. It was more fully developed in my dissertation, "Dialogism, Cultural Narratology, and Contemporary Canadian Novels in English," submitted at the University of British Columbia in 1996.

13 See, for instance, Emerson (1988, 514); Bernstein (1989, 199); Danow (1991, 132); and Gardiner (1992, 182). For a more detailed discussion of this aspect, see Chapter 2.

14 As Söderlind (1991, 229) summarizes it: "The political force of all the novels I have studied ... puts into question the analogy between literary and political radicalism ... The correlation in Deleuze and Guattari's theories between 'minor literatures' and ideological subversion results, I would argue, from an a priori valorization of a certain aesthetics and its subsequent translation/perversion into the realm of politics, a kind of category mistake or wishful thinking which, it seems, every generation insists on repeating." Deer (1994, 133) observes that "the relationship between a novel's propositions concerning authority and its form is not simply complementary." On other literatures see also Gunew and Yeatman (1993, xx); Todd (1992, 76); and Fludernik (1996, 367).

15 For reconceptualizations of resistance, see also Slemon (1990, 36) and Finke (1992, 14).

16 Counter-discourse situates itself as "other" to a dominant discourse that tries to exclude heterogeneous voices. See Terdiman (1985, 25–81) and also Tiffin's explanation (1987, 18): "The operation of post-colonial counter-discourse is dynamic, not static: it does not seek to subvert the dominant with a view to taking its place, but to, in Wilson Harris's formulation, evolve textual strategies which continually 'consume' their 'own biases' at the same time as they expose and erode those of the dominant discourse."

17 Several critics have asked similar questions. See, for example, Grace (1987); New (1990a); Godard (1990a, 1990b); and Emberley (1993).

18 I use the terms "narratology," "narrative theory," and "narrative studies" interchangeably; they describe theories, discourses, and critiques of narratives regardless of the narrative's medium of representation. They study the nature, form, and functioning of narratives and examine what all narratives have in common and what distinguishes them from one another so as to account for our ability to produce and understand them (Prince 1987, 65). My use of the term "narratology" is therefore not limited to what some critics call "narratology proper" (see, for instance, Onega and Landa 1996, 25).

19 My presentation is, of course, simplistic at this point. Medvedev and Bakhtin's (1985, 30) concept itself is rooted in a "sociological poetics" that combines theoretical and historical approaches.

20 Nünning's (2000) recent article overlaps with what I propose here; unfor-

tunately, it was not available to me early enough to give it fuller recognition in my discussion.

21 For more extensive historical overviews of the field of narratology, see Ryan and van Alphen (1993); Onega and Landa (1996), especially for a detailed account of the structuralist phase of narrative theory; Herman (1999a); Jahn and Nünning (1994); and Jahn (1995). See also the excellent overview in Nünning (2000), including his enjoyable "short story" of "the rise, fall, and renaissance of narratology" (346–8).

22 Lanser (1986, 342) describes her task as follows: "to ask whether feminist criticism, and particularly the study of narratives by women, might benefit from the methods and insights of narratology and whether narratology, in turn, might be altered by the understandings of feminist criticism and the experience of women's texts." This early essay focuses on the second question. See also Lanser's (1988) response to Diengott's (1988) challenge.

23 For another interesting example of this debate, see the exchange between Dorrit Cohn (1995a, 1995b), Mark Seltzer (1995), and John Bender (1995). Cohn (1995a, 14) argues that the "associations of modal types with ideological positions" lie outside the realm of classical narratology. She claims to fault ideologically oriented critics not for "*using* narratological concepts to construct cultural history but for *misusing* them," and she insists that "persuasive ideological diagnoses of novelistic form cannot be achieved without supreme caution and extensive sensitization to the complexity involved" (Cohn 1995b, 35). Bender (1995, 31), however, suggests that the intensity of Cohn's attack derives from "an intolerable violation of what she [Cohn] seems to take as transhistorical disciplinary and subdisciplinary boundaries."

24 For more examples of such interesting challenges to and expansions of narrative theory, see, for example, Fludernik (1996); O'Neill (1994); the contributions to *Neverending Stories: Toward a Critical Narratology*, edited by Ann Fehn, Ingeborg Hoesterey, and Maria Tatar (1992); and the essays in *Reading Narrative: Form, Ethics, Ideology*, edited by James Phelan (1989). Phelan (1989, xxviii) notes in his introduction that "the findings of the volume most fruitfully intersect with the developments in criticism following upon the Anglo-American discovery of Bakhtin."

25 Lanser (1986, 344) refers to this as the "dual nature of narrative." See also Herring (1985, 43) and Frye (1986, 202), who, in her analysis of women's writing and reading, attempts to show that "novelistic conventions are not fixed but are instead subject to redefinition"; "women's novels alter women's lives; women's lives alter women's novels."

26 See, as examples, the work by Bal (1990 and 1999) as well as many of the essays in Grünzweig and Solbach (1999), and Kafalenos (2001).

27 Similarly, van Toorn (1990, 103) has reminded us that "the speech,

writing and other cultural practices of minority groups are only liberated into the public domain to the extent that the patron discourses succeed in trapping them in the categories which the dominant audience has available to contain them." See also Lenore Keeshig-Tobias (1990, 175).

CHAPTER TWO

1 It is important to note, as Emerson (1995, 1) points out, "that the Bakhtin boom in post-Communist Russia has had a different trajectory from our own domestic American one." In a very useful way, she introduces the essays in *Bakhtin in Contexts*, edited by Amy Mandelker (1995), by juxtaposing the issues they raise "to a debate or a representative essay among Russian scholars also at work on Bakhtin's legacy" (Emerson 1995, 5). For a more comprehensive assessment of Bakhtin's place in Russian and Western thought, see Emerson (1997).

2 This does not come as a surprise, considering that much of Bakhtin's work cannot easily be said to belong to one specific field of study. Consider his own explanation: "our study will move in the liminal spheres, that is, on the borders of all the aforementioned disciplines [the linguistic, philological, and literary], at their junctures and points of intersection" (Bakhtin 1986, 103).

3 Consider the concerns of Frank Davey (1988, 2–3), who criticizes scholars of Canadian literature who use Bakhtinian theory for not recognizing the dialogic nature of Bakhtin's own work and for ignoring its overtly political character. See also Grace (1987, 134), who recognizes a trend in criticism "to call any experimental postmodern text carnivalesque, or even polyphonic."

4 What follows is only a very brief introduction to the concept of dialogism. For useful and more extensive introductions to his life and work, see Clark and Holquist (1984); Morson and Emerson (1990); Holquist (1990); and Danow (1991). See also Simon Dentith's (1995, 3–104) overview of the writings of Bakhtin and his circle, which serves as an introduction to his Bakhtinian reader.

5 These three are among the texts whose authorship has been attributed to Bakhtin. However, for a number of early works this question has not yet been, and may never be, resolved. These texts include *The Formal Method in Literary Scholarship* (1985, 1928) by P.N. Medvedev, *Marxism and the Philosophy of Language* (1973, 1929) and *Freudianism: A Marxist Critique* (1976, 1927) by V.N. Voloshinov. The debate was initiated by an article by V.V. Ivanov (1976), first published in 1973, in which he claimed that the three texts were written by Bakhtin himself. This opinion was also promoted by Clark and Holquist (1984, 146–70) in Chapter 6 ("The Disputed Texts") of their biography of Bakhtin. For a

rejection of this view see Irwin R. Titunik (1984, 1986) and Chapter 3 in Morson and Emerson (1990, 103–19). To acknowledge the dispute, I will refer to Bakhtin where his authorship is unquestioned; otherwise, I refer to Voloshinov/Bakhtin or Medvedev/Bakhtin.

6 Bakhtin (1986, 118–19) further explores the artistic "transformations" of languages into world views or social voices in "The Problem of the Text."

7 Consider also Bakhtin's (1981, 262–3) description of the novel:
   as a diversity of social speech types (sometimes even diversity of languages) and a diversity of individual voices, artistically organized. The
   internal stratification of any single national language into social
   dialects, characteristic group behaviour, professional jargons, generic
   languages, languages of generations and age groups, tendentious languages, languages of the authorities, of various circles and of passing
   fashions, languages that serve the specific sociopolitical purposes of the
   day, even of the hour (each day has its own slogan, its own vocabulary,
   its own emphases) – this internal stratification present in every language at any given moment of its historical existence is the indispensable prerequisite for the novel as a genre.

8 In his study of Dostoevsky's novels, Bakhtin (1984a, 22–32) discusses the reasons and factors that contributed to the rise of the polyphonic novel. He argues that Dostoevsky "found and was capable of perceiving multi-leveledness and contradictoriness not in the spirit, but in the objective social world" (27), that the epoch itself plus Dostoevsky's vision of coexistence and interaction, not evolution, made the polyphonic novel possible. In "Discourse in the Novel," he also connects the rise of the novel with centrifugal forces (Bakhtin 1981, 272–3, 370). Todorov (1984, 58) summarizes Bakhtin's explanations by saying that "the periods in which the novel flourishes are periods of weakening central power."

9 A clarification of Bakhtin's notion of independence and autonomy may be helpful here. Independence, or relative freedom, characterizes the characters' relationships "vis-à-vis the author – or, more accurately, their freedom vis-à-vis the usual externalizing and finalizing authorial definitions" (Bakhtin 1984a, 13). Their relationship with the other voices in the novel, however, is one of interdependence and mutual influence (Bakhtin 1984a, 36; 1986, 91).

10 Young (1985/86, 92), for instance, argues that Bakhtin's liberalism makes his writings dubious material for radicals, especially those of Marxist provenance, to adopt. Finke (1992, 16) identifies a "liberal humanist misreading of the dialogic" that makes Bakhtin into "a weak-kneed pluralist" who underestimates elements of coercion, constraint, and power. Hirschkop (1986, 79) warns of Bakhtin's assimilation into a liberal schema, drawing attention to questions of oppression and power (75).

See also Stallybrass and White (1986, 26), who treat carnival as a wider phenomenon of transgression in order to "move beyond Bakhtin's troublesome *folkloric* approach to a political anthropology of *binary extremism* in class society." Pechey (1989, 40) wants to rescue Bakhtin "from the cold storage of intellectual history and from the politically compromised liberal academy." And Suzanne Rosenthal Shumway (1994, 168) suggests that Bakhtin can be appropriated even, and I would add especially, by those "who argue most fervently against Marxism and feminism" because his writings constitute a "descriptive theoretical system" rather than a normative plan of action that would threaten the status quo.

11 See Stallybrass and White (1986, 198); Fogel (1989, 180); and Hitchcock (1993, xviii).

12 Bakhtin discusses struggle and conflict within and between discourses especially in "Discourse in the Novel" and with Voloshinov in *Marxism and the Philosophy of Language*. In one of his most notable statements regarding the necessity of conflict, he explains that "it is necessary that heteroglossia wash over a culture's awareness of itself and its language, penetrate to its core, relativize the primary language system underlying its ideology and literature and deprive it of its naive absence of conflict" (Bakhtin 1981, 368).

13 See also Thomson (1989); M. Pollock (1993); Yaeger (1988); Jefferson (1986); and Zavala (1990).

14 Numerous studies have suggested that Foucault's work could be of assistance in further exploring Bakhtin's concepts. See, for example, Stallybrass and White (1986, 201); Pechey (1989, 52); Gardiner (1992, 141–66); Young (1985/86, 84–5); Amigoni (1993, 25–34); and Jefferson (1986, 174–7).

15 The engagement of critics with feminist theory and Bakhtinian concepts is well under way. Consider, for instance, the work of Booth (1982); Berrong (1985); Russo (1986); Bauer (1988); Yaeger (1988); Glazener (1989); Herrmann (1989); Thomson (1989, 1990, 1993); Diaz-Diocaretz (1989a, 1989b); Wills (1989); Cave (1990); Hadjukowski-Ahmed (1990); O'Connor (1990); Zavala (1990); Bauer and McKinstry (1991); Halasek (1992); M. Pollock (1993); and Hohne and Wussow (1994). Most of these critics would not actually want to claim Bakhtin as a feminist; rather, their starting point is usually to acknowledge that Bakhtin omitted gender issues in his discussions of linguistic stratification. Then, recognizing the explanatory and activist potential of many of his concepts, they appropriate his ideas for their analyses of cultural marginalization, subversion, or power relations.

16 Diaz-Diocaretz (1989a, 131); Zavala (1990, 86); Zavala (1993, 262, 270–1); Yelin (1989); Thomson (1993, 227); Harvie and Knowles (1994,

20); Mercer (1988, 59); and Godard (1990a, 159, 161). See also Thomson and Dua (1995, v), who explain that each article in their collection "explores how cultural forces work in society to allow for or to prevent the production of knowledge."

17 A "nod" in the direction of conflict and risk is a common characteristic in Bakhtin criticism; however, critics usually abstain from addressing the implications of contest or violence in any detail. Holquist (1990, 181), for example, frequently mentions struggle in his discussion but does not go beyond a closing gesture indicating that the darker sides of dialogue require more exploration than they have so far received. Danow (1991, 134) acknowledges Bakhtin's omission of violence from his discussion of dialogue but does not see this as an impediment to "Bakhtin's positive view regarding its potential." Both Kershner (1989, 21) and Schultz (1990, 148–50) acknowledge opposition and risk in dialogic struggle but ultimately affirm dialogism's joy and the potential it offers for change.

18 Bakhtin's comments on violence are contradictory. While violence may be destructive in the dialogic sphere (Bakhtin 1986, 150), he nevertheless talks about "justified revolutionary violence" in the context of class oppression (Bakhtin 1984a, 298). In his discussion of confession in Dostoevsky, Bakhtin avoids addressing the issues of violence or torture altogether. He defines confession as "a higher form of a person's *free* self-revelation *from within* (and not his finalizing from without)" (294).

19 For further contributions to this discussion, see especially the groundbreaking work by Stallybrass and White (1986, 14) on carnival. See also White (1987/88, 238); Gardiner (1992, 182, 231, nn. 26 and 29); Stam (1989, 94–6); Hitchcock (1993, 8); Howard (1994, 51); and Crowley (1989, 89).

20 I have formulated the idea of strategic monologism as an analogy to Fuss's discussion of strategic essentialism in the essentialism versus constructionism debate. The most useful way of approaching monologism may be the double gesture of theorizing monologic spaces while at the same time deconstructing them to keep them from solidifying (Fuss 1989, 118). See also the arguments of Bauer (1988, 166), Palmer (1990, 104), and Zavala (1993, 263), who indicate that monologism and dialogism are not separable but, rather, are always already implicated in each other. Palmer (1990, 106) argues that Bakhtin seems to give priority to centrifugal tendencies within a language, which leaves monologism an error to be corrected.

21 This point has also been raised by Hitchcock (1993, 1, 86) and Gardiner (1992, 192–4). See also Gardiner's (1993, 47) critique of Morson and Emerson's treatment of utopian elements in Bakhtin's work as well as his discussion of Bakhtin's "critical utopia," which "must be linked to an anti-hegemonic or transformative politics." Shumway (1994, 155)

explains that "Bakhtinian theory leaves little room for actual practice; it is concerned only with detecting the weaker voices in a text, and not with creating and implementing plans for strengthening such voices."

22 See Garrett (1980, 10) and Howells (1993, 438) as examples of the many ways of approaching dialogic relations that have been addressed within one study.

23 The term "perspective structure" is used by Pfister (1988, 57–68) and Nünning (1989, 76–83).

24 I understand "the text as a whole" as an abstract level of the text that is defined by the relations of contrast and correspondence between the levels of characters and narrators. This structural level is created during the actual reading process. Other elements that can be situated on this level are suspense, time structure, irony, chapter divisions, epigraphs, and so on. Nünning (1989, 31–40) suggests this level as an alternative conceptualization to what has been and still is frequently referred to as "implied author" and "implied reader."

25 Concerning the problematic relationship between narrative techniques of multiplication and fragmentation and notions of change and transformations, see Malcuzynski (1984, 80, 83); Malcuzynski (1990, 94); Bond (1989, 878); and van Toorn (1995, 15–16, 202–3).

26 See, for instance, the work of Ginsburg (1980) and Clark-Beattie (1985) on the internal dialogization of the narrator's perspective.

27 Bakhtin (1984a, 75) describes Raskolnikov's interior dialogue as follows: "nothing incorporated into its [the novel's] content ... remains external to Raskolnikov's consciousness; everything is projected against him and dialogically reflected in him ... All others' perception of the world intersects with his perception. Everything that he sees and observes ... is drawn into dialogue, responds to his questions and puts new questions to him, provokes him, argues with him, or reinforces his own thoughts."

CHAPTER THREE

1 See, for instance, the *Canadian Who's Who* (1991, 552) for the same assessment. For brief overviews of critical responses to *Obasan*, see Davidson (1993, 17–23); Chua (1992, 106–7); Harris (1996, 154–61); and Miki (1998, 155 n. 15).

2 For historical information about Japanese immigration to Canada and the wrongful treatment of Japanese Canadians during and after the Second World War, see, for instance, Adachi (1991); Bolaria and Li (1985); Broadfoot (1977); Miki and Kobayashi (1991); Omatsu (1992); Sunahara (1981); Roy (1989); and Roy et al. (1990). I do not think of these texts as unproblematic representations of history but as partial constructions; the same applies to my own summaries of historical events in this and later chapters.

3 A similar suggestion has been made by Goellnicht (1989); Rose (1987); and Hutcheon (1988b, 198).

4 Diana Brydon (1994, 468–9), however, has been critical of using Hutcheon's term to describe *Obasan* because the suspension of values that characterizes postmodern fiction in general and historiographic metafiction in particular does not apply to the "committed fiction" of *Obasan*. See also Rachelle Kanefsky (1996) for a humanist approach to Kogawa's novels; she disagrees with readings of Kogawa's novels as historiographic metafiction. However, following critics such as Elizabeth Wesseling (1991), Nünning (1995), and many of those represented in Bernd Engler and Kurt Müller (1994), I would argue that historiographic metafiction can indeed be ideologically committed and political.

5 A homodiegetic narrator is a narrator who is also a character in the situation and events s/he narrates; s/he is to be distinguished from a heterodiegetic narrator, who is not part of the narrated world (Prince 1987, 40–1; Nünning 1989, 306).

6 The tension between "home," "native," and "land" in the anthem is also evoked in quotations from Emily's manuscript entitled "The Story of the Nisei in Canada: A Struggle for Liberty" (Kogawa 1981, 38–42). Emily engages dialogically with a line from Sir Walter Scott's (1909, 39) "The Lay of the Last Minstrel": "Breathes there the man, with soul so dead, / Who never to himself hath said, / This is my own, my native land!" Challenging her identification as a Canadian in different contexts, Emily tries to change the sentence by emphasizing different parts and transforming it into a question, but her re-accentuations only confirm what she already felt: "I am Canadian" (Kogawa 1981, 40). Kogawa has adopted Emily's text in *Obasan* from a manuscript by Muriel Kitagawa (Kogawa 1995a, 22), whose writings Kogawa acknowledges in her preface to the novel. In his introduction to Kitagawa's work, Roy Miki (1985, 22–3) highlights the importance to Kitagawa of Scott's poem and its sentiments. For the complete manuscript, see Kitagawa (1985, 286–8). As far as I know, Kamboureli (2000, 187–90) is the first critic who briefly discusses Kitagawa's writing in connection with *Obasan* to show "the historical chain of ideas and ideologies that Emily's position represents" (241 n. 17).

7 Kogawa (1993, 152) has commented that "one has to acknowledge that another person's expressed reality is her reality, and that's hers." In another interview, she has commented that the problem she has "with trying to write The Truth, The Real Live Thing, is that I don't think you ever get it. You never get it" (Kogawa 1995a, 34).

8 I have consulted the following sources for this all too brief and selective historical overview: Anderson (1991); Bolaria and Li (1985, 81–104); Dawson (1991); Li (1988, 1992); Roy (1989); Wickberg (1982); and Yee (1988).

9 Consult Li (1988, 27–8) for more details from a much longer list: "Between 1884 and 1923 the British Columbia legislature successfully passed numerous bills restricting the political and social rights of the Chinese. For example, a bill in 1884 disallowed Chinese from acquiring Crown lands and diverting water from natural channels ... The Coal Mines Regulation Amendment Act of 1890 prevented them from working underground ... The Provincial Home Act of 1893 excluded Chinese from admission to the provincially established home for the aged and infirm."

10 The history of Chinese immigration to Canada is most often written in legal and, therefore, male terms; for attempts to correct this picture, see especially the interviews collected in *Jin Guo* by the Women's Book Committee (1992); Yee (1988); and, to a lesser extent, Evelyn Huang with Lawrence Jeffery (1992).

11 See Liam Lacey (1990) on Lee's historical research. Lee uses material surrounding the Janet Smith murder case and incorporates information about everything from immigration procedures (such as detention camps) to architectural details in Chinatown (such as cheater floors) to the expeditions organized by the Chinese Benevolent Association in Victoria to retrieve the bones of missing railroad workers. He also includes references to telephones as "crying lines."

12 For Sheldon Goldfarb (1990) the exotic does not work. He describes the novel as "a lot of sound and fury, of Victorian-style melodrama, along with Victorian-style sentimentality about the noble Chinese workers, the goodness of Mother Earth and the joys of women together." His review serves as an excellent example of a White male critic imposing Western literary criteria on a text. Goldfarb's comments say more about him than they do about *Disappearing Moon Cafe*.

13 The genealogical imperative "equates the temporal form of the classical novel ... with the dynastic line that unites the diverse generations of the genealogical family ... By an analogy of function, events in time come to be perceived as begetting other events within a line of causality similar to the line of generations, with the prior event earning a special prestige as it is seen to originate, control, and predict future events" (Tobin 1978, 6–7).

14 See Chalykoff (1998) for a discussion of *Disappearing Moon Cafe* and Denise Chong's *The Concubine's Children* in terms of Foucault's "general history." Chalykoff focuses on the evidence that these two texts provide "to counter the hegemonic credo that Canada was the desired home of early Chinese migrants" (163), a belief she identifies in the 1885 *Report of the Royal Commission on Chinese Immigration*.

15 In his history of dialogic prose, Bakhtin (1984a, 111) identifies the threshold situation as a characteristic of the Socratic dialogue. He

explains that "its most fundamental instance is as the chronotope of *cri-sis* and *break* in a life. The word 'threshold' itself already has a metaphorical meaning in everyday usage ... and is connected with the breaking point of a life, the moment of crisis, the decision that changes a life (or the indecisiveness that fails to change a life, the fear to step over the threshold)" (Bakhtin 1981, 248).

16 Graham Huggan (1994a, 145–6), for example, describes one paragraph as "Beatrice Wong's interpretation," presumably because the section is headed by her name. However, the first person singular pronoun in the last few paragraphs of the section should be attributed to the homodiegetic narrator Kae reflecting on her telling of the Wong family stories (Lee 1990, 41). Gary Draper (1990) makes a similar mistake when he refers to "a variety of narrators." I would argue that he means a variety of focalizers.

17 For examples, see 8, 25, 26, 29, 49, 92, 140, 147, 159, 164, 165, 223, 228.

18 See examples on 16, 50, 159, 234.

19 For examples, see 16, 24, 28, 32, 74, 77, 93, 94, 130, 140, 147, 221, 224, 232.

20 For examples, see 6, 10, 14, 49, 115, 123, 136, 139, 180, 221.

21 Consider the following examples. Gwei Chang thinks of Kelora during Wong Foon Sing's interrogation in 1924: "For a precious instant, he remembered another smooth caress. One he once cherished. For a brief moment, he remembered a time when he had soared beyond all human reach. But the feeling passed as it always did, and he was again left behind, always disappointed, always dazed" (Lee 1990, 78). He remembers her also before his death in 1939: "Funny, how he could just be sitting there and the feeling of her lips brushing against his would take him by surprise ... But just for a second. Then it would be gone, leaving him to agonize alone. Funny, wasn't it, how she could still do that to him" (235).

22 For an explanation of free indirect discourse, see Cohn (1978).

23 Consider also: "When she had first approached him, he couldn't believe his good fortune – a wife and a whore! However, now that he was fast on his way to becoming the biggest laugh in Chinatown, he couldn't help but get a little clouded over, because it woke him up at night now, dripping with sweat, gasping for breath, groping for deliverance" (Lee 1990, 100); and "It felt good to talk in the dark, because it was faceless. 'You'll have to get pregnant, A Song. If not by me, by somebody else. But you must have a baby.' His voice stripped as bare as a beggar" (110).

24 I would argue that Kae is not just ventriloquizing in these sections narrated by Suzie but that she is always already ventriloquized herself. For an interesting discussion of Holquist's notion of "ventriloquization," see David Carroll (1983, 72–4).

25 See, for example, the following introductory remarks: "I could begin with Suzanne" (Lee 1990, 185); "Beatrice (if she was willing to talk, I'm sure would respond in a brief, essential way)" (186); "I bet Chi's answer would, as a matter of fact, be very uncharacteristic of her" (186); "I gulp, but I'm afraid I still feel obliged to give Fong Mei the last word" (187).

26 Such weeping would traditionally consist of sobs and sighs along with "speeches expressing affection for the dead, hope that his soul would ascend to Heaven, and glorification of his past deeds" (Yang 1967, 35). These speeches confirm the ties between the dead and the living.

27 Yang (1967, 40) explains: "As in many other cultures, the offering of food and drink to the dead and later the sharing of them by the entire family group had serious social implications. Food was the supreme factor in the sustenance of life, and man's struggle for it had always involved the social group. By offering it at the sacrifice, an effort was made to share it between the living and the dead, thus maintaining contact between the two."

28 Thompson (1988, 74) also points out that a male chief mourner (preferably a son) and a daughter (or female substitute) are needed to make the offerings to the dead. This could be one reason for Morgan's presence in "Feeding the Dead."

29 See also Wong (1995, 143); Wong (1990, 137); M. Andrews (1990); Chong (1990); Lacey (1990); and Chao (1997, 102–3). Draper (1990), however, criticizes Lee's prose for being unidiomatic and over-modified.

30 Other critics have discussed similar strategies under the concept of an "interlanguage" within which the linguistic structures of two languages are fused. Ashcroft, Griffiths, and Tiffin (1989, 68) see interlanguages as potentially "paradigmatic of all cross-cultural writing, since the development of a creative language is not a striving for competence in the dominant tongue, but a striving towards appropriation, in which the cultural distinctiveness can be simultaneously overridden – overwritten."

31 See Wickberg (1982, 7, 9): "The Canton delta, as the heartland of Cantonese Guangdong, is distinct ... From a northern Chinese perspective Guangdong was at the margins of the Chinese cultural system ... But the Cantonese are self-consciously distinct. They regarded themselves as 'people of the Tang,' in contrast to the more typical term for ethnic Chinese, 'people of the Ha.'" I follow Lee, who refers to the novel's characters and their language as Chinese.

32 In British Columbia, Henry Stevens, Conservative member for Vancouver Centre, "built a prominent political profile around the 'Yellow Peril' slogan" in the 1910s and 1920s (Anderson 1991, 135).

33 The salmon-canning industry was one of the primary employers of Chinese Canadians; usually 75 per cent of a plant crew were Chinese (Yee

1988, 59–62). At the beginning of the twentieth century the "Iron Chink," a butchering machine, was introduced to mechanize salmon-canning plants and thus to reduce labour costs. One machine could replace about thirty skilled workers. Obviously, the phrase dehumanized Chinese labour.

34 Compare how Suzie uses "chinks," with intonational quotation marks, ironically: "I bet he [the policeman] would have been too impressed by rich chinks to see anything else" (Lee 1990, 198).

35 See Li (1988, 35) for the definition of "Chinaman" in the Statutes of British Columbia in 1920. For the use of the term in a *Province* editorial in 1937, see Anderson (1991, 167). On 9 January 1886 the ten-stanza poem "John Chinaman" was printed in Nanaimo's *Free Press* (Roy 1989, 64–5). See also W. Peter Ward's (1990, 3–22) chapter on "John China-man."

36 See Bakhtin (1981, 294; 1984a, 195), and Morson and Emerson (1990, 325–9).

37 Anderson (1991, 179) has explored how the Chinese Canadian community has used such phrases or classifications of "Chinese/Chineseness" "in part to offset the history of negative stereotyping and as a means of self-identification and economic gain." See also Heesok Chang's (1994, 225–6) comments on Sharen Yuen's *John Chinaman* installation, which was part of the *Self Not Whole: Cultural Identity and Chinese-Canadian Artists in Vancouver* exhibit at the Chinese Cultural Centre, 2–30 November 1991. Lee (1994, 225–6) offered a literary reading at the event. The sometimes heated debates over the appropriation of terms with racist implications and Asian stereotypes on such clothing items as T-shirts reinforces the importance of audience, intent, and context (Noyes 2002).

CHAPTER FOUR

1 A number of critics have used alternative descriptors for Marlatt's novel. Pamela Banting (1991, 125), for example, has discussed *Ana Historic* in connection with her reading of Marlatt's translation poetics; Manina Jones (1993, 141) focuses her discussion of the novel around the notion of a documentary collage; Stan Dragland (1991, 176–7) considers the text as "historiographic metafiction" but ultimately finds Marlatt's own concept of "fictionalysis" (for a hybrid text that is part fiction and part autobiography) more suitable. Peggy Kelly (1995) reads *Ana Historic* and Gail Scott's *Heroine* as examples of fiction theory.

2 Many critics use other, more familiar, genre labels to discuss *Places Far from Ellesmere*: "collage," "geographically located, feminist-literary fantasy" (Kirkwood 1991, 29); "autobiographical text" (Buss 1993, 200);

"autobiographical essays" (Wilson 1991, 43; Buss 1993, 200); and "an autobiography, a travel narrative, and an act of feminist critical reading" (Neuman 1996, 221). The narrator is self-conscious about not following conventions of novelistic discourse: "if this were a novel," she says, she could predict the narrative development (van Herk 1990, 106). The narrator also reflects on being a character in a larger novel (118).

3 Consider also van Herk's (1992, 58) comment in the same essay: "the only way a country can be truly mapped is with its stories." In his conversation with Margaret Laurence, Kroetsch (1970, 63) similarly explains that "we haven't got an identity until somebody tells our story. The fiction makes us real." Four years later, however, Kroetsch (1983, 17) revisits this idea in "Unhiding the Hidden": "At one time I considered it the task of the Canadian writer to give names to his experience, to be the namer. I now suspect that on the contrary, it is his task to un-name." The relevance of these ideas is obvious in Robert Lecker's *Making It Real* (1995).

4 See Bakhtin (1981, 252) on the interrelation of chronotopes: "Chronotopes are mutually inclusive, they co-exist, they may be interwoven with, replace or oppose one another, contradict one another or find themselves in ever more complex relationships ... The general characteristic of these interactions is that they are dialogical (in the broadest use of the word)."

5 Note the cross-referencing to Edberg (van Herk 1990, 79, 83, 86, 113, 140), Edmonton (79, 81, 83, 86, 113, 141), and Calgary (83, 86, 113, 141).

6 In her interview with George Bowering, Marlatt (1989, 97) has pointed out that she used many archival sources but that Mrs Richards's journal was her own invention. I see Marlatt's inclusion of passages from Mrs Richards's journal as an interesting exploration of the roles of public versus private genres.

7 See, for instance, Dragland (1991, 178); Lowry (1991, 94); and Davey (1993, 199).

8 Consider also Marlatt's (1990a, 188) explanation in "Difference (em)bracing," which contributes to her understanding of these relations: "[words] set up currents of meaning that establish this you i also am (not third person, as in totally other, and not quite the same as me). 'You' is a conduit, a light beam to larger possibility, so large it fringes on the other without setting her apart from me."

9 I take issue, however, with Banting's (1991, 125) suggestion that these documents are "being quoted and collaged into this unfamiliar context ... without being altered or transformed in any way." With Bakhtin (1981, 340), I would argue "that the speech of another, once enclosed in a context, is – no matter how accurately transmitted – always subject to certain semantic changes ... The formulation of another's speech as well as

its framing ... both express the unitary act of dialogic interaction with that speech, a relation determining the entire nature of its transmission and all the changes in meaning and accent that take place in it during transmission."

10 Annie's rereading of sections from *Woodsmen of the West*, which was originally printed in a very limited edition that sold slowly, also questions the public recognition Grainger himself has received. He is still remembered today for his contribution to the Forestry Act, 1912, which is considered to have laid the foundations for the forestry policies in British Columbia – policies that have led to serious environmental problems caused by the logging industry. Joel Martineau (1996) argues, however, that *Woodsmen of the West* is more critical of the turn-of-the-century ideologies of gender and ecology than Marlatt's quotations suggest. Martineau emphasizes the narrator's "self-awareness and his ironic perspective on the masculine culture of agency" (4) as well as Grainger's attempt to shift the focus of the frontier discourse from commodity to community (10).

11 Marlatt incorporates another quotation from Lawson and Young, in which they describe the red cedar (Lawson and Young 1906, 98; Marlatt 1988, 19–20). The quotation highlights the usefulness of red cedars, for example, in house finishings; the trees serve men and could be called "the settler's friend" (Marlatt 1988, 20). In her journal, Mrs Richards puts this observation into perspective: compared to the Earth, "Man ... is afterall dwarf in such green fur, mere Insect only. – It comforts me'" (20).

12 For further discussion, see, for example, Susan Sherwin (1992, 84–8), who points out that feminist criticism needs to look at all modern medical practices, from its institutional structures, to its treatment of patients, to reproductive technologies, to research, and medical practitioners. See also Joan Tronto (1993), who argues for a paradigm shift to an ethic of care, and many of the essays collected in *A Reader in Feminist Ethics*, edited by Debra Shogan (1992).

13 Once hysteria had been made into a "nervous type" discourse, it became a disorder of sympathy, thereby linking suffering, sympathy, and women. For brief overviews, see Foucault (1965, 136–58) and Hillman (1972, 251–8).

14 The term "ecofeminism" was coined by the French writer Françoise d'Eaubonne (1974) to indicate women's potential to bring about an ecological revolution. Ecofeminist discourse has developed with incredible speed across many disciplines. For introductory essays, see "Ecological Feminism"; a special issue of *Hypatia* (1991); Plant (1989); Diamond and Orenstein (1990); Alaimo (1994); and, for specifically literary approaches, the essays in Gaard and Murphy (1998).

15 Van Herk's (1992, 84–5) comment in "Desire in Fiction: De-siring Realism" is illuminating in this context:

Desire moves us forward, incites change, asks for *more* ... The true
measure of human beings is not what they know, but what they long
for, what they strive to attain despite its inaccessibility. And yet, it is
not the result that is important, for when one goal is reached, there
will be another. What is important is the striving, prompted by desire.
Finally ... de-sire will force us to abandon the well-known context for
a better one, even if it is not so safe, desire will give us courage to
explore the fullest range of human possibility, desire prompts us to
make fiction after fiction and make them good.

16 In her crypto-friction that explores her trip to the Arctic, van Herk
(1991, 2) identifies being "free of words" as her greatest desire: "This
hereness, this nowness, and nothing else. I am suspended in an Arctic,
not near Arctic or high Arctic but extreme Arctic, beyond all writing ... I
am simply here, reduced to *being* ... I am at last beyond language, at last
literately invisible" (3).

17 Ken Coates (1993/94, 25) has commented that one of the patterns of
southern control of the north is the government's treatment of the latter
as a tabula rasa for government action. The relocation of Inuit families
and communities, and the declaration of the Yukon and Northwest Terri-
tories as bilingual are well known examples. See also Louis-Edmond
Hamelin (1988, 15) on the precedence of Aboriginal peoples and their
colonization: "Those who were already on the land were denied any title
to that land, and this permitted the European settlers to consider the land
as vacant, appropriate it and then consolidate the land grab by means of
new cartography and place naming, the only official version."

18 Van Herk (1991, 3–4) has commented on her own experience of travelling to Ellesmere Island: "The time I spent at Lake Hazen in the northern
part of Ellesmere Island taught me unreading, the act of dismantling a
text past all its previous readings and writings ... enabling me to untie all
the neatly laced up expectations of words and their printing, their
arrangement on the page, the pages bound together into a directive narrative, that then refused to be static, but turned and began to read back,
to read me, to unread my very reading and my personal geography."

CHAPTER FIVE

1 I use "Aboriginal" (as well as First Nations) as a general term that refers
to status and non-status Indians, Métis, Dene, and Inuit. I realize that the
issue of naming is complex and that I cannot do it justice in the space
available.

2 For critical studies on representations of Aboriginal characters in Canadian literature, see Dumont (1993); Fee (1984); Francis (1992); Goldie
(1989); Hoy (2001); Monkman (1981); and King (1984).

3 In his attempt to avoid using the term "postcolonial," "polemical" and "associational" are two of the four terms King suggests to describe Aboriginal literature; the other two are "tribal" and "interfusional." Tribal refers to literature that exists primarily within a tribe or community and is usually presented in an Aboriginal language; interfusional describes Aboriginal literature that blends oral and written literature (King 1990a, 12–13).

4 Both Theytus Books and Pemmican Publications were founded in 1980 in response to the problems Aboriginal writers were experiencing in the Canadian publishing industry. Theytus Books became a part of the En'owkin Centre in Penticton in 1982; it only publishes Aboriginal authors. Pemmican Publications in Winnipeg is a Métis publishing house, which also supports non-Aboriginal authors whose writing is related to Aboriginal issues. Seventh Generation Books (Toronto), Moonprint Press (Winnipeg), and Rez (Langley) are smaller Aboriginal presses.

5 See Derrida's (1976, 44) explanation: "now from the moment one considers the totality of determined signs, spoken, and a fortiori written, as unmotivated institutions, one must exclude any relationship of natural subordination, any natural hierarchy among signifiers or orders of signifiers."

6 See Hunter (1996, 159–63) and Hoy (2001) for their self-reflexive readings of *Slash*, in which they foreground their responses and literary criteria as being those of non-Aboriginals. See Renée Hulan (1998) for her discussion of teaching "Native Literature" as a non-Native.

7 The textual examples are too numerous to list them here, but it is worth noting that Slash usually begins paragraphs with the observation that he was listening (Armstrong 1985, 42, 54, 81, 119, 133, 145, 184, 191, 193, 209, 210). This kind of repetition, of course, also contributes to the didacticism that Jones (2000) identifies as one of the major criticisms of the book.

8 Armstrong (1991, 16) has commented on the strong desire for community that drives the narrative, even when Slash is not aware of it: "In the writing process I couldn't isolate the character and keep the character in isolation from the development of the events in the community, and the whole of the people ... Everything is a part of something else. Everything is a part of a continuum of other things: a whole." In an interview with Janice Williamson, Armstrong (1993a, 13–14) comments on the notion of relatedness and community with reference to the lack of gendered pronouns in Okanagan: "If I don't know the name, I would say the person who has been involved in connection with this. I can't say 'he,' or 'she.' A person is always connected or related to something, and we must always refer to that connection or that relationship."

9 While Fee (1990, 177) reads the novel's ending as showing "the potential

of the future" in which "people can and do change," Hunter's (1996,
161) misgivings are unmistakable as she describes the "proto-Messianic
ending" as "most problematic of all" and "embarrassing."

10 Godard (1990, 218) also chooses the adjective "flat" to describe Armstrong's *Slash*: "There has been no progress, no development and almost
no action: the narrative is composed mainly of reported speech. In short,
this has been a 'flat' book not likely to make the best-seller list in Canada." Canadian readers, according to Godard, seek out books that con-
form to Western genre conventions rather than those that are different.
"Flat" becomes a pejorative term; that such evaluation may be problematic is signalled by Godard's use of quotation marks.

11 Only once does the narrator play a joke on Coyote. When Coyote calls
him/her, the narrator answers with "First Nations' Pizza" (see Flick
1999, 160) and pretends not to know who Thought Woman is (King
1993, 300).

12 The narrator repeatedly tells Coyote to forget about something and refo-
cus (King 1993, 38, 195, 229, 323, 349), do things later (38, 70, 229),
listen up (38), calm down (40, 324), sit down and listen (41, 229), and
think about something (417). Needless to say, Coyote is not easily controlled.

13 King's reference to the "sacred clown" reminds me of Bakhtin's discussions of folkloric forms in the Middle Ages, which tended towards satire
and parody and which often took cyclical forms. In these forms Bakhtin
identifies the figures of the rogue, the clown, and the fool as central to
the later development of the European novel. One of their features and
privileges is "the right to be 'other' in this world, the right not to make
common cause with any single one of the existing categories that life
makes available; none of these categories quite suits them, they see the
underside and the falseness of every situation" (Bakhtin 1981, 159). In
the struggle against conventions and fixed categories, these figures have
"the right *not* to understand, the right to confuse, to tease, to hyperbolize
life; the right to parody others while talking, the right to not be taken literally ... the right to live a life in ... the chronotope of theatrical space,
the right to act life as a comedy" (163).

14 Native American creation stories can vary significantly according to a
people's culture, geography, history, and so on. For the Cherokee, for
example, the world began with water, with the animals living above the
rainbow (Hirschfelder and Molin 1991, 58). Changing Woman and
Thought Woman are central to Navajo stories (Gill and Sullivan 1992,
56; Flick 1999, 152, 159); First Woman is a figure in Earth Diver creation stories, and Old Woman appears in Cherokee and Blackfoot stories
(Flick 1999, 147, 161). As Donaldson (1995, 32) explains, King comical-
ly conflates the "so-called earth diver creation stories ... with the hau-
denosaunee (Iroquois) tale of the woman who fell from the sky."

15 See also Goldman (1999) on the Fort Marion Ledger art.

16 I am thinking here of the names of the Four Indians, named after four familiar pairs of White settlers and their Aboriginal companions in Western literature and movies: the Lone Ranger of western movies with his companion Tonto; Hawkeye, first known as Natty Bumppo in Fenimore Cooper's "Leatherstocking Tales," and his companion Chingachgook; Robinson Crusoe and his helper Friday from Daniel Defoe's *Robinson Crusoe*; and Ishmael of Herman Melville's *Moby Dick* with his friend Queequeg. There are many other intertextual references in the characters' names: Joe Hovaugh plays on the name Jehovah; George Morningstar refers to George Armstrong Custer's nickname "Son of the Morningstar"; Buffalo Bill Bursum recalls Holm O. Bursum, who proposed the Bursum Bill of 1921, which aimed to take large portions of Pueblo lands Pueblos; Clifford Sifton refers to Laurier's superintendent of Indian affairs of the same name, who promoted settling the West by displacing Aboriginal populations; Eli Stands Alone refers to Elijah Harper, who blocked the Meech Lake Constitutional Accord in 1990; and Grand Baleen Dam evokes the James Bay hydroelectric project (see Flick 1999).

17 Some of the allusions are to Timothy Findley's *Not Wanted on the Voyage*, Howard O'Hagan's *Tay John*, Emily Carr's *Klee Wyck*, and Hugh MacLennan's *Barometer Rising* as well as to historical figures such as Ann Hubert, Pauline Johnson, John Richardson, Susanna Moodie, and Archie Belaney.

18 All critical discussions of the novel deal to some extent with King's use of parody, so I do not want to rehash this material here. See especially Andrews (2002); Chester (1999); Donaldson (1995); Goldman (1999); Horne (1995); Matchie and Larson (1996); Peters (1999); and Wyile (1999).

19 King (1990a, 14) has commented on writing for both Aboriginal and non-Aboriginal readers: with regard to the former, he reminds them of the continuing values of their cultures and shows an active present and viable future in addition to a usable past; with regard to the latter, he allows them to associate with the Aboriginal world, but he does not want them to feel encouraged to feel a part of it.

20 For reasons slightly different from those Andrews (2002, 114) notes in her cautionary second footnote, even though I agree with her argument that the limitations of Bakhtin's notion of carnival may undermine Aboriginal peoples' struggle for liberation.

CHAPTER SIX

1 On 1 May, after three months of negotiations with the Winnipeg Builders' Exchange, all the unions grouped together under the Building Trades Council went on strike; they were joined by the Metal Trades

Council the following day. The Winnipeg Trades and Labour Council polled affiliated unions on a general sympathetic strike after it had been informed of the employers' refusal to bargain. The general strike commenced on 15 May at 11:00 AM; within hours almost 30,000 workers, many of whom were unorganized, had left their jobs. The General Strike Committee bargained with the employers and coordinated the provision of essential services. Opposition to the strike was organized by the Winnipeg Citizens' Committee of 1,000, which brushed aside the strikers' demands and declared the strike to be a revolutionary conspiracy. After the arrest of ten strike leaders on 16 and 17 June and the events of "Bloody Saturday" on 21 June (when the Royal North-West Mounted Police charged into a crowd of strikers, killing two people and injuring many others), on 25 June the strike committee announced that the strike would be terminated on the following day. For more detailed discussions see, for instance, McNaught (1959); Penner (1975); Bercuson (1990); and Bumsted (1994).

2 I have only noticed one possible inconsistency in the novel's chronology. Both "Stevie on the bridge" (Sweatman 1991, 122) and the much later "Parade" (162–6) seem to refer to the parade of 4 June when pro-strike soldiers marched south from Victoria Park, crossed the Maryland Bridge over the Assiniboine River and through Crescentwood – the wealthy residential district of South Winnipeg – and recrossed north over Osborne Street Bridge to return to the city centre. At the same time F.G. Thompson had organized a counter-parade of loyalist anti-strikers (Bercuson 1990, 146–48; Bumsted 1994, 46). Mary sees the anti-strikers organized by Drinkwater in the city and compares them to the pro-labour soldiers whom she sees marching through her own part of town when she returns to her father's house.

3 The *Western Labour News* was the official newspaper of the Trades and Labor Council, and it was edited by William Ivens. The Central Strike Committee published a Special Strike Edition from 18 May to 23 June that employed a language of "working class entitlement," which had grown out ot the war that had recently ended (Reimer 1993, 220). The *Winnipeg Citizen* was the daily paper put out by the Citizens' Committee and distributed free on the streets. The *Winnipeg Free Press* and the *Winnipeg Tribune*, which was at times sympathetic to labour but was ultimately opposed to the general strike, are the mainstream newspapers quoted in the novel; these dailies frequently carried full-page advertisements paid for by the Citizens' Committee (Penner 1975, 116).

4 For explanations of psychonarration, free indirect discourse, and interior monologue, see Cohn (1978).

5 As McNaught (1959, 48–9) explains, the Social Gospel emphasized love and proclaimed the principle of cooperation as opposed to that of com-

petition. It also focused on the brotherhood of man and was more interested in the welfare of individuals in this world than in the salvation of immortal souls. Many of the leaders of the Social Gospel were former Methodist ministers active in the labour movement (Bumsted 1994, 119). J.S. Woodsworth, for example, took over the All People's Mission in Winnipeg in 1907 (Bercuson 1990, 5); he was influenced by Rev. Salem Bland, whose *The New Christianity* (1920) Sweatman also lists as a source book for *Fox*.

6 For similar sentiments, see the following examples: "She has begun her reading ... she's at the number zero, she's not at home, and it's perfect, here" (Sweatman 1991, 91); "she doesn't know them [other people], she loves not knowing" (95); "she doesn't know how to cheer but she feels the tight moans of excitement in her throat" (95).

7 The kitchen could serve between 1,200 and 1,500 meals a day. Men could also come to the food kitchen but were expected to pay or make a small donation, thereby recognizing that female workers were paid less than male workers. (Horodyski 1986, 30; Bumsted 1994, 37; L. Kealey 1989, 137–8).

8 Judge Metcalfe made the position of judicial authorities very clear in the post-strike trials: "In these days when women are taking up special obligations and assuming equal privileges with men, it may be well for me to state now that women are just as liable to ill treatment in a riot as men and can claim no special protection and are entitled to no sympathy; and if they stand and resist officers of the law they are liable to be cut down" (quoted in L. Kealey 1989, 141).

9 With increasing immigration in the first decade of this century, immigrants from Eastern Europe became the so-called "new immigrants," or "aliens," many of whom came from regions that were part of Germany or the Austro-Hungarian Empire. When the war began, this made them "enemy aliens" (Bumsted 1994, 10, 76).

CHAPTER SEVEN

1 The title echoes Marlatt's (1988, n.p.) last lines in *Ana Historic*:
   ... the luxury of being
   has woken you, the reach of your desire, reading
   us into the page ahead.

2 For critiques of the neo-conservative argument, see, for example, Brenkman (1993, 89); Cairns (1995, 25, 30); Henry and Tator (1994, 12–13); and Strong-Boag (1994, 6).

3 For a similar argument, see Cheung (1993, 14), who reminds critics "not to drown Asian American texts in contexts, lest we perpetuate what Henry Louis Gates, Jr., calls the 'anthropological fallacy.'"

4 Similar suggestions have been made by Grace (1987), Harvie and
  Knowles (1994), Helene Keyssar (1991), Jennifer Wise (1989), and David
  H. Richter (1990).

5 Bakhtin (1981, 7) describes the features of novelization of other genres as
  follows: "they become more free and flexible, their language renews itself
  by incorporating extraliterary heteroglossia and the 'novelistic' layers of
  literary language, they become dialogized, permeated with laughter, irony,
  humor, elements of self-parody and finally – this is the most important
  thing – the novel inserts into these other genres an indeterminacy, a certain semantic open-endedness, a living contact with unfinished, still-
  evolving contemporary reality (the openended present)."

Works Cited

Aczel, Richard. 1998. "Hearing Voices in Narrative Texts." *New Literary History* 29: 467–500.

Adachi, Ken. 1991 [1976]. *The Enemy That Never Was: A History of the Japanese Canadians*. New ed. Toronto: McClelland and Stewart.

Alaimo, Stacy. 1994. "Cyborg and Ecofeminist Interventions: Challenges for an Environmental Feminism." *Feminist Studies* 20 (1): 133–52.

Amigoni, David. 1993. *Victorian Biography: Intellectuals and the Ordering of Discourse*. New York: Harvester Wheatsheaf.

Anderson, Benedict. 1983. *Imagined Communities: Reflections on the Origin and Spread of Nationalism*. Rev. ed. London: Verso.

Anderson, Kay J. 1991. *Vancouver's Chinatown: Racial Discourse in Canada, 1875–1980*. Montreal: McGill-Queen's University Press.

Andrade, Susan Z. 1990. "Rewriting History, Motherhood, and Rebellion: Naming an African Women's Literary Tradition." *Research in African Literatures* 21 (2): 91–110.

Andrews, Jennifer. 2002. "Reading Thomas King's *Green Grass, Running Water*: Border-Crossing Humour." *English Studies in Canada* 28: 91–116.

Andrews, Mark. 1990. "Breaking the Code of Silence." *Vancouver Sun*, 19 May, D17.

Andrews, Ralph Warren. 1956. *Glory Days of Logging*. Seattle: Superior.

Armstrong, Jeannette. 1985. *Slash*. Penticton: Theytus.

– 1991. Interview with Hartmut Lutz. *Contemporary Challenges: Conversations with Canadian Native Authors*, ed. Hartmut Lutz, 13–32. Saskatoon: Fifth House.

– 1993. "What I Intended Was to Connect ... and It's Happened." Interview with Janice Williamson. In *Sounding Differences: Conversations with Seventeen Canadian Women Writers*, ed. Janice Williamson, 7–26. Toronto: University of Toronto Press.

– 2000. *Whispering in Shadows*. Penticton: Theytus.

Ashcroft, Bill, Gareth Griffiths, and Helen Tiffin. 1989. *The Empire Writes Back: Theory and Practice in Post-Colonial Literatures*. New York: Routledge.

– 1998. *Key Concepts in Post-Colonial Studies*. London Routledge.

Atwood, Margaret. 1970. *The Journals of Susanna Moodie*. Toronto: Oxford University Press.

– 1979. *Life before Man*. Toronto: McClelland and Stewart.

Avery, Donald. 1976. "The Radical Alien and the Winnipeg General Strike of 1919." In *The West and the Nation: Essays in Honour of W.L. Morton*, ed. Carl Berger and Ramsay Cook, 209–31. Toronto: McClelland and Stewart.

Bakhtin, Mikhail M. 1929. *Problemy tvorčestva Dostoevskogo [Problems of Dostoevsky's Creative Works]*. Leningrad: Priboj.

– 1981. *The Dialogic Imagination*. Trans. Caryl Emerson and Michael Holquist. Austin: University of Texas Press.

– 1984a [1972]. *Problems of Dostoevsky's Poetics*. Trans. Caryl Emerson. Minneapolis: University of Minnesota Press.

– 1984b [1968]. *Rabelais and His World*. Trans. Helene Iswolsky. Bloomington: Indiana University Press.

– 1986. *Speech Genres and Other Late Essays*. Trans. Vern W. McGee. Austin: University of Texas Press.

– 1990. *Art and Answerability: Early Philosophical Essays*. Trans. Vadim Liapunov. Ed. Michael Holquist and Vadim Liapunow. Austin: University of Texas Press.

– 1993. *Toward a Philosophy of the Act*. Trans. Vadim Liapunov. Ed. Michael Holquist and Vadim Liapunov. Austin: University of Texas Press.

Bal, Mieke. 1985. *Narratology: Introduction to the Theory of Narrative*. Trans. Christine van Boheemen. Toronto: University of Toronto Press.

– 1990. "The Point of Narratology." *Poetics Today* 11 (4): 727–53.

– 1995. *Narratology: Introduction to the Theory of Narrative*. 2nd ed. Trans. Christine van Boheemen. Toronto: University of Toronto Press.

– 1996. *Double Exposure: The Subject of Cultural Analysis*. New York: Routledge.

– 1999. "Close Reading Today: From Narratology to Cultural Analysis." In *Grenzüberschreitungen: Narratologie im Kontext (Transcending Boundaries: Narratology in Context)*, ed. Walter Grünzweig and Andreas Solbach, 19–40. Tübingen: Gunter Narr Verlag.

– and Inge E. Boer, eds. 1994. *The Point of Theory: Practices of Cultural Analysis*. New York: Continuum.

Bannerji, Himani. 1993. "Returning the Gaze: An Introduction." In *Returning the Gaze: Essays on Racism, Feminism and Politics*, ed. H. Bannerji, xiii–xxiv. Toronto: Sister Vision.

Banting, Pamela. 1991. "Translation A to Z: Notes on Daphne Marlatt's *Ana Historic*." In *Beyond Tish*, ed. Douglas Barbour, 123–9. Edmonton: NeWest.

Barthes, Roland. 1974 [1970]. *S/Z: An Essay*. New York: Hill and Wang.

Bauer, Dale. 1988. *Feminist Dialogics: A Theory of Failed Communities*. New York: State University of New York Press.

– and Susan Janet McKinstry, eds. 1991. *Feminism, Bakhtin, and the Dialogic*. Albany: State University of New York Press.

Beauregard, Guy. 2002. "After *Obasan*: Kogawa Criticism and Its Futures." *Studies in Canadian Literature* 26 (2): 1–18.

Bender, John. 1995. "Making the World Safe for Narratology: A Reply to Dorrit Cohn." *New Literary History* 26: 29–33.

Bennett, Donna. 1993/94. "English Canada's Postcolonial Complexities." *Essays on Canadian Writing* 51/52: 164–210.

Bercuson, David Jay. 1990 [1974]. *Confrontation at Winnipeg: Labour, Industrial Relations, and the General Strike*. Rev. ed. Montreal: McGill-Queen's University Press.

Bernstein, Michael André. 1989. "The Poetics of *Ressentiment*." In *Rethinking Bakhtin: Extensions and Challenges*, ed. Gary Saul Morson and Caryl Emerson, 197–224. Evanston: Northwestern University Press.

– 1992. *Bitter Carnival: Ressentiment and the Abject Hero*. Princeton: Princeton University Press.

Berrong, Richard M. 1985. "Finding Antifeminism in Rabelais; or, A Response to Wayne Booth's Call for an Ethical Criticism." *Critical Inquiry* 11 (4): 687–97.

Bhabha, Homi K., ed. 1990. *Nation and Narration*. London: Routledge.

– 1994. *The Location of Culture*. New York: Routledge.

Billson, Janet Mancini. 1991. "Interlocking Identities: Gender, Ethnicity and Power in the Canadian Context." *International Journal of Canadian Studies* 3: 49–67.

Bland, Salem Goldworth. 1973 [1920]. *New Christianity, or the Religion of the New Age*. Toronto: McClelland and Stewart.

Bolaria, B. Singh, and Peter S. Li. 1985. *Racial Oppression in Canada*. Toronto: Garamond.

Bond, D.G. 1989. "The Dialogic Form of Uwe Johnson's *Mutmaßungen über Jakob*." *Modern Language Review* 84 (4): 874–84.

Booth, Wayne C. 1961. *The Rhetoric of Fiction*. Chicago: University of Chicago Press.

- 1982. "Freedom of Interpretation: Bakhtin and the Challenge of Feminist Criticism." *Critical Inquiry* 9: 45–76.
- 1989. "Are Narrative Choices Subject to Ethical Criticism?" In *Reading Narrative: Form, Ethics, Ideology*, ed. James Phelan, 57–78. Columbus: Ohio State University Press.

Branham, Robert Bracht. 2001. *Bakhtin and the Classics*. Evanston: Northwestern University Press.

Brenkman, John. 1993. "Multiculturalism and Criticism." In *English Inside and Out: The Places of Literary Criticism*, ed. Susan Gubar and Jonathan Kamholtz, 87–101. New York: Routledge.

Brennan, Timothy. 1989. *Salman Rushdie and the Third World: Myths of the Nation*. London: Macmillan

Bright, William. 1993. *A Coyote Reader*. Berkeley: University of California Press.

Broadfoot, Barry. 1977. *Years of Sorrow, Years of Shame: The Story of the Japanese Canadians in World War II*. Toronto: Doubleday.

Browning, Elizabeth Barrett. 1992 [1900]. *Sonnets from the Portuguese and Other Poems*. New York: Dover.

Brydon, Diana. 1987. "Discovering 'Ethnicity': Joy Kogawa's *Obasan* and Mena Abdullah's *Time of the Peacock*." In *Australian/Canadian Literatures in English*, ed. Russell McDougall and Gillian Whitlock, 94–110. Melbourne: Methuen.
- 1994. "*Obasan*: Joy Kogawa's 'Lament for a Nation.'" *Kunapipi* 16 (1): 465–70.
- 1995. "Introduction: Reading Postcoloniality, Reading Canada." *Essays on Canadian Writing* 56: 1–19.

Bumsted, J.M. 1994. *The Winnipeg General Strike of 1919: An Illustrated History*. Winnipeg: Watson and Dwyer.

Buss, Helen. 1993. *Mapping Ourselves: Canadian Women's Autobiography in English*. Montreal: McGill-Queen's University Press.

Butler, Judith. 1990. *Gender Trouble: Feminism and the Subversion of Identity*. New York: Routledge.

Cairns, Alan C. 1995. "Whose Side Is the Past on?" In *Reconfigurations: Canadian Citizenship and Constitutional Change – Selected Essays by Alan C. Cairns*, ed. Douglas E. Williams, 15–30. Toronto: McClelland and Stewart.

Calinescu, Matei. 1993. "Orality in Literacy: Some Historical Paradoxes of Reading." *Yale Journal of Criticism* 6 (2): 175–90.

The Canadian Encyclopedia. 1988. Ed. James H. Marsh. 2nd ed. Edmonton: Hurtig.

Campbell, Maria. 1995. "Memory is Community." In *Realizing Community: Multidisciplinary Perspectives*, ed. L.M. Findlay and Isobel M. Findlay, 86–9. Saskatoon: Humanities Research Unit and Centre for the Study of Co-operatives, University of Saskatchewan.

The Canadian Who's Who. 1991. Ed. Kieran Simpson. Vol. 26. Toronto: University of Toronto Press.

Carroll, David. 1983. "The Alterity of Discourse: Form, History, and the Question of the Political in M.M. Bakhtin." *Diacritics* 13 (2): 65–83.

Cave, Marianne. 1990. "Bakhtin and Feminism: The Chronotopic Female Imagination." *Women's Studies* 18: 117–27.

Cavell, Richard. 1987. "Bakhtin Reads De Mille: Canadian Literature, Postmodernism, and the Theory of Dialogism." In *Future Indicative: Literary Theory and Canadian Literature,* ed. John Moss, 205–11. Ottawa: University of Ottawa Press.

– 1993. "Antonio Gramsci." In *Encyclopedia of Contemporary Literary Theory: Approaches, Scholars, Terms,* ed. Irena R. Makaryk, 344–5. Toronto: University of Toronto Press.

Chalykoff, Lisa. 1994. "Undocumenting Selfhood: Sky Lee's *Disappearing Moon Cafe* and Daphne Marlatt's *Ana Historic.*" Unpublished manuscript.

– 1998. "Encountering Anomalies: A Cultural Study of Chinese Migrants to Early Canada." In *Painting the Maple: Essays on Race, Gender and the Construction of Canada,* ed. Veronica Strong-Boag, Sherrill Grace, Avigail Eisenberg, and Joan Anderson, 155–69. Vancouver: UBC Press.

Chan, Céline. 1992. "Lesbian Self-Naming in Daphne Marlatt's *Ana Historic.*" *Canadian Poetry* 31: 68–74.

Chang, Heesok. 1994. "Allegories of Community: Chinese-Canadian Art in Vancouver." In *Vancouver: Representing the Postmodern City,* ed. Paul Delany, 217–41. Vancouver: Arsenal Pulp.

Chao, Lien. 1995. "Constituting Minority Canadian Women and our Sub-Cultures: Female Characters in Selected Chinese Canadian Literature." In *The Other Woman: Women of Colour in Contemporary Canadian Literature,* ed. Makeda Silvera, 332–54. Toronto: Sister Vision.

– 1997. *Beyond Silence: Chinese Canadian Literature in English.* Toronto: TSAR, 1997.

Chatman, Seymour. 1990. "What Can We Learn from Contexualist Narratology?" *Poetics Today* 11 (2): 309–28.

Chester, Blanca. 1999. "*Green Grass, Running Water*: Theorizing the World of the Novel." *Canadian Literature* 161/2: 44–61.

Cheung, King-Kok. 1993. *Articulate Silences: Hisaye Yamamoto, Maxine Hong Kingston, Joy Kogawa.* Ithaca: Cornell University Press.

Chong, Denise. 1990. Rev. of *Disappearing Moon Cafe,* by Sky Lee. *Quill and Quire,* 23 May, 23.

– 1994. *The Concubine's Children.* Toronto: Penguin.

Chow, Rey. 1993. *Writing Diaspora: Tactics of Intervention in Contemporary Cultural Studies.* Bloomington: Indiana University Press.

Choy, Wayson. 1995. *The Jade Peony.* Vancouver: Douglas and McIntyre.

– 1999. *Paper Shadows: A Chinatown Childhood.* Toronto: Viking.

Chua, Cheng Lok. 1992. "Witnessing the Japanese Canadian Experience in World War II: Processual Structure, Symbolism, and Irony in Joy Kogawa's *Obasan*." In *Reading the Literatures of Asian America*, ed. Shirley Geoklin Lim and Amy Ling, 97–108. Philadelphia: Temple University Press.

Clark, Katerina, and Michael Holquist. 1984. *Mikhail Bakhtin*. Cambridge: Harvard University Press.

Clark-Beattie, Rosemary. 1985. "*Middlemarch*'s Dialogic Style." *Journal of Narrative Technique* 15 (3): 199–218.

Clarke, George Elliott. 2000 [1990]. *Whylah Falls*. Vancouver: Polestar.

Coates, Ken. 1993/94. "The Rediscovery of the North: Towards a Conceptual Framework for the Study of Northern/Remote Regions." *Northern Review* 12–13: 15–43.

Cobley, Evelyn. 1993. *Representing War: Form and Ideology in First World War Narratives*. Toronto: University of Toronto Press.

Cohn, Dorrit. 1978. *Transparent Minds: Narrative Modes for Presenting Consciousness in Fiction*. Princeton: Princeton University Press.

– 1995a. "Optics and Power in the Novel." *New Literary History* 26: 3–25.

– 1995b. "Reply to John Bender and Mark Seltzer." *New Literary History* 26: 35–37.

Coleman, Daniel. 1998. *Masculine Migrations: Reading the Postcolonial Male in "New Canadian" Narratives*. Toronto: University of Toronto Press.

Corbeil, Carole. 1992. *Voice-Over*. Toronto: Stoddart.

Crowley, Tony. 1989. "Bakhtin and the History of the Language." In *Bakhtin and Cultural Theory*, ed. Ken Hirschkop and David Shepherd, 68–90. Manchester: Manchester University Press.

Cruikshank, Julie, with Angela Sidney, Kitty Smith, and Annie Ned. 1990. *Life Lived Like a Story: Life Stories of Three Yukon Native Elders*. Vancouver: UBC Press.

Culler, Jonathan. 1994. "Introduction: What's the Point?" In *The Point of Theory: Practices of Cultural Analysis*, ed. Mieke Bal and Inge E. Boer, 13–17. New York: Continuum.

Culleton, Beatrice. 1983. *In Search of April Raintree*. Winnipeg: Pemmican.

Currie, Elizabeth Noel. 1990. "Jeannette Armstrong and the Colonial Legacy." In *Native Writers and Canadian Writing*, ed. W.H. New, 138–52. Vancouver: UBC Press.

Damm, Kateri. 1993. "Says Who: Colonialism, Identity and Defining Indigenous Literature." In *Looking at the Words of Our People: First Nations Analysis of Literature*, ed. Jeannette Armstrong, 9–26. Penticton: Theytus.

Danow, David K. 1991. *The Thought of Mikhail Bakhtin: From Word to Culture*. New York: St. Martin's.

Davey, Frank. 1988. *Reading Canadian Reading*. Winnipeg: Turnstone.

– 1993. *Post-National Arguments: The Politics of the Anglophone-Canadian Novel since 1967*. Toronto: University of Toronto Press.

Davidson, Arnold. 1993. *Writing against the Silence: Joy Kogawa's* Obasan. Toronto: ECW.

Davidson, Michael. 1983. "Discourse in Poetry: Bakhtin and Extensions of the Dialogic." In *Code of Signals: Recent Writing in Poetics*, ed. Michael Palmer, 143–50. Berkeley: North Atlantic.

Dawson, Brian J. 1991. *Moon Cakes in Gold Mountain: From China to the Canadian Plains*. Calgary: Detselig.

d'Eaubonne, Françoise. 1980. "Feminism or Death." Trans. Betty Schmitz. In *New French Feminisms: An Anthology*, ed. Elaine Marks and Isabella de Courtivron, 64–7. Amherst: University of Massachusetts Press. (From *Le féminisme ou la mort*. 1974. Paris: Pierre Horay.)

Deer, Glenn. 1994. *Postmodern Canadian Fiction and the Rhetoric of Authority*. Montreal: McGill-Queen's University Press.

Delbaere, Jeanne, ed. 1990. *Multiple Voices: Recent Canadian Fiction*. Sydney: Dangaroo.

de Man, Paul. 1983. "Dialogue and Dialogism." *Poetics Today* 4: 99–107.

Dentith, Simon. 1995. *Bakhtinian Thought: An Introductory Reader*. London: Routledge.

Derrida, Jacques. 1976. [1967]. *Of Grammatology*. Trans. Gayatri Chakravorty Spivak. Baltimore: Johns Hopkins University Press.

Diamond, Irene, and Gloria Orenstein, eds. 1990. *Reweaving the World: The Emergence of Ecofeminism*. San Francisco: Sierra Club.

Díaz-Diocaretz, Myriam. 1989a. "Bakhtin, Discourse, and Feminist Theories." *Critical Studies* 1 (2): 121–39.

– 1989b. "Sieving the Matriheritage of the Sociotext." *The Difference Within: Feminism and Critical Theory*, ed. Elizabeth Meese and Alice Parker, 115–47. Amsterdam: John Benjamins.

Dickinson, Harley, and Terry Wotherspoon. 1992. "From Assimilation to Self-Government: Towards a Political Economy of Canada's Aboriginal Policies." In *Deconstructing a Nation: Immigration, Multiculturalism and Racism in '90s Canada*, ed. Vic Satzewich, 405–21. Halifax: Fernwood.

Dickinson, Peter. 1994. "'Orality in Literacy': Listening to Indigenous Writing." *Canadian Journal of Native Studies* 14 (2): 319–40.

– 1999. *Here Is Queer: Nationalisms, Sexualities, and the Literatures of Canada*. Toronto: University of Toronto Press.

Diengott, Nilli. 1988. "Narratology and Feminism." *Style* 22 (1): 42–51.

Donaldson, Laura E. 1995. "Noah Meets Old Coyote, or Singing in the Rain: Intertextuality in Thomas King's *Green Grass, Running Water*." *Studies in American Indian Literatures* 7 (2): 27–43.

Dragland, Stan. 1991. "Out of the Blank: Daphne Marlatt's *Ana Historic*." In *The Bees of the Invisible: Essays in Contemporary English Canadian Writing*, ed. Stan Dragland, 173–90. Toronto: Coach House.

Draper, Gary. 1990. "The Making of Legends." Rev. of *Disappearing Moon Cafe*, by Sky Lee. *Books in Canada*, June/July, 49–50.

Dumont, Marilyn. 1993. "Popular Images of Nativeness." In *Looking at the Words of Our People: First Nations Analysis of Literature*, ed. J. Armstrong, 45–50. Penticton: Theytus.

Durkin, Douglas. 1974. *The Magpie*. 1923. Toronto: University of Toronto Press.

Eagleton, Terry. 1989. "Bakhtin, Schopenhauer, Kundera." In *Bakhtin and Cultural Theory*, ed. Ken Hirschkop and David Shepherd, 178–88. Manchester: Manchester University Press.

"Ecological Feminism." 1991. Special Issue. *Hypatia* 6 (1).

Ellis, Scott. 1991. Rev. of *Fox*, by Margaret Sweatman. *Prairie Fire* 12 (2): 71–3.

Emberley, Julia V. 1993. *Thresholds of Difference: Feminist Critique, Native Women's Writings, Postcolonial Theory*. Toronto: University of Toronto Press.

Emerson, Caryl. 1988. "Problems with Baxtin's Poetics." *Slavic and East European Journal* 32 (4): 503–25.

– 1995. "Introduction: Dialogue on Every Corner, Bakhtin in Every Class." In *Bakhtin in Contexts: Across the Disciplines*, ed. Amy Mandelker, 1–30. Evanston: Northwestern University Press.

– 1997. *The First Hundred Years of Mikhail Bakhtin*. Princeton: Princeton University Press.

Engler, Bernd, and Kurt Müller, eds. 1994. *Historiographic Metafiction in Modern American and Canadian Literature*. Paderborn: Schöningh.

Farrell, Thomas J., ed. 1995. *Bakhtin and Medieval Voices*. Gainesville: University Press of Florida.

Fee, Margery. 1984. "Romantic Nationalism and the Image of Native People in Contemporary English-Canadian Literature." In *The Native in Literature*, ed. Thomas King, Cheryl Calver, and Helen Hoy, 15–33. Toronto: ECW.

– 1990. "Upsetting Fake Ideas: Jeannette Armstrong's *Slash* and Beatrice Culleton's *April Raintree*." In *Native Writers and Canadian Writing*, ed. W.H. New, 168–80. Vancouver: UBC Press.

– 1995. "What Use is Ethnicity to Aboriginal Peoples in Canada?" *Canadian Review of Comparative Literature* 22 (3–4): 683–91.

– and Jane Flick. 1999. "Coyote Pedagogy: Knowing Where the Borders Are in Thomas King's *Green Grass, Running Water*." *Canadian Literature* 161/2: 131–9.

Fehn, Ann, Ingeborg Hoesterey, and Maria Tatar, eds. 1992. *Neverending Stories: Toward a Critical Narratology*. Princeton: Princeton University Press.

Finke, Laurie. 1992. *Feminist Theory, Women's Writing*. Ithaca: Cornell University Press.

Finnegan, Ruth. 1988. *Literacy and Orality: Studies in the Technology of Communication*. London: Blackwell.

Fischlin, Daniel. 1995. "'As Sparrows Do Fall': Sweatman's *Fox* and Transforming the Socius." *Open Letter* 9 (4): 57–68.

FitzHugh, Terrick. 1985. *Dictionary of Genealogy*. Sherborne: Alphabooks.

Flick, Jane. 1999. "Reading Notes for Thomas King's *Green Grass, Running Water*." *Canadian Literature* 161/2: 140–72.

Fludernik, Monika. 1996. *Towards a "Natural" Narratology*. London: Routledge.

Fogel, Aaron. 1985. *Coercion to Speak: Conrad's Poetics of Dialogue*. Cambridge: Harvard University Press.

– 1989. "Coerced Speech and the Oedipus Dialogue Complex." In *Rethinking Bakhtin: Extensions and Challenges*, ed. Gary Saul Morson and Caryl Emerson, 173–96. Evanston: Northwestern University Press.

Foucault, Michel. 1965 [1961]. *Madness and Civilization: A History of Insanity in the Age of Reason*. Trans. Richard Howard. New York: Random.

– 1972 [1969]. *The Archaeology of Knowledge*. Trans. A.M. Sheridan Smith. London: Routledge.

– 1978 [1976]. *The History of Sexuality*. Vol. 1: *An Introduction*. Trans. Robert Hurley. New York: Random.

Francis, Daniel. 1992. *The Imaginary Indian: The Image of the Indian in Canadian Culture*. Vancouver: Arsenal.

Frank, Leonard Roy, ed. 1978. *The History of Shock Treatment*. San Francisco: Frank.

Friedman, Susan Stanford. 1989. "Lyric Subversion of Narrative in Women's Writing: Virginia Woolf and the Tyranny of Plot." In *Reading Narrative: Form, Ethics, Ideology*, ed. James Phelan, 162–85. Columbus: Ohio State University Press.

Frye, Joanne S. 1986. *Living Stories, Telling Lives: Women and the Novel in Contemporary Experience*. Ann Arbor: University of Michigan Press.

Frye, Northrop. 1971 [1965]. "Conclusion to a Literary History of Canada." In *The Bush Garden: Essays on the Canadian Imagination*, ed. N. Frye, 213–51. Toronto: Anansi.

Fuss, Diana. 1989. *Essentially Speaking: Feminism, Nature and Difference*. New York: Routledge.

Gaard, Greta Claire, and Patrick D Murphy, eds. 1998. *Ecofeminist Literary Criticism: Theory, Interpretation, Pedagogy*. Urbana: University of Illinois Press.

Gardiner, Michael. 1992. *The Dialogics of Critique: M.M. Bakhtin and the Theory of Ideology*. London: Routledge.

– 1993. "Bakhtin's Carnival: Utopia as Critique." *Critical Studies* 3.2–4.1/2: 20–47.

Garrett, Peter K. 1980. *The Victorian Multiplot Novel: Studies in Dialogical Form*. New Haven: Yale University Press.

Gates, Henry Louis, Jr. 1985. "Introduction: Writing 'Race' and the Difference It Makes." In *"Race," Writing, and Difference*, ed. Henry Louis Gates, Jr, 1–20. Chicago: University of Chicago Press.

Genette, Gérard. 1980 [1972]. *Narrative Discourse: An Essay in Method*. Trans. Jane E. Lewin. Oxford: Blackwell.

Gill, Sam D., and Irene F. Sullivan. 1992. *Dictionary of Native American Mythology*. Santa Barbara: ABC-CLIO.

Ginsburg, Michael Peled. 1980. "Pseudonym, Epigraphs, and Narrative Voice: *Middlemarch* and the Problem of Authority." *English Literary History* 47: 542–58.

Glazener, Nancy. 1989. "Dialogic Subversion: Bakhtin, the Novel and Gertrude Stein." In *Bakhtin and Cultural Theory*, ed. Ken Hirschkop and David Shepherd, 109–29. Manchester: Manchester University Press.

Godard, Barbara. 1984/85. "World Wonders: Robertson Davies' Carnival." *Essays on Canadian Writing* 30: 239–86.

– 1987. "Robertson Davies' Dialogic Imagination." *Essays on Canadian Writing* 34: 64–80.

– 1990a. "The Discourse of the Other: Canadian Literature and the Question of Ethnicity." *Massachusetts Review* 31 (1–2): 153–84.

– 1990b. "The Politics of Representation: Some Native Canadian Women Writers." In *Native Writers and Canadian Writing*, ed. W.H. New, 183–225. Vancouver: UBC Press.

– 1997. "F(r)ictions: Feminists Re/Writing Narrative." In *Gender and Narrativity*, ed. Barry Rutland, 115–45. Ottawa: Carleton University Press.

– ed. 1994. *Collaboration in the Feminine: Writings on Women and Culture from Tessera*. Toronto: Second Story.

Goellnicht, Donald C. 1989. "Minority History as Metafiction: Joy Kogawa's *Obasan*." *Tulsa Studies in Women's Literature* 8 (2): 287–306.

Goldberg, Theo. 1993. *Racist Culture: Philosophy and the Politics of Meaning*. Oxford: Blackwell.

Goldfarb, Sheldon. 1990. "Into Chinatown for a Saga Full of Sound and Fury." Rev. of *Disappearing Moon Cafe*, by Sky Lee. *Vancouver Sun*, 19 May, D19.

Goldie, Terry. 1989. *Fear and Temptation: The Image of the Indigene in Canadian, Australian and New Zealand Literatures*. Kingston: McGill-Queen's University Press.

Goldman, Marlene. 1992. "Daphne Marlatt's *Ana Historic*: A Genealogy for Lost Women." *Resources for Feminist Research* 21 (3–4): 33–8.

– 1993. "Earth-Quaking the Kingdom of the Male Virgin: A Deleuzian Analysis of Aritha van Herk's *No Fixed Address* and *Places Far from Ellesmere*." *Canadian Literature* 137: 21–38.

– 1997a. "Go North Young Woman: Representations of the Arctic in the Writings of Aritha van Herk." In *Echoing Silence: Essays on Arctic Narratives*, ed. John Moss, 153–62. Ottawa: Ottawa University Press.

– 1997b. *Paths of Desire: Images of Exploration and Mapping in Canadian Women's Writing.* Toronto: University of Toronto Press.

– 1999. "Mapping and Dreaming Native Resistance in *Green Grass, Running Water.*" *Canadian Literature* 161/2: 18–41.

Goto, Hiromi. 1994. *Chorus of Mushrooms.* Edmonton: NeWest.

Grace, Sherrill E. 1987. ""Listen to the Voice": Dialogism and the Canadian Novel." In *Future Indicative: Literary Theory and Canadian Literature*, ed. John Moss, 117–36. Ottawa: University of Ottawa Press.

– 1990. ""A Sound of Singing": Polyphony and Narrative Decentring in Malcolm Lowry's *Hear Us O Lord.*" In *Modes of Narrative*, ed. Reingard Nischik and Barbara Korte, 129–40. Würzburg: Königshausen and Neumann.

– 1991. "Comparing Mythologies: Ideas of West and North." In *Borderlands: Essays in Canadian-American Relations*, ed. Robert Lecker, 243–62. Toronto: ECW.

– 1995. "Canada Post: – Modern? – Colonial? – National?" Paper presented to the Royal Society of Canada. Ottawa, 24 November.

– 1997. "Gendering Northern Narrative." In *Echoing Silence: Essays on Arctic Narratives*, ed. John Moss, 163–81. Ottawa: Ottawa University Press.

Grainger, M. Allerdale. 1964 [1908]. *Woodsmen of the West.* Toronto: McClelland and Stewart.

Green, Keith, and Jill LeBihan. 1994. "The Speaking Object: Daphne Marlatt's Pronouns and Lesbian Poetics." *Style* 28 (3): 432–44.

Gregory, Steven. 1994. "'We've Been Down This Road Already.'" In *Race*, ed. Steven Gregory and Roger Sanjek, 18–38. New Brunswick: Rutgers University Press.

Gregory, Steven, and Roger Sanjek, eds. 1994. *Race.* New Brunswick: Rutgers University Press.

Greimas, A.J. 1983 [1966]. *Structural Semantics: An Attempt at a Method.* Trans. Daniele McDowell, Ronald Schleifer, and Alan Velie. Lincoln: University of Nebraska Press.

Griffin, Susan. 1978. *Woman and Nature: The Roaring Inside Her.* New York: Harper.

– 1982. *Made from This Earth: An Anthology of Writings.* New York: Harper.

Griffiths, Linda, and Maria Campbell. 1989. *The Book of Jessica: A Theatrical Transformation.* Toronto: Coach House.

Grisé, C. Annette. 1993. "'A Bedtime Story for You, Ina': Resisting Amnesia of the Maternal in Daphne Marlatt's *Ana Historic.*" *Tessera* 15: 90–8.

Grünzweig, Walter, and Andreas Solbach, ed. 1999. *Grenzüberschreitungen: Narratologie im Kontext (Transcending Boundaries: Narratology in Context).* Tübingen: Gunter Narr Verlag.

Guba, Egon C., and Yvonne S. Lincoln. 1989. "What Is This Constructivist Paradigm Anyway?" In *Fourth Generation Evaluation*, 79–116. Newbury Park: Sage.

Gunew, Sneja, and Anna Yeatman. 1993. "Introduction." In *Feminism and the Politics of Difference*, ed. S. Gunew and A. Yeatman, xiii-xxv. Halifax: Fernwood.

Hadjukowski-Ahmed, Maroussia. 1990. "Bakhtin and Feminism: Two Solitudes?" *Critical Studies* 2 (1–2): 153–63.

Halasek, Kay. 1992. "Feminism and Bakhtin: Dialogic Reading in the Academy." *Rhetoric Society Quarterly* 22 (1): 63–75.

Hamelin, Louis-Edmond. 1988. *About Canada: The Canadian North and Its Conceptual Referents*. Ottawa: Supply and Services.

Haraway, Donna J. 1991. *Simians, Cyborgs, and Women: The Reinvention of Nature*. New York: Routledge.

Harlow, Barbara. 1987. *Resistance Literature*. New York: Methuen.

Harris, Mason. 1990. "Broken Generations in *Obasan*: Inner Conflict and the Destruction of Community." *Canadian Literature* 127: 41–57.

– 1996. "Joy Kogawa (1935–)." *Canadian Writers and Their Works: Fiction Series*, ed. Robert Lecker, Jack David, and Ellen Quigley, 139–211. Toronto: ECW.

Harris, Wendell V. 1990. "Bakhtinian Double Voicing in Dickens and Eliot." *English Literary History* 57 (2): 445–58.

Harris, Wilson. 1985. "Adversarial Contexts and Creativity." *New Left Review* 154: 124–8.

Harvie, Jennifer, and Richard Paul Knowles. 1994. "Dialogic Monologue: A Dialogue." *Theatre Research in Canada* 15 (2): 136–63.

Hay, Elizabeth. 1992. *The Only Snow in Havana*. Dunvegan: Cormorant.

Helms, Gabriele, Matt James, and Paddy Rodney. 1996. "Multifarious, Processual, and Pervasive: Towards an Interdisciplinary Dialogue on Constructions." In *Race, Gender, and the Construction of Canada: Conference Proceedings, 19–22 October 1995*. Vol. 2, n.p. Vancouver: University of British Columbia, Centre for Women's Studies and Gender Relations.

Henderson, Mae Gwendolyn. 1989. "Speaking in Tongues: Dialogics, Dialectics, and the Black Woman Writer's Literary Tradition." In *Changing Our Own Words: Essays on Criticism, Theory, and Writing by Black Women*, ed. Cheryl A. Wall, 16–37. New Brunswick: Rutgers University Press.

Henry, Ann. 1975. *Lulu Street*. Vancouver: Talonbooks.

Henry, Frances, and Carol Tator. 1994. "The Ideology of Racism: 'Democratic Racism.'" *Canadian Ethnic Studies* 26 (2): 1–14.

Herman, David. 1999a. "Introduction: Narratologies." In *Narratologies: New Perspectives on Narrative Analysis*, ed. D. Herman, 1–30. Columbus: Ohio State University Press.

– ed. 1999b. *Narratologies: New Perspectives on Narrative Analysis*. Columbus: Ohio State University Press.

Herring, Henry D. 1985. "Constructivist Interpretation: An Alternative to Deconstruction." *Bucknell Review* 29 (2): 32–46.

Herrmann, Anne. 1989. *The Dialogic and Difference: "An/Other Woman" in Virginia Woolf and Christa Wolf.* New York: Columbia University Press.

Highway, Tomson. 1998. *Kiss of the Fur Queen.* Toronto: Doubleday.

Hillman, James. 1972. *The Myth of Analysis: Three Essays in Archetypal Psychology.* Evanston: Northwestern University Press.

Hirschfelder, Arlene, and Paulette Molin. 1991. *The Encyclopedia of Native American Religions.* New York: Facts on File.

Hirschkop, Ken. 1986. "A Response to the Forum on Mikhail Bakhtin." In *Bakhtin: Essays and Dialogues on His Work,* ed. Gary Saul Morson, 73–9. London, Chicago: University of Chicago Press.

– 1989a. "Critical Work on the Bakhtin Circle: A Bibliographical Essay." In *Bakhtin and Cultural Theory.* ed. Ken Hirschkop and David Shepherd, 195–212. Manchester: Manchester University Press

– 1989b. "Introduction: Bakhtin and Cultural Theory." In *Bakhtin and Cultural Theory.* ed. Ken Hirschkop and David Shepherd, 1–38. Manchester: Manchester University Press.

Hitchcock, Peter. 1993. *The Dialogics of the Oppressed.* Minneapolis: University of Minnesota Press.

Hohne, Karen, and Helen Wussow, eds. 1994. *A Dialogue of Voices: Feminist Literary Theory and Bakhtin.* Minneapolis: University of Minnesota Press.

Holquist, Michael. 1990. *Dialogism: Bakhtin and His World.* London: Routledge.

Horne, Dee. 1995. "To Know the Difference: Mimicry, Satire, and Thomas King's *Green Grass, Running Water.*" *Essays on Canadian Writing* 56: 255–73.

Horodyski, Mary. 1986. "Women and the Winnipeg General Strike of 1919." *Manitoba History* 11: 28–37.

Howard, Jacqueline. 1994. *Reading Gothic Fiction: A Bakhtinian Approach.* Oxford: Clarendon.

Howells, Coral Ann. 1996. "Disruptive Geographies: or, Mapping the Region of Woman in Contemporary Canadian Women's Writing in English." *Journal of Commonwealth Literature* 31 (1): 115–27.

– and Lynette Hunter, eds. 1991. *Narrative Strategies in Canadian Literature: Feminism and Postcolonialism.* Buckingham: Open University Press.

Howells, Robin. 1993. "Dialogism in Canada's First Novel: *The History of Emily Montague.*" *Canadian Review of Comparative Literature* 20 (3–4): 437–50.

Hoy, Helen. 2001. *How Should I Read These?: Native Women Writers in Canada.* Toronto: University of Toronto Press.

Huang, Evelyn, with Lawrence Jeffery. 1992. *Chinese Canadians: Voices from a Community.* Vancouver: Douglas and McIntyre.

Huggan, Graham. 1994a. "The Latitudes of Romance: Representations of Chinese Canada in Bowering's *To All Appearances a Lady* and Lee's *Disappearing Moon Cafe.*" *Canadian Literature* 140: 34–48.

– 1994b. *Territorial Disputes: Maps and Mapping Strategies in Contemporary Canadian and Australian Fiction.* Toronto: University of Toronto Press.

Hulan, Renée. 1998. "Some Thoughts on 'Integrity and Intent' and Teaching Native Literature." *Essays on Canadian Writing* 63: 210–30.

Hunter, Lynette. 1996. *Outsider Notes: Feminist Approaches to Nation State Ideology, Writers/Readers and Publishing.* Vancouver: Talonbooks.

Hutcheon, Linda. 1988a. *The Canadian Postmodern: A Study of Contemporary English-Canadian Fiction.* Toronto: Oxford University Press.

– 1988b. *A Poetics of Postmodernism: History, Theory, Fiction.* New York: Routledge.

– 1988c. "Telling Accounts." Rev. of *Ana Historic* by Daphne Marlatt. *Brick* 34: 17–19.

– 1990. "The Novel." In *Literary History of Canada: Canadian Literature in English* (2nd ed., vol. 4), ed. W.H. New. 73–96. Toronto: U of Toronto P.

Ignatieff, Michael. 1993. *Blood and Belonging: Journeys into the New Nationalism.* New York: Farrar, Straus and Giroux.

– 2000. *The Rights Revolution.* Toronto: Anansi.

Irvine, Lorna. 1986. *Sub/Version: Canadian Fictions by Women.* Toronto: ECW.

Itwaru, Arnold Harrichand. 1994. *Closed Entrances: Canadian Culture and Imperialism.* Toronto: Tsar.

Ivanov, Vyacheslav Vs. 1976 [1973]. "The Significance of M.M. Bakhtin's Ideas on Sign, Utterance, and Dialogue for Modern Semiotics." In *Semiotics and Structuralism: Readings from the Soviet Union*, ed. Henryk Baran, 310–76. White Plains: International Arts and Sciences.

Jahn, Manfred. 1995. "Narratologie: Methoden und Modelle der Erzähltheorie." In *Literaturwissenschaftliche Theorien, Modelle und Methoden: Eine Einführung*, ed. Ansgar Nünning, 29–50. Trier: Wissenschaftlicher Verlag.

– 1997. "Frames, Preferences, and the Reading of Third-Person Narratives: Towards a Cognitive Narratology." *Poetics Today* 18 (4): 441–68.

– 1999. "'Speak, Friend, and Enter': Garden Paths, Artificial Intelligence, and Cognitive Narratology." In *Narratologies: New Perspectives on Narrative Analysis*, ed. David Herman, 167–94. Columbus: Ohio State University Press.

– and Ansgar Nünning. 1994. "A Survey of Narratological Models." *Literatur in Wissenschaft und Unterricht* 27.4: 283–303.

James, Matt. 1995. "Symbolic Capital and the Social Alchemy of Redress Politics." Unpublished manuscript.

Jameson, Frederic. 1981. *The Political Unconscious: Narrative as a Socially Symbolic Act.* Ithaca: Cornell University Press.

JanMohammed, Abdul, and David Lloyd. 1987. "Introduction: Toward a Theory of Minority Discourse." *Cultural Critique* 6: 5–12.

Jefferson, Ann. 1986. "Realism Reconsidered: Bakhtin's Dialogism and the 'Will to Reference.'" *Australian Journal of French Studies* 23 (2): 169–84.

Jones, Manina. 1990. "The Avenues of Speech and Silence: Telling Difference in Joy Kogawa's *Obasan*." *Theory between the Disciplines: Authority/Vision/ Politics*, ed. Martin Kreiswirth and Mark A. Cheetham, 213–29. Ann Arbor: University of Michigan Press.

– 1993. *That Art of Difference: "Documentary-Collage" and English Canadian Writing*. Toronto: University of Toronto Press.

– 2000. "*Slash* Marks the Spot: 'Critical Embarrassment' and Activist Aesthetics in Jeannette Armstrong's *Slash*." *West Coast Line* 33 (3): 48–62.

Kafalenos. Emma, ed. 2001. *Contemporary Narratology*. Special issue of *Narrative* 9 (2).

Kamboureli, Smaro. 2000. *Scandalous Bodies: Diasporic Literature in English Canada*. Oxford: Oxford University Press.

Kanefsky, Rachelle. 1996. "Debunking a Postmodern Conception of History: A Defence of Humanist Values in the Novels of Joy Kogawa." *Canadian Literature* 148: 11–36.

Kealey, Gregory. 1984. "1919: The Canadian Labour Revolt." *Labour/Le Travail* 13: 11–44.

Kealey, Linda. 1989. "No Special Protection – No Sympathy: Women's Activism in the Canadian Labour Revolt of 1919." In *Class, Community and the Labour Movement: Wales and Canada, 1850–1930*, ed. Deian R. Hopkin and Gregory S. Kealey, 134–59. St John's: LLAFUR/CCLH.

Kearns, Michael. 1999. *Rhetorical Narratology*. Lincoln: University of Nebraska Press.

Keeshig-Tobias, Leonore. 1990. "The Magic of Others." In *Language in Her Eye: Views on Writing and Gender by Canadian Women Writing in English*, ed. Libby Scheier, Sarah Sheard, and Eleanor Wachtel, 173–7. Toronto: Coach House.

Kelly, Peggy. 1995. "Fiction Theory as Feminist Practice in Marlatt's *Ana Historic* and Scott's *Heroine*." *Open Letter* 9 (4): 69–98.

Kershner, R.B. 1989. *Joyce, Bakhtin, and Popular Literature: Chronicles of Disorder*. Chapel Hill: University of North Carolina Press.

Kertzer, Jonathan. 1998. *Worrying the Nation: Imagining a National Literature in English Canada*. Toronto: University of Toronto Press.

Keyssar, Helene. 1991. "Drama and the Dialogic Imagination: *The Heidi Chronicles* and *Fefu and Her Friends*." *Modern Drama* 34 (1): 88–106.

King, Thomas. 1989. *Medicine River*. Toronto: Penguin.

– 1990a. "Godzilla vs. Post-Colonial." *World Literature Written in English* 30 (2): 10–16.

– 1990b. "Interview with Thomas King." With Constance Rooke. *World Literature Written in English* 30 (2): 62–76.

– 1993. *Green Grass, Running Water*. Toronto: HarperCollins.
– 1994. "Interview with Thomas King." With Jeffrey Canton. *Paragraph* 16 (1): 2–6.
– 1999. "Peter Gzowski Interviews Thomas King on *Green Grass, Running Water*." *Canadian Literature* 161/2: 65–76.
– Cheryl Calver, and Helen Hoy, eds. 1984. *The Native in Literature*. Toronto: ECW.

Kirkwood, Hilda. 1991. "Geografictione." Rev. of *Places Far from Ellesmere*, by Aritha van Herk. *Canadian Forum*, April, 29–30.

Kitagawa, Muriel. 1985. *This Is My Own: Letters to Wes and Other Writings on Japanese Canadians, 1941–1948*. Ed. Roy Miki. Vancouver: Talonbooks.

Knowles, Richard Paul. 1995. "Representing Canada: Teaching Canadian Studies in the United States." *American Review of Canadian Studies* 25 (1): 9–26.

Kogawa, Joy. 1981. *Obasan*. London: Penguin.
– 1984. "Is There a Just Cause?" *Canadian Forum*, March, 20+.
– 1992. *Itsuka*. Toronto: Penguin.
– 1993. "'In Writing I Keep Breathing, I Keep Living ...'" In *Sounding Difference: Conversations with Seventeen Canadian Women Writers*, ed. Janice Williamson, 148–59. Toronto: University of Toronto Press.
– 1995a. "Joy Kogawa Talks to Karlyn Koh: The Heart-of-the-Matter Questions." In *The Other Woman: Women of Colour in Contemporary Canadian Literature*, ed. Makeda Silvera, 19–41. Toronto: Sister Vision.
– 1995b. *The Rain Ascends*. Toronto: Knopf.

Kramer, Reinhold. 1999. "The 1919 Winnipeg General Strike and Margaret Sweatman's *Fox*." *Canadian Literature* 160: 50–70.

Kroetsch, Robert. 1970. "A Conversation with Margaret Laurence." In *Creation*, ed. Robert Kroetsch, 53–63. Toronto: New Press.
– 1983. "Unhiding the Hidden." 1974. *Open Letter* 5 (4): 17–21.

Krupat, Arnold. 1989. "The Dialogic of Silko's Storyteller." In *Narrative Chance: Postmodern Discourse on Native American Indian Literature*, ed. Gerald Vizenor, 55–68. Albuquerque: University of New Mexico Press.

Kuester, Martin. 1992. *Framing Truths: Parodic Structures in Contemporary English-Canadian Historical Novels*. Toronto: University of Toronto Press.

Kulchyski, Peter. 1995. "Aborginal Peoples and Hegemony in Canada." *Journal of Canadian Studies* 30 (1): 60–8.

Lacey, Liam. 1990. "Writer Tries to Make Chinatown Come Alive." Rev. of *Disappearing Moon Cafe*, by Sky Lee. *Globe and Mail*, 19 May, C9.

Lai, Larissa. 1995. *When Fox Is a Thousand*. Vancouver: Press Gang.

Lanser, Susan Sniader. 1986. "Toward a Feminist Narratology." *Style* 20 (3): 341–63.
– 1988. "Shifting the Paradigm: Feminism and Narratology." *Style* 22.1: 52–60.

- 1992. *Fictions of Authority: Women Writers and Narrative Voice*. Ithaca: Cornell University Press.
- 1996. "Queering Narratology." In *Ambiguous Discourse: Feminist Narratology and British Women Writers*, ed. Kathy Mezei, 250–61. Chapel Hill: University of North Carolina Press.
- 1999. "Sexing Narratology: Toward a Gendered Poetics of Narrative Voice." In *Grenzüberschreitungen: Narratologie im Kontext (Transcending Boundaries: Narratology in Context)*, ed. Walter Grünzweig and Andreas Solbach 167–83, Tübingen: Gunter Narr Verlag.
- 2001. "(Im)plying the Author." *Contemporary Narratology*. Special issue of *Narrative* 9 (2): 153–60.
Lau, Evelyn. 1989. *Runaway*. Toronto: Harper.
- 2001. *Inside Out: Reflections on a Life so Far*. Toronto: Anchor.
Lawson, Alan. 1991. "A Cultural Paradigm for the Second World." *Australian-Canadian Studies* 9 (1–2): 67–78.
- 1995. "Postcolonial Theory and The 'Settler' Subject." *Essays on Canadian Writing* 56: 20–36.
Lawson, Maria, and Rosalind Watson Young. 1906. *A History and Geography of British Columbia: For Use in Public Schools*. Toronto: Gage.
Lecker, Robert. 1995. *Making It Real: The Canonization of English-Canadian Literature*. Toronto: Anansi.
Lee, Bennett, and Jim Wong-Chu, eds. 1991. *Many-Mouthed Birds: Contemporary Writing by Chinese Canadians*. Seattle: University of Washington Press.
Lee, Sky. 1990. *Disappearing Moon Cafe*. Vancouver: Douglas and McIntyre.
- 1995. "Sky Lee Talks to C. Allyson Lee: Is There a Mind without Media Any More?" In *The Other Woman: Women of Colour in Contemporary Canadian Literature*, ed. Makeda Silvera, 382–403. Toronto: Sister Vision.
Lévi-Strauss, Claude. 1963 [1958]. *Structural Anthropology*. Trans. Claire Jacobson and Brooke G. Schoepf. New York: Basic Books.
Li, Peter S. 1988. *The Chinese in Canada*. Toronto: Oxford University Press.
- 1992. "The Chinese Minority in Canada, 1858–1992: A Quest for Equality." In *Chinese Canadians: Voices from a Community*, ed. Evelyn Huang with Lawrence Jeffery, 264–75. Vancouver: Douglas and McIntyre.
Lill, Wendy. 1987. *The Occupation of Heather Rose*. In *NeWest Plays by Women*, ed. Diane Bessai and Don Kerr, 63–94. Edmonton: NeWest.
Lim, Shirley Geok-lin. 1991. "Asian American Daughters Rewriting Asian Maternal Text." In *Asian Americans: Comparative and Global Perspectives*, ed. Shirley Hune, Hyung-Chan Kim, Stephen S. Fugita, and Amy Ling, 239–48, Pullman: Washington State University Press.
Linton, Patricia. 1999. "'And Here's How It Happened': Trickster Discourse in Thomas King's *Green Grass, Running Water*." *Modern Fiction Studies* 45 (1): 213–34.
Lowry, Glen. 1991. "Risking Perversion and Reclaiming Our Hysterical

Mother: Reading the Material Body in *Ana Historic* and *Double Standards.*" *West Coast Line* 5 (25/2): 83–96.

MacEwen, Gwendolyn. 1989. "The Disovery." In *Poetry by Canadian Women*, ed. Rosemary Sullivan, 163. Toronto: Oxford University Press.

Malcuzynski, M.-Pierrette. 1984. "Polyphonic Theory and Contemporary Literary Practices." *Studies in Twentieth Century Literature* 9 (1): 75–87.

– 1990. "Mikhail Bakhtin and the Sociocritical Practice." *Discours social/Social Discourse* 3 (1–2): 83–97.

Mandelker, Amy, ed. 1995. *Bakhtin in Contexts: Across the Disciplines.* Evanston: Northwestern University Press.

Manera, Matthew. 1995. "The Act of Being Read: Fictional Process in *Places Far from Ellesmere.*" *Canadian Literature* (146): 87–94.

Maracle, Lee. 1990. "You Become the Trickster." In *Sojourner's Truth and Other Stories*, 11–13. Vancouver: Press Gang.

– 1992a. "Oratory: Coming to Theory." In *Give Back: First Nations Perspectives on Cultural Practice*, 85–93. North Vancouver: Gallerie Publications.

– 1992b. *Sundogs.* Penticton: Theytus.

Marlatt, Daphne. 1988. *Ana Historic: A Novel.* Toronto: Coach House.

– 1989. "On *Ana Historic*: An Interview with Daphne Marlatt." With George Bowering. *Line* 13: 96–107.

– 1990a. "Difference (Em)bracing." In *Language in Her Eye: Views on Writing and Gender by Canadian Women Writing in English*, ed. Libby Scheier, Sarah Sheard, and Eleanor Wachtel, 188–93. Toronto: Coach House.

– 1990b. "Self-Representation and Fictionalysis." *Tessera* 8: 13–17.

– 1991a. "Between Continuity and Difference: An Interview with Daphne Marlatt." With Brenda Carr. In *Beyond Tish*, ed. Douglas Barbour, 99–107. Edmonton: NeWest.

– 1991b. *Salvage.* Red Deer: Red Deer College.

– 1993. "When We Change Language." Interview with Janice Williamson. In *Sounding Differences: Conversations with Seventeen Canadian Women Writers*, ed. Janice Williamson, 181–93. Toronto: University of Toronto Press.

– 1998. *Readings from the Labyrinth.* Edmonton: NeWest.

– 2001 [1974]. *Steveston.* Vancouver: Ronsdale.

– Barbara Godard, Kathy Mezei, and Gail Scott. 1986. "Theorizing Fiction Theory." *Tessera* 3 / *Canadian Fiction Magazine* 57: 6–12. Reprinted in *Collaboration in the Feminine: Writings on Women and Culture from Tessera*, ed. Barbara Godard, 53–62. Toronto: Second Story, 1994.

Martineau, Joel. 1996. "Ecology and Community in *Woodsmen of the West.*" Unpublished manuscript.

Matchie, Thomas, and Brett Larson. 1996. "Coyote Fixes the World: The Power of Myth in Thomas King's *Green Grass, Running Water.*" *North Dakota Quarterly* 63 (2): 153–68.

Matthews, Major J.S. 1932. *Early Vancouver: Narratives of Pioneers of Vancouver, BC.* Vancouver: Matthews.

McFarlane, Scott. 1995a. "Covering *Obasan* and the Narrative of Internment." In *Privileging Positions: The Sites of Asian American Studies,* ed. Gary Y. Okihiro, Marilyn Alquizola, Dorothy Fujita Rony, K. Scott Wong, 401–11. Pullman: Washington State University Press.

– 1995b. "The Haunt of Race: Canada's Multiculturalism Act, the Politics of Incorporation, and Writing Thru Race." *Fuse* 18 (3): 18–31.

McHale, Brian. 1987. *Postmodernist Fiction.* New York: Methuen.

McNaught, Kenneth. 1959. *Prophet in Politics: A Biography of J.S. Wordsworth.* Toronto: University of Toronto Press.

Medvedev, P.N. / M.M. Bakhtin. 1985 [1928]. *The Formal Method in Literary Scholarship.* Trans. Albert J. Wehrle. Cambridge: Harvard University Press.

Mercer, Kobena. 1988. "Diaspora Culture and the Dialogic Imagination: The Aesthetics of Black Independent Film in Britain." In *Blackframes: Critical Perspectives on Black Independent Cinema,* ed. Mybe B. Cham and Claire Andrade-Watkins, 50–61. Cambridge: MIT Press.

Mezei, Kathy, ed. 1996. *Ambiguous Discourse: Feminist Narratology and British Women Writers.* Chapel Hill: University of North Carolina Press.

Miki, Roy. 1985. "Introduction: The Life and Times of Muriel Kitagawa." In *This Is My Own: Letters to Wes and Other Writings on Japanese Canadians, 1941–1948,* ed. R. Miki, 1–64. Vancouver: Talonbooks.

– 1998. "Asiancy: Making Space for Asian Canadian Writing." In *Broken Entries: Race, Subjectivity, Writing,* 101–24. Toronto: Mercury Press.

Miki, Roy, and Cassandra Kobayashi. 1991. *Justice in Our Time: The Japanese Canadian Redress Settlement.* Vancouver: Talonbooks.

Mohanty, Chandra Talpade. 1991. "Introduction: Cartographies of Struggle: Third World Women and the Politics of Feminism." In *Third World Women and the Politics of Feminism,* ed. Chandra Talpade Mohanty, Ann Russo, and Lourdes Torres, 1–47. Bloomington: Indiana University Press.

Mojica, Monique. 1991. *Princess Pocahontas and the Blue Spots.* Toronto: Women's Press.

Monkman, Leslie. 1981. *A Native Heritage: Images of the Indian in English-Canadian Literature.* Toronto: University of Toronto Press.

More, Hannah. 1799. *Strictures on the Modern System of Female Education.* 2 vols. London: T. Cadell Jun. and W. Davies.

Morley, Alan. 1961. *Vancouver: From Milltown to Metropolis.* Vancouver: Mitchell.

Morson, Gary Saul. 1986. "The Baxtin Industry." *Slavic and East European Journal* 30 (1): 81–90.

– and Caryl Emerson, eds. 1989. *Rethinking Bakhtin: Extensions and Challenges.* Evanston: Northwestern University Press.

– and Caryl Emerson. 1990. *Mikhail Bakhtin: Creation of a Prosaics.* Stanford: Stanford University Press.

Mukherjee, Arun P. 1990. "Whose Post-Colonialism and Whose Postmodernism?" *World Literature Written in English* 30 (2): 1–9.

– 1995a. "Bessie Head's Dialogue with India." In *Dialogism and Cultural Criticism*, ed. Clive Thomson and Hans Raj Dua, 217–35. London: Mestengo.

– 1995b. "Canadian Nationalism, Canadian Literature and Racial Minority Women." In *The Other Woman: Women of Colour in Contemporary Canadian Literature*, ed. Makeda Silvera, 421–44. Toronto: Sister Vision.

Murphy, Patrick D. 1988. "Sex-Typing the Planet: Gaia Imagery and the Problem of Subverting Patriarchy." *Environmental Ethics* 10 (2): 155–68.

– 1991. "Prolegomenon for an Ecofeminist Dialogics." In *Feminism, Bakhtin, and the Dialogic*, ed. Dale Bauer and Susan Janet McKinstry, 39–56. Albany: State University of New York Press.

Neuman, Shirley. 1996. "Writing the Reader, Writing the Self in Aritha van Herk's *Places Far from Ellesmere.*" *Essays on Canadian Writing* 60: 215–34.

New, W.H. 1990a. "Studies in English Canadian Literature." *International Journal of Canadian Studies* 1–2: 97–114.

– ed. 1990b. *Native Writers and Canadian Writing.* Vancouver: UBC Press.

– 1998. *Borderlands: How We Talk about Canada.* Vancouver: UBC Press.

Newton, Adam Zachary. 1995. *Narrative Ethics.* Cambridge, MA: Harvard University Press.

Ng, Maria Noëlle. 1999. "Representing Chinatown: Dr. Fu-Manchu at the Disappearing Moon Cafe." *Canadian Literature* 163: 157–75.

Ng, Roxanna. 1993. "Sexism, Racism, Canadian Nationalism." In *Returning the Gaze: Essays on Racism, Feminism and Politics*, ed. Himani Bannerji, 182–96. Toronto: Sister Vision.

Noyes, Stacey. 2002. "Dressed for Conversation: Albert Liao Knocks a Chink in the Armour of Cultural Stereotypes." *Vancouver Sun*, 27 April, D2.

Nünning, Ansgar. 1989. *Grundzüge eines kommunikationstheoretischen Modells der erzählerischen Vermittlung: Die Funktionen der Erzählinstanz in den Romanen George Eliots.* Trier: Wissenschaftlicher Verlag.

– 1992. "Narrative Form und fiktionale Wirklichkeitskonstruktion aus der Sicht des New Historicism und der Narrativik: Grundzüge und Perspektiven einer kulturwissenschaftlichen Erforschung des englischen Romans im 18. Jahrhundert." *Zeitschrift für Anglistik und Amerikanistik* 40 (1): 197–213.

– 1994. "Gender and Narratology: Kategorien und Perspektiven einer feministischen Narrativik." *Zeitschrift für Anglistik und Amerikanistik* 42 (2): 102–23.

– 1995. *Von historischer Fiktion zu historiographischer Metafiktion.* 2 vols. Trier: Wissenschaftlicher Verlag.
– 1999. "Unreliable, Compared to What? Towards a Cognitive Theory of Unreliable Narration: Prolegomena and Hypotheses." In *Grenzüberschreitungen: Narratologie im Kontext (Transcending Boundaries: Narratology in Context)*, ed. Walter Grünzweig and Andreas Solbach, 53–73. Tübingen: Gunter Narr Verlag.
– 2000. "Towards a Cultural and Historical Narratology: A Survey of Diachronic Approaches, Concepts, and Research Projects." In *Anglistentag 1999 Mainz. Proceedings*, ed. Bernhard Reitz and Sigrid Rieuwerts, 345–73. Trier: Wissenschaftlicher Verlag.
O'Brien, Susie. 1995. "'Please Eunice, Don't Be Ignorant': The White Reader as Trickster in Lee Maracle's Fiction." *Canadian Literature* 144: 82–96.
O'Connor, Mary. 1990. "Chronotopes for Women under Capital: An Investigation into the Relation of Women to Objects." *Critical Studies* 2 (1–2): 137–51.
Omatsu, Maryka. 1992. *Bittersweet Passage: Redress and the Japanese Canadian Experience.* Toronto: Between the Lines.
Onega, Susana, and José Angel García Landa. 1996. Introduction. In *Narratology: An Introduction*, 1–41. London: Longman.
O'Neill, Patrick. 1994. *Fictions of Discourse: Reading Narrative Theory.* Toronto: University of Toronto Press.
Ong, Walter J. 1982. *Orality and Literacy: The Technologizing of the Word.* London: Routledge.
The Oxford English Dictionary. 1989. 2nd ed. Oxford: Clarendon.
Palmer, Bryan D. 1983. *Working-Class Experience: The Rise and Reconstitution of Canadian Labour, 1800–1980.* Toronto: Butterworths.
Palmer, R. Barton. 1990. "Languages and Power in the Novel: Mapping the Monologic." *Studies in the Literary Imagination* 23 (1): 99–127.
Parks, Ward. 1991. "The Textualization of Orality in Literary Criticism." In *Vox intexta: Orality and Textuality in the Middle Ages*, ed. A.N. Doane and Carol Braun Pasternack, 46–61. London: University of Wisconsin Press.
Pechey, Graham. 1989. "On the Borders of Bakhtin: Dialogisation, Decolonisation." In *Bakhtin and Cultural Theory*, ed. Ken Hirschkop and David Shepherd, 36–67. Manchester: Manchester University Press.
Penner, Norman. 1975. *Winnipeg 1919: The Strikers' Own History of the Winnipeg General Strike.* 2nd ed. Toronto: James Lorimer.
Peters, Darrell Jesse. 1999. "Beyond the Frame: Tom King's Narratives of Resistance." *Studies in American Indian Literatures* 11 (2): 66–79.
Petrone, Penny. 1990. *Native Literature in Canada: From the Oral Tradition to the Present.* Toronto: Oxford University Press.
Pfister, Manfred. 1988. *The Theory and Analysis of Drama.* Cambridge: Cambridge University Press.

Phelan, James. 1989. "Introduction: Diversity and Dialogue in Narrative Theory." In *Reading Narrative: Form, Ethics, Ideology*, ed. J. Phelan, ix-xix. Columbus: Ohio State University Press.

– 1996. *Narrative as Rhetoric: Technique, Audiences, Ethics, Ideology.* Columbus, Ohio State University Press.

Philip, Marlene Nourbese. 1989. *She Tries Her Tongue, Her Silence Softly Breaks*. Chalottetown: Ragweed.

Pianos, Tamara. 1995. "Aritha van Herk's *Places Far from Ellesmere* as 'geografictione.'" *Zeitschrift der Gesellschaft für Kanada-Studien* 15 (1): 94–101.

Plant, Judith, ed. 1989. *Healing the Wounds: The Promise of Ecofeminism.* Philadelphia: New Society.

Pollock, Mary S. 1993. "What Is Left Out: Bakhtin, Feminism, and the Culture of Boundaries." *Critical Studies* 3.2–4.1/2: 229–41.

Pollock, Sharon. 1981. *Blood Relations*. In *Blood Relations and Other Plays*, 11–70. Edmonton: NeWest.

– 1992. *Getting It Straight*. In *Heroines: Three Plays*, ed. Joyce Doolittle, 85–126. Red Deer: Red Deer College.

Porteous, J. Douglas. 1990. *Landscapes of the Mind: Worlds of Sense and Metaphor*. Toronto: University of Toronto Press.

Prince, Gerald. 1987. *A Dictionary of Narratology*. Lincoln: University of Nebraska Press.

– 1995. "On Narratology: Criteria, Corpus, Context." *Narrative* 3 (1): 73–84.

Propp, Vladimir. 1958 [1928]. *Morphology of the Folktale*. Bloomington: Indiana University Press.

Quan, Andy, and Jim Wong-Chu. 1999. *Swallowing Clouds: An Anthology of Chinese-Canadian Poetry*. Vancouver: Arsenal Pulp.

Rabasa, José. 1987. "Dialogue as Conquest: Mapping Spaces for Counter-Discourse." *Cultural Critique* 6: 131–59.

Rabinowitz, Peter J. 1987. *Before Reading: Narrative Conventions and the Politics of Interpretation*. Ithaca: Cornell University Press.

Reed, Walter L. 1993. *Dialogues of the Word: The Bible as Literature According to Bakhtin*. New York: Oxford University Press.

Reimer, Chad. 1993. "War, Nationhood and Working-Class Entitlement: The Counterhegemonic Challenge of the 1919 Winnipeg General Strike." *Prairie Forum* 18 (2): 219–37.

Richler, Mordecai. 1989. *Solomon Gursky Was Here*. Toronto: Penguin.

Richter, David H. 1990. "Dialogism and Poetry." *Studies in the Literary Imagination* 23 (1): 9–27.

Rimmon-Kenan, Shlomith. 1983. *Narrative Fiction: Contemporary Poetics*. London: Methuen.

Robinson, Eden. 2000. *Monkey Beach*. Toronto: Knopf.

Robinson, Sally. 1991. *Engendering the Subject: Gender and Self-Representa-*

tion in *Contemporary Women's Fiction*. New York: State University of New York Press.

Rose, Marilyn Russell. 1987. "Hawthorne's 'Custom House,' Said's *Orientalism* and Kogawa's *Obasan*: An Intertextual Reading of an Historical Fiction." *Dalhousie Review* 67 (2–3): 286–96.

– 1988. "Politics into Art: Kogawa's *Obasan* and the Rhetoric of Fiction." *Mosaic* 21.2–3: 215–26.

Ross, A.M. 1971. "The Romance of Vancouver's Schools." In *Schools of Old Vancouver*, ed. James M. Sandison, 11–25. Vancouver: Vancouver Historical Society.

Roy, Patricia E. 1989. *A White Man's Province: British Columbia Politicians and Chinese and Japanese Immigrants, 1858–1914*. Vancouver: UBC Press.

– J.L. Granatstein, Masako Iino, and Hiroko Takamura. 1990. *Mutual Hostages: Canadian and Japanese during the Second World War*. Toronto: University of Toronto Press.

Royal Commission on Aboriginal Peoples. 1996. *Report of the Royal Commission on Aboriginal Peoples*. Ottawa: The Commission.

Russo, Mary. 1986. "Female Grotesques: Carnival and Theory." In *Feminist Studies: Critical Studies*, ed. Teresa de Lauretis, 213–19. Bloomington: Indiana University Press.

Rutland, Barry, ed. 1997. *Gender and Narrativity*. Ottawa: Carleton University Press.

Ryan, Marie-Laurie, and Ernst van Alphen. 1993. "Narratology." In *Encyclopedia of Contemporary Literary Theory: Approaches, Scholars, Terms*, ed. Irena R. Makaryk, 110–16. Toronto: University of Toronto Press.

Said, Edward W. 1993. *Culture and Imperialism*. New York: Vintage Books.

San Juan, E., Jr. 1992. *Racial Formations/Critical Transformations: Articulations of Power in Ethnic and Racial Studies in the United States*. New Jersey: Humanities.

Sasaki, Betty. 1998. "Reading Silence in Joy Kogawa's *Obasan*." In *Analyzing the Different Voice: Feminist Psychological Theory and Literary Texts*, ed. Jerilyn Fisher and Ellen S. Silber, 117–39. Lanham: Rowman and Littlefield.

Schmidt, Siegfried J. 1992. "The Logic of Observation: An Introduction to Constructivism." *Canadian Review of Comparative Literature* 19 (3): 295–311.

Schueller, Malini Johar. 1994. "Multiculturalism as a Strategy of Reading." *Prose Studies* 17 (1): 1–19.

Schultz, Emily A. 1990. *Dialogue at the Margins: Whorf, Bakhtin, and Linguistic Relativity*. Madison: University of Wisconsin Press.

Schwandt, Thomas A. 1994. "Constructivist, Interpretivist Approaches to Human Inquiry." In *Handbook of Qualitative Research*, ed. Norman K. Denzin and Yvonne S. Lincoln, 118–37. Thousand Oaks: Sage.

Scollon, Ron, and Suzanne B.K. Scollon. 1984. "Cooking It Up and Boiling

It Down: Abstracts in Athabaskan Children's Story Retellings." In *Coherence in Spoken and Written Discourse*, ed. Deborah Tannen, 173–97. Norwood: ABLEX.

Scott, Joan W. 1986. "Gender: A Useful Category of Historical Analysis." *American Historical Review* 91: 1053–75.

– 1988. *Gender and the Politics of History*. New York: Columbia University Press.

– 1992 "Experience." *Feminists Theorize the Political*, ed. Judith Butler and Joan W. Scott, 22–40. New York: Routledge.

Scott, Sir Walter. 1909. "The Lay of the Last Minstrel." In *The Poetical Works of Sir Walter Scott*, ed. J. Logie Robertson, 1–88. London: Oxford University Press.

Seaman, Donna. 1991. Rev. of *Disappearing Moon Cafe*, by Sky Lee. *Booklist*, 15 October, 408.

Seltzer, Mark. 1995. "The Graphic Unconscious: A Response." *New Literary History* 26: 21–8.

Sherwin, Susan. 1992. *No Longer Patient: Feminist Ethics and Health Care*. Philadelphia: Temple University Press.

Shogan, Debra A., ed. 1992. *A Reader in Feminist Ethics*. Toronto: Canadian Scholars' Press.

Shumway, Suzanne Rosenthal. 1994. "The Chronotope of the Asylum: *Jane Eyre*, Feminism, and Bakhtinian Theory." In *A Dialogue of Voices: Feminist Literary Theory and Bakhtin*, Karen Hohne and Helen Wussow, 152–70. Minneapolis: University of Minnesota Press.

Slemon, Stephen. 1987. "Monuments of Empire: Allegory/Counter-Discourse/Post-Colonial Writing." *Kunapipi* 9 (3): 1–16.

– 1990. "Unsettling the Empire: Resistance Theory for the Second World." *World Literature Written in English* 30 (2): 30–41.

– 1995. "Afterword: The English Side of the Lawn." *Essays on Canadian Writing* 56: 274–86.

Slipperjack, Ruby. 1992. *Silent Words*. Saskatoon: Fifth House.

Söderlind, Sylvia. 1991. *Margin/Alias: Language and Colonization in Canadian and Québécois Fiction*. Toronto: University of Toronto Press.

Spivak, Gayatri Chakravorty. 1987. *In Other Worlds: Essays in Cultural Politics*. New York: Routledge.

Stallybrass, Peter, and Allon White. 1986. *The Politics and Poetics of Transgression*. London: Methuen.

Stam, Robert. 1989. *Subversive Pleasures: Bakhtin, Cultural Criticism, and Film*. Baltimore: Johns Hopkins University Press.

St Andrews, B.A. 1986. "Reclaiming a Canadian Heritage: Kogawa's *Obasan*." *International Fiction Review* 13 (1): 29–31.

Stanzel, Eberhard. 1979 [1955]. *Narrative Situations in the Novel*. Bloomington: Indiana University Press.

Sternberg, Meir. 1982. "Proteus in Quotation-Land: Mimesis and the Forms of Reported Discourse." *Poetics Today* 3 (2): 107–56.

Strong-Boag, Veronica. 1994. "Contested Space: The Politics of Canadian Memory." *Journal of the Canadian Historical Association* 5: 3–17.

– Sherrill Grace, Avigail Eisenberg, and Joan Anderson, eds. 1998. *Painting the Maple: Essays on Race, Gender and the Construction of Canada*. Vancouver: UBC Press.

Sunahara, Ann Gomer. 1981. *The Politics of Racism: The Uprooting of Japanese Canadians during the Second World War*. Toronto: James Lorimer.

Sweatman, Margaret. 1991. *Fox*. Winnipeg: Turnstone.

– 1993. "Dialogue and Difficulty: Narrative as Performance." *Studying and Writing the Difference: Essays in Canadian Culture(s) and Society*, ed. Hans Braun and Wolfgang Kloos, 159–64. Trier: Zentrum für Kanada-Studien.

Terdiman, Richard. 1985. *Discourse/Counter-Discourse: The Theory and Practice of Symbolic Resistance in Nineteenth-Century France*. Ithaca: Cornell University Press.

Thibault, Paul. 1984. "Narrative Discourse as a Multi-Level System of Communication: Some Theoretical Proposals Concerning Bakhtin's Dialogic Principle." *Studies in Twentieth Century Literature* 9 (1): 89–118.

Thomas, Joan. 1991. Rev. of *Places Far from Ellesmere*, by Aritha van Herk. *Prairie Fire* 12 (2): 68–70.

Thompson, Stuart E. 1988. "Death, Food, and Fertility." In *Death Ritual in Late Imperial and Modern China*, ed. James L. Watson and Evelyn S. Rawski, 71–108. Berkeley: University of California Press.

Thomson, Clive. 1989. "Mikhail Bakhtin and Contemporary Anglo-American Feminist Theory." *Critical Studies* 1 (2): 141–61.

– 1990. "Introduction: Mikhail Bakhtin and Shifting Paradigms." *Critical Studies* 2 (1–2): 1–12.

– 1993. "Bakhtin and Feminist Projects: Judith Butler's *Gender Trouble*." *Critical Studies* 3.2 (4.1/2): 210–28.

– and Hans Raj Dua. 1995. Preface. In *Dialogism and Cultural Criticism*, ed. C. Thomson and H.R. Dua, v–xi. London: Mestengo.

Thornton, William H. 1994. "Cultural Prosaics as Counterdiscourse: A Direction for Cultural Studies after Bakhtin." *Prose Studies* 17 (2): 74–97.

Tiffin, Helen. 1983. "Commonwealth Literature: Comparison and Judgement." In *The History and Historiography of Commonwealth Literature*, ed. Dieter Riemenschneider, 19–35. Tübingen: Gunter Narr Verlag.

– 1987. "Post-Colonial Literatures and Counter-Discourse." *Kunapipi* 9 (3): 17–34.

Titunik, Irwin R. 1984. "Baxtin and/or Volosinov and/or Medvedev: Dialogue and/or Doubletalk." In *Language and Literary Theory*, ed. Benjamin

A. Stolz, Irwin R. Titunik, and Lubomir Dolezel, 535–64. Ann Arbor: University of Michigan Press.

– 1986. "The Baxtin Problem: Concerning Katerina Clark and Michael Holquist's *Mikhail Bakhtin.*" *Slavic and East European Journal* 30.1 (1986): 91–5.

Tobin, Patricia Drechsel. 1978. *Time and the Novel: The Genealogical Imperative.* Princeton: Princeton University Press.

Todd, Loretta. 1992. "What More Do They Want?" In *Indigena: Contemporary Native Perspectives,* ed. Gerald McMaster and Lee-Ann Martin, 71–9. Vancouver: Douglas and McIntyre.

Todorov, Tzvetan. 1969. *Grammaire du Décameron.* The Hague: Mouton.

– 1984. *Mikhail Bakhtin: The Dialogical Principle.* Trans. Wlad Godzich. Minneapolis: University of Minnesota Press.

Tolstoy, L.N. 1978 [1874–76]. *Anna Karenin.* Trans. and ed. Rosemary Edmonds. Toronto: Penguin.

Tompkins, Joanne. 1995. "'The Story of Rehearsal Never Ends': Rehearsal, Performance, Identity in Settler Culture Drama." *Canadian Literature* 144: 142–61.

Tostevin, Lola Lemire. 1989. "Daphne Marlatt: Writing in the Space That Is Her Mother's Face." *Line* 13: 32–9.

Tranfield, Pam. 1989. "Girl Strikers." *NeWest Review* 14 (5): 29+.

Trinh T. Minh-ha. 1991. *When the Moon Waxes Red: Representation, Gender and Cultural Politics.* New York: Routledge.

Tronto, Joan C. 1993. *Moral Boundaries: A Political Argument for an Ethic of Care.* New York: Routledge.

Turner, Margaret. 1995. *Imagining Culture: New World Narrative and the Writing of Canada.* Montreal: McGill-Queen's University Press.

van Herk, Aritha. 1987. "Interview with Aritha van Herk." With Dorothy Jones. *SPAN* 25: 1–15.

– 1990. *Places Far from Ellesmere: A Geografictione.* Red Deer: Red Deer College.

– 1991. *In Visible Ink: (Crypto-Frictions).* Edmonton: NeWest.

– 1992. *A Frozen Tongue.* Sydney: Dangaroo.

– 1993. "Spectral Tattoo: Reconstructive Fictions." *SPAN* 36 (1): 15–24.

– 1996. "The Map's Temptation or the Search for a Secret Book." *Journal of Commonwealth Literature* 31 (1): 129–36.

van Toorn, Penny. 1990. "Discourse/Patron Discourse: How Minority Texts Command the Attention of Majority Audiences." *SPAN* 30: 102–15.

– 1995. *Rudy Wiebe and the Historicity of the Word.* Edmonton: University of Alberta Press.

Vautier, Marie. 1998. *New World Myth: Postmodernism and Postcolonialism in Canadian Fiction.* Montreal: McGill-Queen's University Press.

Verdecchia, Guillermo. 1993. *Fronteras Americanas (American Borders).* Toronto: Coach House.

Voloshinov, V.N. / M.M. Bakhtin. 1973. [1929]. *Marxism and the Philosophy of Language*. Trans. Ladislav Matejka and Irwin R. Titunik. Cambridge: Harvard University Press.

Voloshinov, V.N. 1976 [1927]. *Freudianism: A Marxist Critique*. New York: Academic Press.

Wall, Anthony. 1989. "Silence as Weapon of Authoritarian Discourse." *Critical Studies* 1 (2): 211–29.

Ward, W. Peter. 1990 [1978]. *White Canada Forever: Popular Attitudes and Public Policy toward Orientals in British Columbia*. Montreal: McGill-Queen's University Press.

Warhol, Robyn R. 1989. *Gendered Interventions: Narrative Discourse in the Victorian Novel*. New Brunswick: Rutgers University Press.

– 1999. "Guilty Cravings: What Feminist Narratology Can Do for Cultural Studies." In *Narratologies: New Perspectives on Narrative Analysis*, ed. David Herman, 340–55. Columbus: Ohio State University Press.

Watson, James L. 1988. "The Structure of Chinese Funerary Rites: Elementary Forms, Ritual Sequence, and the Primacy of Performance." In *Death Ritual in Late Imperial and Modern China*, ed. James L. Watson and Evelyn S. Rawski, 3–19. Berkeley: University of California Press.

Watzlawick, Paul, ed. 1984. *The Invented Reality*. New York: Norton.

Wesseling, Elisabeth. 1991. *Writing History as a Prophet: Postmodernist Innovations of the Historical Novel*. Amsterdam: John Benjamins.

Wharton, Thomas. 1995. *Icefields*. Edmonton: NeWest.

White, Allon. 1987/88. "The Struggle Over Bakhtin: Fraternal Reply to Robert Young." *Cultural Critique* 8: 217–41.

Wickberg, Edgar, ed. 1982. *From China to Canada: A History of the Chinese Communities in Canada*. Toronto: McClelland and Stewart.

Wiebe, Rudy. 1994. *A Discovery of Strangers*. Toronto: Vintage.

Williams, Raymond. 1977. *Marxism and Literature*. New York: Oxford University Press.

– 1989. "Appendix: Media, Margins and Modernity." In *The Politics of Modernism: Against the New Conformists*. 177–97. London: Verso.

Wills, Clair. 1989. "Upsetting the Public: Carnival, Hysteria and Women's Texts." In *Bakhtin and Cultural Theory*, ed. Ken Hirschkop and David Shepherd, 130–51. Manchester: Manchester University Press.

Wilson, John. 1991. "Literary Explorations." Rev. of *Places Far from Ellesmere*, by Aritha van Herk. *Western Report*, 14 January, 42–3.

Wise, Jennifer. 1989. "Marginalizing Drama: Bakhtin's Theory of Genre." *Essays in Theatre* 8 (1): 15–22.

Women's Book Committee of the Chinese Canadian National Council. 1992. *Jin Guo: Voices of Chinese Canadian Women*. Toronto: Women's Press.

Wong, Rita. 1990. Rev. of *Disappearing Moon Cafe*, by Sky Lee. *West Coast Line* 24: 135–7.

– 1995. "Jumping on Hyphens: A Bricolage Receiving 'Genealogy/Gap,'

'Goods,' 'East Asian Canadian,' 'Translation,' and 'Laughter.'" In *The Other Woman: Women of Colour in Contemporary Canadian Literature*, ed. Makeda Silvera, 117–53. Toronto: Sister Vision.

Wright, Raymond S. 1995. *The Genealogist's Handbook: Modern Methods for Researching Family History*. American Library Association.

Wyile, Herb. 1999. "'Trust Tonto': Thomas King's Subversive Fictions and the Politics of Cultural Literacy." *Canadian Literature* 161/2: 105–24.

Yang, C.K. 1967. *Religion in Chinese Society*. Berkeley: University of California Press.

Yaeger, Patricia S. 1988. *Honey-Mad Women: Emancipatory Strategies in Women's Writing*. New York: Columbia University Press.

Yee, Paul. 1988. *Saltwater City: An Illustrated History of the Chinese in Vancouver*. Vancouver: Talonbooks.

Yelin, Louise. 1989. "Problems of Gordimer's Poetics: Dialogue in *Burger's Daughter*." In *Feminism, Bakhtin, and the Dialogic*, ed. Dale Bauer and Susan Janet McKinstry, 219–38. Albany: State University of New York Press.

Young, Robert. 1985/86. "Back to Bakhtin." *Cultural Critique* 1–2: 71–92.

Young-Ing, Greg. 1993. "Aboriginal Peoples' Estrangement: Marginalization in the Publishing Industry." In *Looking at the Words of Our People: First Nations Analysis of Literature*, ed. Jeannette Armstrong, 177–87. Penticton: Theytus.

Zavala, Iris M. 1990. "Bakhtin and Otherness: Social Heterogeneity." *Critical Studies* 2 (1–2): 77–89.

– 1993. "Notes on the Cannibalistic Discourse of Monologism." *Critical Studies* 3.2–4.1/2: 261–76.

Index